D1738579

GARLAND STUDIES IN

AMERICAN POPULAR HISTORY AND CULTURE

edited by

JEROME NADELHAFT
UNIVERSITY OF MAINE

A GARLAND SERIES

Garland Studies in American Popular History and Culture
Jerome Nadelhaft, series editor

Political Cartoons in the 1988 Presidential Campaign: Image, Metaphor, and Narrative
Janis L. Edwards

The Origins and Early Development of Professional Football
Marc S. Maltby

Seduction, Prostitution, and Moral Reform in New York, 1830–1860
Larry Whiteaker

Hollywood's Vision of Team Sports: Heroes, Race, and Gender
Deborah V. Tudor

The Flamingo in the Garden: American Yard Art and the Vernacular Landscape
Colleen J. Sheehy

Textual Vehicles: The Automobile in American Literature
Roger N. Casey

Film and the Nuclear Age: Representing Cultural Anxiety
Toni A. Perrine

Lesbian and Gay Memphis: Building Communities Behind the Magnolia Curtain
Daneel Buring

Making Villains, Making Heroes: Joseph R. McCarthy, Martin Luther King, Jr., and the Politics of American Memory
Gary Daynes

America Under Construction: Boundaries and Identities in Popular Culture
Kristi S. Long and Matthew Nadelhaft, editors

AIDS, Social Change, and Theater: Performance as Protest
Cindy J. Kistenberg

"When the Spirit Says Sing!": The Role of Freedom Songs in the Civil Rights Movement
Kerran L. Sanger

African American Nationalist Literature of the 1960s: Pens of Fire
Sandra Hollin Flowers

The Rehabilitation of Richard Nixon: The Media's Effect on Collective Memory
Thomas J. Johnson

Chicano Images: Refiguring Ethnicity in Mainstream Film
Christine List

At a Theater or Drive-in Near You: The History, Culture, and Politics of the American Exploitation Film
Randall Clark

Teatro Hispano: Three Major New York Comapnies
Elisa de la Roche

Lolita in Peyton Place: Highbrow, Lowbrow, and Middlebrow Novels of the 1950s
Ruth Wood

Contra Dance Choreography: A Reflection of Social Change
Mary Dart

Public Discourse and Academic Inquiry
William Craig Rice

TEXTUAL VEHICLES

THE AUTOMOBILE IN AMERICAN LITERATURE

ROGER N. CASEY

GARLAND PUBLISHING, INC.
NEW YORK & LONDON / 1997

Library of Congress Cataloging-in-Publication Data

Casey, Roger N., 1961–
    Textual vehicles : the automobile in American literature /
Roger N. Casey.
        p.   cm. — (Garland studies in American popular history
and culture)
    Includes bibliographical references and index.
    ISBN 0-8153-3050-2 (alk. paper)
    1. American literature—20th century—History and criticism.
2. Automobile travel in literature. 3. Automobiles in literature. I.
Title. II. Series.
PS228.A95C37 1997
810.9'355—dc21

                                            97-39735

Printed on acid-free, 250-year-life paper
Manufactured in the United States of America

To my father, Ruskin, for teaching me how to drive,
and
to Robyn, for driving along with me

Contents

Preface   xi

Acknowledgments   xv

INTRODUCTION. Textual Vehicles: The Automobile and
American Literature   3

CHAPTER 1. Romancing the Machine: America Courts
the Auto   13

Automobility Before the Automobile   13

The Automobile Age Arrives   19

The Car Comes to Broadway   23

Sinclair Lewis and America's Marriage to the
Automobile   24

Free Air   26

A Six-Cylinder Courtship   34

"Speed"   35

CHAPTER 2. From Romantic to Rogue: Satire and the
Auto   41

Altering Our Ideals: *The Magnificent Ambersons*   41

The Car Comes to Main Street   43

Main Street   44

Babbitt   46

Dodsworth   47

Gatsby and "The Arrogance of Wealth"   51

CHAPTER 3. An Intricate Relationship: The Car as
          Complex Signifier   57

   "Discipline Perfectly Embroidered": Ford as Fiction   58

      The Flivver King   64

      Ragtime   67

      John Dos Passos   69

   "The Inescapable Destiny": Cars and Rural America   71

      Erskine Caldwell   72

      John Steinbeck   76

      William Faulkner   84

CHAPTER 4. Permanent Union/Impossible Escape: Post-
          War Literature and Automobility   97

   Driving Miss Flannery   99

   The Road as Life   110

      Jack Kerouac   110

      Vladimir Nabokov   118

   Rabbit in Traffic   121

   Crossing the White Line   131

      Arna Bontemps   132

      Richard Wright   134

      Ralph Ellison   136

      E. L. Doctorow   137

CHAPTER 5. "Where We Are in America":

      Contemporary Representations of Automobility   141

   Rotting Birds and Blue Convertibles: Joy Williams's
      Failed Escapes   142

   "Useful Junk": Louise Erdrich's Mystical Vehicles   150

   Ann Beattie's Shifting Symbols   156

   On the Road— Revisited   163

   Harry Crews's *Car*   166

A Complex and Inescapable Symbol   175

Contents *ix*

Notes	175
Bibliography	185
Index	195

Preface

In this study I am concerned with two objects (texts): the automobile and selected works of American literature; yet both of these objects/texts are elusive. What does one envision through the word *automobile*? A Ferrari, a Volkswagen Beetle, a Ford Thunderbird? And what year model? A stripped-down 1922 Model T or perhaps a high-tech 1997 BMW? *American literature* is even more elusive as a signifier, for its model years and makes are as diverse as the number of writers in the country's literary culture, and no cataloging can easily encompass all that have been produced. Even the term *American* proves to be ethnocentric nomenclature because my study focuses on what in actuality should be called United States literature, or, at the least, literature produced in the United States and primarily about this country. As for the label *literature*, post-structuralist critics have appropriately informed us of the privileging of certain texts into this sacred category. What makes *The Great Gatsby* any more a piece of literature than the *1997 New Car Pricing Guide*? Hence, in line with some current literary theory, the focus of this study might be on "texts" rather than on the privileged domain of nationalistic "literature." However, in narrowing the field of focus, I approached the topic wanting to know what some texts that *have been* privileged as "American literature" reveal about America's number-one privileged machine—the car, and how this machine so privileged has made an impact on the content and style of these literary texts.

My first task was to locate as many works of American literature as I could find which made use of automobiles. I found that I had begun a gargantuan undertaking, although the very fact that this task proved thus solidified my perception that the automobile had indeed profoundly affected the making of this nation's poetry, drama, and, especially, fiction. After isolating and reading a great number of such works, I then examined studies of automobiles and automobility, both academic and "popular." The next task was to overlap the matrices of these two domains and attempt to discover if a paradigm developed through which I could postulate some conclusions.

I discovered through a roughly chronological approach that representative writers and their texts could be isolated to illustrate diverse and changing perceptions and uses of the automobile in American culture. Therefore, this study does not attempt to address or include every work of American literature that contains a textual vehicle, but rather to deal with a smaller number of writers and most often to examine the treatment of automobility in several of their works, not just a single text. An occasional digression from this pattern does in fact, nevertheless, occur when a single work proves illustrative.

I also discovered that no single methodological approach allowed sufficient latitude for elaborating on my findings. Therefore, several approaches are used in the study: structural, material cultural, and new historical. The structural is evident in that the study endeavors to describe the grammar of automobility as it has been presented in American literature, not unlike the approach of Roland Barthes in *Mythologies*, except rather than deal with numerous cultural "myths," I focus on one—the automobile (a myth which also concerned Barthes). Second, the notion of myth led me to the so-called "myth and symbol" school of material-cultural studies, a school perhaps best represented by Leo Marx, whose *The Machine in the Garden* is of primary concern, or by Alan Trachtenberg, whose study of the Brooklyn Bridge my work somewhat resembles in approach and intention. These texts, like mine, attempt to locate the importance of one object within the American psyche. Third, the new historicist revision is significant in showing how in examining the impact of an object on American culture one must also place that object within the context of other objects (or texts, as the case may be). By placing a text such as Sinclair Lewis's *Free Air* against other writings of its day—for example, automobile ads, drivers' handbooks, tour guides, *et al*—one can uncover corroborations and collisions among texts and perhaps ultimately ascertain the positioning of the primary text within the culture.

A material culturalist study that privileges the literary artifact would perhaps be an accurate theoretical description of the agenda in this work. It is an agenda which hopefully leads to a persuasive rereading of certain texts in light of the material culture of their origin, opens them up to new and variant interpretive possibilities, and concludes that the automobile is a pervasive textual vehicle in the composition of American literature.

Acknowledgments

While it might seem more appropriate to acknowledge tribute to some well-known scholar for his or her ultimate inspiration in giving me the idea for this work, the actual source of this project probably lies in the fact that my hometown, Woodruff, South Carolina, had no zoning laws when I was an adolescent, thereby making possible, in the heart of town, my backyard—a junk-car lot, a conglomeration of wrecked and rusted models ranging from a 1952 Ford to a nearly brand-new, but quite demolished 1966 Volkswagen. The garage of Ruskin Casey, my mechanic father, was no more than a hundred yards from our back door, and as early as I can remember, I crawled under Fords beside him, getting grease on my trouser seats and oil on my shoes. His world, and the world of my family, revolved (and still revolves) around automobiles. Thus my ultimate thanks for the idea behind this project must go to Ruskin Casey for the many hours he spent with me under the hood of a car and behind the wheel of his old Ford pick-up teaching me how to drive and to Barbara Casey for washing the grease out of my jeans every day.

For the scholarly side of this project, I am eternally grateful to Professor Fred Standley of Florida State University, who has served as my professional mentor. I cannot praise enough his support, advice, cooperation, and demeanor. I would also like to thank Professors John Fenstermaker, David Kirby, Karen Laughlin, and Alan Mabe of Florida State for their generous suggestions and editorial advice. Also, thanks must go to my faculty colleagues and the administration, students, and staff of Birmingham-Southern College who have generously supported my efforts to complete this book, especially President Neal Berte, Provost Irvin Penfield, Professors Susan Hagen and Sandra Sprayberry, my student assistant, Ginny Phillips, and secretary, Grace Burns. I especially want to thank all my acquaintances who have at one time or another stopped me in the hall and said: "I'm reading this book that has a car in it . . . ."

An especial debt of gratitude must go to Garland Press for encouraging me to publish this work, particularly to Professor Jerome Nadelhaft, Chuck Bartelt, and my editor, Kristi Long.

Lastly, my deepest appreciation goes to Robyn Allers for tolerating me while I have immersed myself in automobility and spouted forth more automotive trivia than anyone should have to endure in her lifetime, for taking sidetrips in the middle of the West so that I could locate old U.S. 90, the Wigwam Motel, the largest roadrunner statue in America, or whatever automotive nonsense I happened to be researching at the time. Most of all I thank her for listening and for reading and for being my best friend.

Textual Vehicles

Textual Vehicles:
The Automobile and American Literature

Over one hundred years have passed since Charles E. and J. Frank
Duryea built and tested their first gasoline-powered horseless carriage
on the streets of Springfield, Massachusetts, and in that century the
automobile has come to dominate the lives of most Americans. Today
it seems retrospectively inevitable that the automobile would prosper in
the United States because it brings together two fundamentals of the
American way: individualism and movement—auto-mobility. The car
allows Americans to be on the go, to "go West" on Whitman's open
road, and it allows them to do so at their own pace with Emersonian
self-reliance, to remain unconfined by train or bus schedules and
limited only by the expanse of highway before them (and, with the
advent of off-road vehicles, perhaps not even to be limited by that).

Already by 1933, forty years after the Duryea, the President's
Research Committee on Social Trends reported: "It is probable that no
invention of such far reaching importance was ever diffused with such
rapidity or so quickly exerted influences that ramified through the
national culture, transforming even habits of thought and language"
(*Recent Social Trends* 172). President Warren G. Harding called the
motorcar "an indispensable instrument in our political, social, and
industrial life" (Kihlsted, "Auto" 4). It would seem he was correct,
because now, slightly more than one hundred years after its
introduction to America, this invention fundamentally controls our
culture. We drive to work. We drive to play. We drive to eat. We take
vacations in the family station wagon. Our banks, restaurants, liquor
stores, dry cleaners, and even churches have drive-in windows. Service
stations crowd our intersections. Small towns have grown up around
interstate exits. Everywhere we drive, uniformity follows—a freeway

exchange in California looks exactly like one in Florida: the same
Exxon, Burger King, Holiday Inn, and Subway, all adjoining the same
cloverleaf. Everywhere we go we see parking lots. Our major shopping
areas have moved from downtown to suburban malls or Wal-Marts,
which from overhead look like huge temples surrounded by faithfully
devoted automobiles. The suburbs have become our neighborhoods,
except we no longer have to be neighborly with the folks next door
because the car allows us to drive to be with our scattered friends. And
if we live in the country, the car has brought us closer to the city, away
from isolation, so that rural and urban have become less distinct.
America has truly become a vast motorscape.

The car is the driving machine of America, the machine that
affects and has affected the lives of Americans more than any other.
Perhaps this will not always be true. Even as I write on my word
processor, the computer is replacing the auto as the machine on which
we most depend. But the computer is a silent machine, its workings
invisible. We do not see computer junkyards on the outskirts of small
towns. We will not build our house with a two-computer garage in
mind. And most teenagers still dream of their first Corvette more than
their first PC. Perhaps, though, we may soon no longer need the car's
"conveniences": the bank drive-in window may be replaced by the
internet modem, for example. This point suggests that as we look at the
place of the car in society, we are looking from an age of the car's
waning control; therefore, today we are standing at yet another
important juncture in the evolution of automobility in American life.
Nevertheless, the car is still an indispensable component in the lives of
the majority of Americans.

The focus of this study is on the automobile's depiction in one
aspect of American culture, its literature, and the effects of the culture
of automobility on that literature. First I must define what I mean by
literature. In this study I will concentrate on selected writers of poetry,
drama, and, particularly, fiction. This arbitrary specification omits a
host of other automotive texts. Any magazine rack or bookstore
displays plenty of such works: for example, *Motor Trend, Car and
Driver, Chilton's Automotive Repair Manual for the 1996 Ford
Thunderbird, The Automotive Pricing Guide.* Almost as soon as cars
appeared in America, magazines appeared to talk about them:
Horseless Age and *Motocycle,* for example, were already being
published in the 1890s. One could easily write a book focusing on
these and other such sources.

In addition, the textual vehicles of all American cultures are not found solely on the page. The clearest example of such non-literary textual vehicles can be found in the contemporary Mexican-American cultural practice of low riding. Low riding is the art of turning an ordinary automobile into an artistic creation through additions, alterations, and artistic applications to the body of the car. According to Brenda Jo Bright, low riders can transform the automobile "through the skills of symbolic manipulation, money, hard work, and creativity into a vehicle of possibility, pleasure, and resistance" to mainstream culture. Most often, low riders cover their cars with murals which tell stories. Like written literature, "Car murals locate truth not in actual objects or events, but in the retelling or simulation of these objects and events" (96). These cars thus serve as "both vehicles and metaphor for cultural travel" (Bright 109). Bright concludes that these cars provide "a mobile canvas for cultural representation and critique" (91), a role not unlike what one might consider more traditional literature to play.

Thus, not only must a manageable study of textual vehicles be limited to a prescribed type of literature, it must be limited to a certain production of text as well. In my case, I have chosen to focus on works more traditionally considered as American *belles-lettres*, not necessarily literature in the sanctity of the American canon, but works predominantly by commonly assumed mainstream writers. And with a few exceptions, duly noted, I will limit my specification of "text" to that of the written page. My concerns in examining such literary textual vehicles are two-fold: 1. How has the automobile been treated in American literature? and 2. How has the presence of the automobile affected the creation of American literary texts? This line of questioning is central to a material-cultural study, and, in essence, the methodology of this study is a material-culturalist one drawing not only on literary studies, but also on sociology, anthropology, psychology, history, and other fields that illuminate the place of the automobile and the concept of automobility within society. As for theoretical stance, this work is most compatible with that articulated by Ihab Hassan, who declares unequivocally in *Selves at Risk*:

> I neither argue for or against theory nor address a particular "community of scholars." ... I concern myself urgently with meanings, stable, shifty, or complex. Not Deconstructionist, Marxist even less, not a "straight" Humanist reader, I construe the books of our time with the discipline of my experience, construe them finally

as they move me and as I imagine they move some readers. . . . I
confess: my bias is for an independent critical stance. (15)

The examination of texts herein will take a roughly chronological
approach, exploring the complex changing relationship between
automobility and American culture. Automotive historian James Flink
describes the development of this relationship by identifying three
stages of American "automobile consciousness":

> The first stage, from the introduction of the motor vehicle to the
> opening of the Ford Highland Park plant in 1910, was characterized
> by the rapid development of an attitudinal and institutional context
> that made the domination of the American civilization by the
> automobile inevitable. The second stage involved mass idolization of
> the motorcar and a mass accommodation to automobility that
> transformed American institutions and lifeways. Automobile
> Consciousness III was inaugurated in the late 1950s, when it first
> became apparent that automobility was no longer an historically
> progressive force for change in American civilization. Since then the
> motorcar increasingly has been conceived of as a major social
> problem. ("Three Stages" 451-52)

These stages characterizing the role of the car—rapid development,
mass idolization, and increasing decline—have often been compared to
a romance, America's love affair with the automobile. In fact, in book
after book and article after article, the metaphor of romance is the most
common one used to describe the relationship between Americans and
their cars. For example, in a recent *New York Times* article about "Car
Culture: The Automobile in 20th-Century Photography," an exhibition
at the Howard Greenberg Gallery in Manhattan, Vicki Goldberg writes:
"[M]odern life and the car are joined in holy matrimony. Or is it illicit
passion? Anyway, no earthly force can put the two asunder" (B1). It's
not so surprising that the auto and marriage should be metaphorically
connected: a *Motor Trend* survey in 1967 reported that nearly 40% of
marriage proposals in America take place in a car (Flink, *Automobile
Age* 162).

In *The Insolent Chariots* John Keats also writes about this love
story:

Once upon a time, the American met the automobile and fell in love.
Unfortunately, ... he did not live happily ever after.... [H]e
joyfully leaped upon her, and she responded to his caresses by
bolting about the landscape.... Quickly the automobile became a
nagging wife, demanding rubbings and shinings and gifts.... She
grew sow-fat ... and the fatter she grew, the greater her
demands.... (11-13)

With the inherent sexist imagery bracketed, Keats's metaphorical
romance serves well as a framework for this study.

First, I will set the stage for this courtship by examining the
literary groundwork for automobility prior to the automotive age:
America's enchantment with technology and the desire for individual
mobility. Next, following Flink's first stage, I will examine the
romance and marriage of the automobile and America: the nascent
automobile industry and the rapid development of a new category of
citizenry—the automobilist. Many works from this first period,
including numerous Broadway melodramas and romances like Sinclair
Lewis's *Free Air*, feature the automobile as a central romantic figure.
The innocent romance did not last long, however. Lewis himself, along
with Booth Tarkington and other writers, began to use the automobile
as a satirical embodiment of the conspicuous consumption of
America's growing bourgeoisie. At first a plaything for the rich, like
Fitzgerald's Gatsby, the car gradually became a liberator of the masses,
a common sight on every Main Street, and the mythic proportions of
Henry Ford are central in this evolution. Upton Sinclair's *The Flivver
King* and John Dos Passos's *U.S.A.* (and later E. L. Doctorow's
Ragtime), however, look beneath the veneer of Ford and his age to
expose the realities of mass production and assembly-line technology.

By the Thirties, the second stage, mass idolization, became
commonplace. The car had become essential to most Americans, like
Steinbeck's Joad family, and it had changed the face of the rural, and
particularly Southern, landscape, as evidenced in the works of Caldwell
and Faulkner. During this period the car became an increasingly
complex signifier in American fiction. Not satirized, not exalted, the
automobile in literature came to be the center of an intricate
relationship of attraction and repulsion. After World War II, idolization
continued as style reigned supreme, and autos resembled missiles and
airplanes, monstrous machines of chrome and steel. The automobile
also assumed a mythic prominence, as obviously evinced in Jack

Kerouac's cultic *On the Road*, but not so obviously, and not so favorably, in the works of his contemporary, Flannery O'Connor. In spite of such idolization, increasing decline occurred in the third stage of automotive development as the car's mid-life crisis set in. Escape became a central concern in many literary works. The social revolutions of the Sixties and Seventies continued to deflate the image of the great wheeled god, replacing it with an image of car as polluter and murderer—both a gradual destroyer of the environment and an instantaneous destroyer of lives, as seen vividly in the works of a number of African-American fiction writers: Bontemps, Wright, and Ellison, in particular. During these automotive divorce proceedings, Ralph Nader became a household name, as did the words *seat belt*, *catalytic converter*, *smog control*, and *unleaded gas*. Next, the petroleum crises of the 1970s brought American automotive giants to their knees as Americans literally ran out of gas. John Updike grasps these manifold changes perspicaciously in his Rabbit tetralogy.

The differing responses to automobility have never been so multifarious as in the present era. In the last decade of the century, Americans view the car with ambiguity and complexity, nostalgia and bad feeling, contemplating the difficult choice of reconciliation with the car or life without vehicles. Americans need the automobile, yet they are cognizant of the high cost of the relationship. Several contemporary works, such as Harry Crews's *Car* and Joy Williams's *Escapes*, present this paradoxical role automobility has assumed in our lives. And interestingly, women writers, such as Williams, Ann Beattie, and Louise Erdrich have seemingly superseded their male counterparts in recent years at foregrounding the car in their fiction.

Throughout the evolution of the automobile in American culture, novelists, playwrights, and poets have been at work. Some writers, such as Edith Wharton, cite the automobile as directly responsible for the creation of some of their works, *Ethan Frome* being one (Wharton, *Backward* 153-54). Others, such as Gertrude Stein, even used the auto as a site for composing their works. In *The Autobiography of Alice P. Toklas*, she writes:

> One cold dark afternoon she went out to sit with her ford car and
> while she sat on the steps of another battered ford watching her own
> being taken to pieces and put together again [by mechanics], she
> began to write. She stayed there several hours and when she came

back chilled, with the ford repaired, she had written the whole of Composition As Explanation. (286)

Few writers make the car the main focus of their work, as, for instance, Harry Crews does in *Car*; yet the automobile habitually surfaces in American literature. *Textual Vehicles* will thus foreground and scrutinize the presence of the automobile in the works of certain writers to see how the automobile is "driving" them. Would American literature be possible without these textual vehicles? Were the Italian Futurists correct in upholding the car as the modern artist's muse?

Unfortunately, I cannot discuss every textual vehicle in American literature in this study. Additional texts that I could have written about include William Carlos Williams's *The Great American Novel*, Larry McMurtry's *The Last Picture Show*, John Hawkes's *Second Skin*, Robert Penn Warren's *All the King's Men*, Steve Heller's *The Automotive History of Lucky Kellerman*, Thomas Pynchon's *V*, Paul Auster's *The Music of Chance*, and James Agee's *A Death in the Family*, to name only a few. But I have attempted to address a representative sampling of works that illustrate significant conclusions about the car's importance as a textual signifier in our national literature. Perusing the list of authors covered also leads one quickly to see that far more male writers than female have employed the auto as a device in their literary creations. Historically and mythically, the car has been seen as a male domain. The facts do not always support the myth, however. For example, while one myth perpetuated in our culture is that men make better drivers than women, since 1925, accident statistics and studies of drivers' habits show that female drivers in fact hold the advantage (Flink, *Automobile Age* 163). So why such myths?

Historian Clay McShane offers one opinion. In a chapter entitled "Gender Wars" from his book *Down the Asphalt Path*, he theorizes that the new organization of work dominated by the corporate and industrial models emerging at the turn of the century required men to create new institutions and models to salvage the traditional notions of masculinity that called for brute force or domination. Since maintaining an auto in the early days of motorcars did require considerable physical strength, men quickly began to see automobiling as inherently masculine. With the car, a man could be in control of a machine, the opposite of what he often experienced at work in an industrial job. Thus, the car became an important contributor to the psyche of male dominance (154-55). Cars themselves were thus often equated with the feminine. For example, an article in the *Daily Mail* of 6 Feb. 1908 declares that "the motor car, after woman, is the most fragile and capricious thing on earth" (Anderson 157). Articles with titles like "Why Women Are, or Are Not, Good Chauffeuses" (*Outing* 1904) were common place. These articles argued that women "suffer from natural impulsiveness and timidity, inability to concentrate and single-mindedness, indecisiveness and foolhardiness, weakness, and other estrangement from things mechanical" (Scharff 26).

McShane continues:

> Men defined driving in terms of values that they proclaimed as masculine. When men claimed mechanical ability as a gender trait, implicitly they excluded women from automobility. Men claimed that the key emotional traits needed to drive—steady nerves, aggression, and rationality—were masculine. . . . This process of coopting relevant physical and emotional traits was crucial to dominating the car culture. (156)

And since men also controlled the media, "newspapers, magazines, popular songs, and films customarily portrayed drivers as men and described drivers generically with masculine pronouns" (McShane 157). The sport of motor racing became the main arena through which the media focused on automobiling, and women were early on banned from competing with men. Some cities even considered banning women motorists altogether. Moreover, in the early years of automobiling, famous women motorists such as Emily Post, Edith Wharton, and Gertrude Stein were not emphasized in the popular media (McShane 157).

Not until the 1950s, when women began to enter the work force in greater numbers, but especially by the 1970s, when one of every two women was employed outside the home, did automobility begin to lose its gendered identity. Women began to hold positions of authority in the heretofore masculine car culture such that by 1978 Janet Guthrie was qualifying for the Indy 500. General Motors vice president John DeLorean cited as one of the reasons for his resignation in 1973: "The automobile industry has lost its masculinity" (Stern 108). Examining Volkswagen advertisements from 1963 and then 1977 demonstrates this profound change. In 1963, the ads show a picture of a VW and ask, "Do you have the right kind of wife for it?" But by 1977 a woman lying in front of a VW declares: "I bought a wagon out of wedlock." "I love my Dasher. Someday I may load it up with kids. For now, I love to load it up and take off" (Stern 110, 123).

Even with these cultural changes, women do continue to seem less serious about car culture and men more romantic. As Marshall McLuhan noted in 1964, a car seems to be part of a man's dress. Charles Sanford concurs, "And who but men have made cars over into art objects and converted many Sundays into an almost religious ceremony of 'polishing the car'?" ("Woman's" 143-45). Psychologist Jean Rosenbaum believes that many men identify with the car sexually. After an accident, "a crumpled fender affects them as if they have been castrated" (24). She adds that our society does not allow for discussion of the potency or size of the penis in public, so often "car chatter becomes a substitute," especially for adolescents. "Most girls do not understand the real meaning of car chatter and become exasperated" (11). Rosenbaum concludes that the car "has become the means by which man is able to actively express his wishes for power and mastery over nature" (6). Thus, for many men the automobile is a means through which they can transcend time and space.

In conclusion, whether one is male or female, Blaine Brownell argues that "the motor vehicle was a more impressive piece of machinery than a radio, more personal in its impact than a skyscraper or a dynamo, and certainly more tangible than electricity. Thus it was generally more legible as a symbol and more apparent in its consequences" (43). In *Mythologies* Roland Barthes contends about the symbolic value of objects that "Everything, then, can be a myth. . . . Every object in the world can pass from a closed, silent existence to an oral state open to appropriation by society" (109). Elsewhere he states that cars are "consumed in image if not in usage by a whole population which appropriated them as a purely magical object" (88). *Textual Vehicles* thus explores how this magical object—the automobile—has been appropriated into the mythos of American writing as a symbolic, metaphoric, hierophanic, structural, ironic, satiric, sexual, and even unconscious vehicle.

I

Romancing the Machine: America Courts the Auto

... the most important influence on civilization of all time ...
—James Rood Doolittle

Automobility Before the Automobile

Anyone whose perceptions of America were based on an overhead view of Los Angeles would have difficulty imagining America as it entered the last decade of the nineteenth century: no automobiles, no concrete highways, no gasoline stations. Horse and buggy were the most conspicuous sights of transportation. How then ten years later were automobiles proliferating, and twenty years later, commonplace? Though the gasoline-engine automobile had not appeared in America by 1890, American culture had in many ways prepared itself for the car, or rather, a large percentage of the population had. By 1805 Oliver Evans had built a steam-powered vehicle for the city of Philadelphia, and as early as 1825 the magazine *American Mechanics* was promoting the creation of road vehicles of all sorts (Anderson 25).

The concept of mobility is deep-rooted in the American psyche. The United States is a nation populated by movement: the immigration of Europeans, Latin Americans, and Asians and the forced dislocation of Africans. When European immigrants arrived on the eastern shore, they began a movement westward, first to the Mississippi and then to the Pacific. Now, many Americans move southward, away from cold climates or northward, up from their Hispanic roots. On any given day, a steady stream of U-Hauls crisscrosses America's interstates. As Phil

Patton observes in *Open Road: A Celebration of the American Highway*: "The automobile and its highways froze the values of the frontier by making movement a permanent state of mind, turning migration into circulation" (13). From observing this movement, we might conclude that most Americans seem to agree with Willie Nelson when he sings, "On the road again. I can't wait to get on the road again." Drake Hokanson, author of *The Lincoln Highway: Main Street Across America*, corroborates:

> In 1847 the South American statesman Domingo Faustino Sarmiento said, "If God were suddenly to call the world to judgement He would surprise two-thirds of the American population on the road like ants." Our national monuments have been the Conestoga wagon and the steam locomotive, the automobile and the airplane.... American icons of travel replaced the architectural wonders of our European roots. Instead of perfecting a national style of building, we perfected the engines of travel, the machines that nibbled at the frontier until we stood at the western sea. (31)

In addition to boasting of physical mobility, America also acclaims itself as a country of economic mobility, a nation of independent, self-made individualists—do-it-your-own-way-ers. Our poor public transportation system clearly represents this fact. Compared to other industrialized nations, public transit in the United States is pathetically inadequate, yet we commute more miles per person than the citizens of any other nation. This point emphasizes the fact that Americans seem to want to do "it" their own way, whatever "it" is. The automobile united this powerful proclivity toward individuality with the drive for movement by making Americans truly self-mobile—auto-mobile.

Even prior to the advent of the automobile, American literature acclaimed auto-mobility. Huck Finn, one of our archetypal literary heroes, proclaims he must "light out for the Territory"—alone. Emily Dickinson looks at a locomotive and likes "to see it lap the miles." Walt Whitman extols the virtues of "the open road." So how did the invention of the automobile alter this earlier idea of auto-mobility? First and foremost, the automobile is a machine, an invention resulting from "progress." "Walt Whitman said of a great locomotive careening across the landscape, the machine simply *was* the 'Type of the modern—emblem of motion and power—pulse of the continent'" (Marx, *Pilot* 186). Like the locomotive, the auto represented the ingenuity of modern humankind: the creation of a machine that could do the work of one of nature's transportational creations, such as the horse or the river. Yet unlike the locomotive, this machine could be owned, operated, and maintained by an individual. The bicycle could be as well, but it was not self-propelled. With the automobile, owners poured in a little gasoline, and Poof!—they were in motion. There was something almost magical about the auto's powers.

Advocates of progress saw the automobile as yet another step in the progressive evolution of modern life. As early as 1831, Timothy Walker's "Defence of Mechanical Philosophy" had exalted forms of progress which improve on nature's works: "Where she [Nature] denied us rivers, Mechanism has supplied them. Where she left our planet uncomfortably rough, Mechanism has applied the roller. Where her mountains have been found in the way, Mechanism had boldly leveled or cut through them. . . . As if her earth were not good enough for wheels, Mechanism travels upon iron pathways" (Marx, *Machine* 183). Henry Ford agreed with the argument established by Walker when he stated in *Today and Tomorrow* (1926): "The machine is the symbol of man's mastery of his environment" (167). To appropriate Leo Marx's terms, the automobile is a "machine in the garden" of America, a mechanism improving the natural order, which, according to Peter Marsh and Peter Collett, "allowed us to clothe ourselves in the apparel of the machine age" (27). What Marx concludes of the locomotive in his seminal study *The Machine in the Garden* could be applied equally as well to the automobile: "The new mechanical invention had the effect, as nothing else did, of certifying the reality of progress" (Marx, *Pilot* 185).

James Flink, one of the foremost historians of the automobile, asserts that the central positive value associated with automobility was "material prosperity and progress through unlimited production and consumption of consumer goods—and the fusing of rural and urban advantages in a suburban Utopia"—in essence, the bringing together of city and countryside (*Culture* 183). Elsewhere he maintains that the car was viewed as a solution to the major social problems of public health, urban crowding, and rural isolation: "The general adoption of the automobile becomes an important aspect of Progressive reform, one especially attractive to Americans because it did not involve collective political action. Automobility perfectly reconciled the contradictory impulses . . . to achieve a social order based upon technical efficiency

in which traditional cultural values would be preserved and enhanced" ("Three Stages" 457).
However, some did not see the automobile as this type of positive step forward. They saw it as a destroyer: noisy, fast, and dangerous. This polarity of beliefs echoes the dichotomous responses of American culture to many forms of technological change, a tension Marx elaborates on in his work. Late nineteenth-century society was divided between a positive progressivist view of change which "manifest itself in Manifest Destiny—millennial optimism of the country's geopolitical good fortune and pastoral dream of Golden Age state of harmony with nature" and a negative critique of science and technology, a "romantic-pastoral response to the alleged imperialism of instrumental rationality" (Marx, *Pilot* 186-87 & xvii).[1]

Some writers could embrace this attraction/repulsion toward the machine within one paragraph, illustrating Americans' paradoxical response to the automobile, like other similar technological machines. Writing in *Harper's* (Feb. 1902), Maurice Maeterlinck describes an automobile ride:

> The pace goes faster and faster; the delirious wheels send forth a shrill and eager cry. And at first the road comes moving towards me like a bride waving palms, rhythmically keeping time to some melody of gladness. But it soon grows frantic, springs forward, and throws itself madly upon me, rushing under the car like a furious torrent, whose foam dashes over my face; it drowns me beneath its waves; it blinds me with its breath. Oh, that wonderful breath!
> (Schneider, *Quotable* 7)

Is he excited by the vehicle? Terrified? Both?

Perhaps Henry Adams, better than any other writer, encapsulated the polarity between machine and nature through the tensions existing in his own beliefs concerning technological progress. Writing in 1900 Adams proclaimed that the automobile "had become a nightmare at a hundred kilometres an hour, almost as destructive as the electric tram which was ten years older; and threatening to become as terrible as the locomotive steam-engine itself." Yet simultaneously he exalts another machine, the dynamo, as a virtue of progress:

> [T]o Adams the dynamo became the symbol of infinity. . . . [H]e began to feel the forty-foot dynamos as a moral force, much as the

early Christians felt the Cross. The planet itself seemed less impressive, in its old-fashioned, deliberate, annual, or daily revolution, than this huge wheel, revolving within arms'-length at some vertiginous speed, and barely murmuring.... (380)

What seems clear, in spite of his reservations, is Adams's sense of fascination, his desire to experience this new phenomenon of power.[2] Adams is prepared to absorb the dynamo into the dimension of his own spiritual psyche. Later in his essay, Adams comments on how this acceptance is characteristically American:

> When Adams was a boy in Boston, the best chemist in the place had probably never heard of Venus except by way of scandal, or of the Virgin except as idolatry; neither had he heard of dynamos or automobiles; yet his mind was ready to feel the force of it all.... The force of the Virgin was still felt at Lourdes, and seemed to be as potent as X-rays; but in America neither Venus nor the Virgin ever had value as force—at most as sentiment. No American had ever been truly afraid of either. (383)[3]

Adams's observations corroborate with those of Mark Foster, who professes somewhat less elaborately: "Many consumers were simply fascinated with the mechanical appeal of the motor vehicle" ("The Automobile and the City" 25).

Not only had most Americans come not to fear the forces behind the automotive machine, they had actually begun to embrace the industrial apparati of automotive production: mass production and standardization. By the turn of the century, "Machine fabrication of standardized parts was generally referred to as the 'American system of manufacturing'" (Rae 55). However, according to Warren Belasco, early car manufacturing ironically was not viewed as a form of industrial capitalism but as a process of creating a nostalgic mobility which could deliver people from the modern city. Car manufacturing was thus perceived as much more humane than a foundry or sweatshop. In "Commercialized Nostalgia" he argues that the strangest irony surrounding car culture is perhaps that "early on, the automobile industry became the backbone of modern industrial capitalism, yet it was born in a spirit of rebellion against that system" (108).

This system affected not only automobile manufacture but literary output as well, and the poetry of Walt Whitman serves as a prime example of literature conceived of structurally in terms of machine manufacture. Whitman, who died in 1892 at the onset of the automobile age, promoted the literary and aesthetic benefits of the American system of manufacturing in many of the poems in *Leaves of Grass*. In "Starting from Paumanok" he writes:

> I will make the poems of materials, for I think they are to be the
>   most spiritual poems.
> . . . .
> I will not make poems with reference to parts,
> But I will make poems, songs, thoughts, with reference to
>   ensemble . . . . (ll. 71, 172-73)

He continues this tribute to manufacturing in "Song of the Exposition": "Mark the spirit of invention everywhere, thy rapid patents, / Thy continual workshops, foundries, risen or rising" (ll. 195-96). Whitman's analysis of the poetic process—the assemblage of material parts—clearly prefigures and parallels that of automotive manufacturing.

Whitman's connection to automobility is apparently obvious to other writers. Though Whitman never drove an automobile himself, D. H. Lawrence uses automotive metaphors abundantly in his assessment of the poet:

> He drove an automobile with a very fierce headlight, along the track of a fixed idea, through the darkness of this world. And he saw everything that way. Just as a motorist does in the night. . . . ONE DIRECTION! toots Walt in the car, whizzing along it. . . . ONE DIRECTION! whoops America, and sets off also in an automobile. . . . ONE IDENTITY! chants democratic En Masse, pelting behind in motor-cars, oblivious of the corpses under the wheels. God save me, I feel like creeping down a rabbit-hole, to get away from all these automobiles rushing down the ONE IDENTITY track to the goal of ALLNESS. (167)

In addition, according to many scholars, the ideas of the Italian Futurists, who exalted the automobile as the new muse of art, can be traced to the artistic concepts of Whitman. Gerald Silk comments: "The Italian Futurists admired Whitman, and many modernist painters of the urban scene . . . were deeply moved by Whitman's verse" (101). Rosa

Clough agrees that "much of Futurism dated back to Whitman" (34). Perhaps the clearest linkage between the poet and automobility can be found in the naming of the Walt Whitman Rest Area on the Jersey Turnpike. Both in American society and literature, the stage was set for the automobile's arrival. The central concepts of automobility were deep-rooted in the American psyche and also visible in American literature; however, as Adams attests, the acceptance of mechanical automobility was not without tension. Kenneth Schneider encapsulates this tension in *Autokind vs. Mankind*: "Progress of the automobile is thus pockmarked with ironies: its evolution from a romantic toy into a despotic necessity; its ability to grow upon its destructiveness as well as its contributions to society" (143). As Leo Marx explores in *The Machine in the Garden*, the history of the machine in America is a history replete with romance and disillusionment, filled with tensions among desire, necessity, repulsion, and indulgence. The history of the automobile, like the history of other technological achievements in America, mirrors these tensions. Not surprisingly, the history of the automobile in American literature reflects these concerns as well.

The Automobile Age Arrives

Though resistance to technological change has frequently manifested itself as American society has developed, the growth of automobility has tended to be readily accepted, and even eagerly desired. As automobiles became commonplace and then superabundant, they were quickly adopted and adapted by various segments of society, and a brief history of the dispersion of the automobile in America can serve as background for the arrival of the auto on America's stages and into its fiction.[4]

One of the earliest American inventors focusing on the problem of self-propelled transportation was Oliver Evans, who in 1787 obtained a patent from the state of Maryland for the rights to operate a steam-powered vehicle on public roads. His creation in 1805 for the city of Philadelphia, the "Orukter Amphibolos" (Amphibious Digger), attracted large crowds as it moved through the city's streets. Evans proved unsuccessful though in his attempts to start a steam-powered wagon company; most people felt the vehicle too cumbersome for the existing Pennsylvania turnpikes.

Seeds for automobility were also deeply sown in the railroad and bicycle industries. The railroads opened up long-distance travel but operated on fixed schedules (often very inconvenient) and went only to certain towns and cities; thus many people ultimately became dissatisfied with rail service. In spite of dissatisfaction over long-distance rail service, local rail lines in the form of electric streetcars grew to be prevalent by the turn of the century. Street-car lines provided transportation to and from work, thereby making it possible to live farther from the workplace and laying the groundwork for the expansion of suburbia. However, according to Mark Foster, many street-car operators abused both clientele and employees through exorbitant fares, low wages, and hazardous conditions. Accidents and graft were equally common, so eventually reformers led politicians to turn against the street-car companies (27).

The introduction of the safety bicycle in 1885 led to a proliferation of individual transportation affordable to nearly all social classes. Many early American automobile builders, including the Duryeas, were first bicycle manufacturers. Pedaling a bicycle over rough terrain or through the mud was nearly impossible, and as a result, a demand for good roads grew. This desire for roads cultivated the initial consciousness later necessary to undertake the expansive project of building a vast network of paved roads for the automobile, and the construction of these roads subsequently strengthened the escalation of the automobile in this country.

The desire for a self-propelled vehicle, however, was certainly not an exclusively American phenomenon. Literature from the Chou Dynasty proclaims that the Chinese invented a self-propelled vehicle 3000 years ago. (Roger Bacon's translations of these texts into Latin in 1270 precipitated his being imprisoned for fourteen years) (Marsh 1). On a more documentable level, Europeans were roughly a decade ahead of their American counterparts in the field of automotive engineering. Belgian Etienne Lenoir built the first commercially successful two-cycle internal combustion engine in France in 1860, although Stuart Perry of New York had patented, but not built, a model in 1844. Nicolaus Otto's introduction of the four-cycle version in Germany in 1876 was a significant step toward the modern automobile. In 1885 Gottlieb Daimler along with his assistant Wilhelm Maybach modified the four-cycle engine and built the first of four experimental motor cars. German Carl Benz followed with the first commercially successful cars in the early 1890s, a majority of them sold in France. By the mid-1890s automobiles were a common sight on the streets of Paris. In France and Germany, as in America, the development of steam-powered vehicles preceded that of internal combustion ones. The Stanley Steamer, which went into production in 1897, is perhaps the best known of such vehicles in the U.S. Steam engines were dangerous, however. Serious burns and sometimes death occurred when a boiler exploded or leaked. Electric cars also appeared with regularity in the formative years of the auto. William Morrison of Des Moines built an electric vehicle in 1891, and electric cabs built by the Electric Carriage and Wagon Company were experimented with on the streets of New York City. Ultimately, the difficulties of battery charging and size and the inadequacies of storage cells led to the early demise of this form of vehicle (however, in 1990 General Motors once more announced plans to mass produce a battery-powered vehicle).

Although some importation occurred, the United States's automobile industry matured mostly on its own. A laissez-faire governmental attitude encouraged experimentation and development of early automobiles. This attitude clearly contrasted with that of England, whose notorious Red Flag Act, stipulating that a motorized vehicle be preceded by a walking bearer of a red flag, impeded the development of an automobile industry there.

The Duryeas are generally credited as having perfected the first internal-combustion automobile in America in 1893, although less-successful gasoline models had been built before the Duryeas': in 1889 by Henry Nadig of Allentown, in 1890 by Gottfried Schloemer in Milwaukee, and in 1891 by Charles Black of Indianapolis (A. Rose 75). By 1896 Ransom Olds, Alexander Winton, and Henry Ford had all built vehicles, at least eight automobile companies had been formed, and Frank Duryea had sold his first vehicle and built a dozen more. Ohio, Indiana, and Michigan, already centers of carriage production and of manufacture of engines used on mid-western farms, also became the centers of U.S. automobile production. By 1904 French automobile production fell second to American companies, and prior to World War I the U.S. overwhelmingly outproduced all the Europeans combined. The abundant resources of the United States and its lack of interstate tariffs made possible such wide-spread rapid expansion of the industry so that by 1916 James Doolittle could boast about American automotive achievements that "the automobile, Father of the Locomotive; the greatest and most insistent producer of Good Roads; the only improvement in road transportation since Moses, and the most important influence on civilization of all time, has flowered and fruited on American soil" (ix).

By the turn of the century, a major portion of the public foresaw the complete replacement of the horse and buggy. Though cries of "Get a horse!" descended upon motorists who found themselves in mechanical difficulty, the echoes of such cries were short-lived because by 1910 over 458,000 automobiles had been registered in the U.S. Early on, only the wealthy were the buyers. Physicians in particular led the way in purchases, and the automobile contributed to revolutionizing home health care. The motor car made it possible for the local doctor to respond quickly to emergencies and to see many people in a relatively short time, despite inclemency, a frequent detractor to health care in the horse-and-buggy days.

Because of declining production costs, cars soon became attractive to the masses, as evidenced by the proliferation of automotive journals: *Motocycle* and *Horseless Age* (1895), *Cycle and Automobile Trade Journal* (1897), *Automobile* (1899), *Motor Age* (1899), *Motor World* (1900), and *Motor* (1903). Newspaper articles on automobiles proliferated, and newspapers themselves supported the industry; for instance, the *Chicago Times-Herald* race on Thanksgiving Day 1895 did much to promote the growing interest in automobility. Tens of thousands came to the first National Automobile Show at Madison Square Garden in 1900, and the press gave a great deal of publicity to the introduction of new vehicle makes.

Perhaps cross-country tours received the most publicity of all. Alexander Winton's highly publicized seventy-nine-hour drive from Cleveland to New York in 1897 was one of the first such stunts. Track races, too, were important for proving new technologies, but they did not capture the attention of the general public nearly so much as the long journey. Roy D. Chapin's trek from the Oldsmobile plant in Detroit to the New York auto show in a new curved-dash Oldsmobile led to record sales of 1500 vehicles for his relatively inexpensively priced car ($650) which became immortalized in the hit song, "My Merry Oldsmobile." The first successful transcontinental journey is credited to Dr. H. Nelson Jackson of Burlington, Vermont, and his chauffeur, Sewall K. Crocker, who traveled from San Francisco to New York in sixty-three days in 1903, a remarkable achievement considering the poor condition (or the non-existence) of the roads over a great portion of the western part of their trip. The Glidden Tours, sponsored by millionaire Charles Glidden, soon followed. From 1905-13 these distance tours demonstrated the reliability of the car and enhanced its romantic image.

The Car Comes to Broadway

Before long the car made it to the Great White Way. Not only were automobiles seen parked on the streets of Broadway, they were starring on the boards of its theatres as well. A host of Broadway shows featured automobiles; the following are a representative sample: Elmer Vance's *Patent Applied For* (1893), Richard Carroll and William Parry's *Very Little Faust and Much Marguerite* (in which Faust carries off the innocent Marguerite in a taxi-cab) (1897), Clyde Fitch's *The Way of the World* (1901), Theodore Kremer's *The Great Automobile Mystery* (starring John Barrymore) (1904), A. N. and C. N. Williamson's *The Lightning Conductor* (1905), Shaw's *Man and Superman* (1905, New York opening), Lincoln Carter's *Bedford's Hope* (1906), Booth Tarkington and Harry Leon Wilson's *The Man from Home* (1908), Stanislaus Stange's *The Girl in the Taxi* (1910), William Anthony McGuire's *Six Cylinder Love* (1921), and Owen Davis's *The Nervous Wreck* (1921). *The Auto Race* (1907) had twenty-one autos on stage at once. *The Vanderbilt Cup* (1906) had an on-stage automobile race, and *Bedford's Hope* featured a race between car and train. The 1905-06 season alone had eleven plays which featured cars, prompting the *New York World* to proclaim: "It is the auto's day on the stage. No horse need apply." In addition to *Man and Superman* and *Bedford's Hope*, the season featured *The Triumph of Betty*, *Miss Dolly Dollars*, *John Bull's Other Island*, *Motoring*, *The Earl and the Girl*, *The Babes and the Baron*, *The Vanderbilt Cup*, *The Fascinating Mr. Vanderveldt*, and *Der Kilometerfesser* (Anderson 240-72).

As can be deduced from these plays' titles, most were melodramatic pieces starring good guys, bad guys, and gorgeous girls. On occasion the car itself proved to be the evil villain. A *New York Sun* article from 12 December 1904 declares: "There is a new villain in town—a new stage villain, one guilty of infamy and then sliding up on the lowlands of high society again without wrenching a sprocket" (Anderson 247). Not only were automobiles acting, actors were automobiling. Magazines published pictures of stars in their cars. Seeing celebrities motoring about romanticized the car even more in the eyes of the average American (a romanticization which continues even today. Actors Paul Newman and Tom Cruise, part-time race-car drivers, are good examples).

Sinclair Lewis and America's Marriage to the Automobile

As with drama, the earliest fiction featuring automobiles was predominantly romantic and melodramatic, and the early works of Sinclair Lewis insightfully demonstrate this brand of romanticized automobility. In particular, his *Free Air* and "Speed" fit into this pattern, and they also provide additional insight into the rapid cultural changes brought on by automobility as well as the growing tensions created by automobiles in American society once the honeymoon of the motor age began to fade.

Prior to Lewis, American adolescents could read the serialized adventures of the Motor Boys, who, starting in their first book in 1906, traveled across the country solving mysteries and encountering numerous thrilling adventures (Vaughan 74). Many well-known writers had also been fascinated with the automobile. Emily Post drove coast to coast and published the story of her tour under the title, *By Motor to the Golden Gate* (1916). Accompanied by illustrator Franklin Booth and a chauffeur only known as "Speed," Theodore Dreiser made an automobile pilgrimage from New York through Pennsylvania to the Great Lakes and Cleveland, then back down to his hometown of Terre Haute, Indiana. In what historian Douglas Brinkley calls the first American road novel, *A Hoosier Holiday* (1916) presents Dreiser's collected reflections of the journey (4).

Already by the mid-Teens, hordes of Americans had joined Dreiser in hitting the highways and crowding the inconsiderable amount of decent roads that had been built. Dreiser bemoans these throngs:

> But this Hudson-Albany-State-road route irritated me from the very
> first. Everyone traveling in an automobile seemed inclined to travel
> that way. I had a vision of thousands of cars we would have to
> trail. . . . Give me the poor, undernourished routes which the dull,

imitative, rabble shun, and where, because of this very fact, you have some peace and quiet. (21)

In his history of the Lincoln Highway, Drake Hokanson substantiates Dreiser's impression of the effusion of automobile travel:

> In post-World War I America, the notion of automobile touring conquered the nation's imagination. Automobile and auto touring periodicals . . . were full of . . . stories of daring journeys to new, ever more remote places, and encouragement about how easy or cheap or fun it was to climb into your own car and go where fancy may take you. The lure of distant places always had been strong . . . but opportunity for travel heretofore had been limited to the rich. (85)

According to Hokanson, the automobile became "the newest outlet for a national wanderlust" (31).

No writer encompassed this sense of wanderlust as did Sinclair Lewis. In her autobiography, Lewis's wife Grace wrote concerning her husband's first automobile:

> There were to be many thrilling occasions in the life of Sinclair Lewis—seeing an entire bookseller's window on Fifth Avenue devoted to *Main Street*, receiving the Nobel Prize from a king—but it's a safe guess that neither topped that moment when he stopped the Ford [his first car] neatly in front of the old stone carriage step and called out to his father and mother and me sitting on the porch after supper: "How about a ride?" . . . Story-writing was one thing but owning and driving a car was another. (98)

Few things excited Lewis as much as the automobile. He was caught up in the fever of automobility that raged in the early part of the twentieth century, and his early works not only display his excitement over motor transport, they also serve as historical and cultural documents providing valuable insight into the ascent of the automobile age.

As early as his second novel, *The Trail of the Hawk* (1915), Lewis created a character, Carl Ericson, who designs and produces cars for the Van-Zile Motor Corporation. One of his inventions is the Touricar, a vehicle especially designed for auto touring. Though without a Touricar in real life, the Lewises followed the automobile tourism craze of the day and undertook a cross-country trip in 1916, navigating for four months from Sauk Centre, Minnesota, through Seattle to San Francisco. Mrs. Lewis wrote:

> The Lincoln Highway was often only two grooves in a Dakota wheat field, mud holes were frequent. . . . It was foolish to plan a long-distance journey by car unless you took along a shovel, an ax, a steel cable, extra gasoline, water for a boiling radiator, spare tires, and a lantern. . . . The hardships of the journey and the wonder of it were to . . . provide an imperishable background for all his work to come. (99-100)

The experience of the Lewises formed the basis for one of Lewis's earliest novels, *Free Air* (1919), which appeared first as a *Saturday Evening Post* serial.[5]

Free Air

The novel opens as "Miss Boltwood of Brooklyn Is Lost in the Mud," clearly an echo of the comments Mrs. Lewis made concerning her own arduous trip. As writer Edith Wharton recounted in her autobiography, "In those epic days roads and motors were an equally unknown quantity, and one set out on a ten-mile run with more apprehension than one would now attend a journey across Africa" (153). In his history of the National Road (1948) Philip Jordan addressed the difficulties of the pioneer automobile tourist, who

> setting out in his topless, high-wheeled, chain-driven car, gripped the steering lever savagely and braced himself against a curved dashboard. . . . Pitting his driving skill against washed-out roads, chuckholes and boulders, the motorist also gambled that his gears would not strip or the rear end fall out before he reached his destination. A tool kit came with every car. . . . "Get out and get under" was the motorist's motto. (382)

Free Air captures this ruggedly romantic spirit of motoring during the age as it tells of the blooming romance between debutante Claire Boltwood and poor Milton Daggett, a romance which begins with Claire traveling with her wealthy father cross-country by car. Along the way the Boltwoods encounter Daggett, a young mechanic who dreams of becoming an engineer. He falls madly for Claire and follows the Boltwoods across the country, rescuing them from many dangers: roadside desperadoes, con artists, mechanical breakdowns, wild bears, and so forth. In Seattle, Milt enrolls in the university and Claire socializes. Eventually, after a great deal of posturing, the two declare their love for each other and decide to get married.

Though *Free Air* is for the most part a melodramatic romance, the novel provides an excellent view of the status of the automobile in the changing times of the early twentieth century and reflects the growing cultural importance of automobility. It illustrates the exaltation of the car over the train as the public's preferred mode of transport and the sense that the car afforded a return to nature, to health and prosperity. It portrays the extremes of motoring during the age, from the limousines of New York's parkways to the jalopies of mid-western farm roads; and through Claire, it also depicts the changing role of women in society. Thus, it serves to exemplify the role of the automobile in early twentieth-century literature.

A decade before Lewis's romance, *Bedford's Hope* had already dramatically demonstrated the car's rapid replacement of the railroad as the premier method of travel in this country. The climax of Lincoln Carter's drama comes as a racing automobile carrying the play's hero overtakes a train which houses the play's villain. This dramatic scene accentuates the historical shift in transportation from train to car—a fact ironically conveyed also in Lewis's character Henry B. Boltwood. Boltwood is taking time off from his position as vice president of a railroad company to travel, but he is doing so by car, not by train. A related irony appears in an early 1920s' ad for Chevrolet which heralds: "Every owner is in effect a railroad president, operating individually on an elective schedule, over highways built and maintained chiefly at the expense of himself and his fellow motorists!" (Stern 21).

By far, the accentuation of the automobile at the expense of the railroad is conveyed most explicitly in *Free Air* when Claire abandons her automobile tour to take a train. The negative image of the train appears lucidly in Lewis's hellish description of the railway station: "She stood in that cold, swaying, darkling place that was filled with the smell of rubber and metal and grease and the thunderous clash of steel on steel" (243-44). This depiction markedly contrasts with Lewis's endearing descriptions of automobiles: "[S]he thought of the Teal bug as a human thing—as her old friend, to which she had often turned in need" (221).

Others also viewed the automobile as a relief from the evils of trains and train travel. Warren Belasco writes:

> The train, not the car, represented Modern Times: ruthlessly efficient, fast-paced, impersonal, insulated, indifferent to personal schedules and needs. Motoring, on the other hand, seemed more like stage-coach travel: slow, arduous, close to nature, more "intimate." In entering cities trains usually passed through factory and slum districts—ugly reminders of the industrial present. Motorists, however, could enter by imposing avenues . . . or they could avoid big cities altogether and stick to pastoral countryside and picturesque hamlets. (*Americans* 109)

In concert with Belasco's contention, Lewis's automobiles are humanistically personified, natural even, whereas the train is depersonalized, cold, detached, and mechanical.

Dreiser prophetically concurs with this view of trains and cars in *A Hoosier Holiday*:

> [I]t wouldn't surprise me in the least if the automobile, as it is being perfected now, would make over the whole world's railway systems into something very different from what they are today. Already the railways are complaining that the automobile is seriously injuring business, and this is not difficult to understand. It ought to be so. At best the railroads have become huge, clumsy, unwieldy affairs little suited to the temperamental needs and moods of the average human being. . . . Think what you have to endure on the ordinary railroad . . . smoke, dust, cinders, noise, the hurrying. . . . [O]ur huge railways . . . are a nuisance. (92)

Other writers of the day concurred with this view of the unwieldy railroad. The image of the train which Emily Dickinson liked to see "lap the miles" was replaced by an image conveyed in Frank Norris's *The Octopus*, for example, where the train is a death machine which slaughters helpless lambs who stray into its path.

Ironically, though a machine itself, the automobile was seen as pastoral, as a move back to nature. Henry Ford saw the car as a means to enjoy "the blessings of hours of pleasure in God's great open

Spaces" (Nash 158). Herbert Ladd Towle exclaimed in *Scribner's Magazine* (1913): "Greater fruitfulness of time and effort, brighter glimpses of the wide and beautiful world, more health and happiness— these are the lasting benefits of the motor car. . . . We shall thank God that we live in the Motor-Car era" (Schneider, *Autokind* 29). One reason Claire and her father take the trip is for Mr. Boltwood's health and happiness. While the healing powers of such an arduous excursion might be questioned, most health professionals of the day saw the automobile drive as an expedition into the beneficial air of the outdoors, a positive stride toward well-being, and they published pamphlets listing the healthy possibilities afforded through car travel. The Health Commissioner of New York City contended: "Not only does the driver get the full benefit of open road and fresh air, but he gets actual physical exercise in a form best calculated to repair the damages wrought on by our modern existence" (Berger 178). In 1914 an anonymous writer proclaimed: "I do not know of a surer antidote for the nervousness and unrest with which so many modern men are afflicted than the new interest, the enthusiasm, and the hours in the open which are the experience of every automobile owner" (Schneider, *Autokind* 29).

The automobile provided benefits in addition to the advantages of being outdoors. Although speed at first was thought to be a danger to the human system, members of the scientific and medical communities came to consider the sensation of speed to be therapeutic. In fact, speed came to be regarded as a necessity to health and, particularly, success. James Doolittle avowed in 1916:

> Speed is one of the most important factors in the development of humanity. It is becoming more and more important with each progressive step in the life of the world. . . . Nothing more flagrantly false was ever said than that speed is inherently bad. Speed is the difference between doing and not doing. Speed is the measure of efficiency. Speed marks the line between misery and well-being—the difference between civilization of today and the benighted squalor of the Dark Ages. (317, 319)

Automobile advertising also upheld the virtues of speed. A Chevrolet ad from 1924 depicts the blur of passing cars as a man on the street "watches others go by." The caption reads: "If you can move your person twice as fast and apply your personality in twice as many places as some other chap, your chances for success are twice as good as his.... Speed up success! ... Enter the great race against Time!" (Stern 20). A fictional advertisement written by one of Lewis's own characters in *Babbitt* (1922) heralds Zecco cars by proclaiming: "The long white trail is calling—calling—and it's over the hills and far away for every man or woman that has red blood in his veins.... Speed— glorious Speed—it's more than just a moment's exhilaration—it's Life for you and me!" (101). In this ad, speed embodies life itself. Speed was unquestionably the new virtue of the culture.

That Claire drives the car in *Free Air* illustrates yet another facet of the transforming culture, the changing roles of women (though just how respectable it was for a lady to be knee-deep in mud pushing the rear axle of a car is questioned in the chapter entitled "Claire Escapes from Respectability"). Claire's need for daring is summarized in this passage: "She discovered that she again longed to ... conquer new roads. She didn't want all good road. She wanted something to struggle against" (45). Claire desires challenge, so she ultimately chooses the free spirit of Milt and the open road over the confines of high society: "In the Gilsons' huge cars she had been shut off from the road, but in this tiny bug, so close to the earth, she recovered the feeling of style, of triumph over difficulties, of freedom unbounded" (265). Appropriately, Milt and Claire agree to marry, not in the parlor, but while riding in Milt's tiny bug.

Women therefore made significant strides toward freedom thanks to the car. That a woman no less mannered than Emily Post could write about her cross-country travels in *By Motor to the Golden Gate* illustrates this fact well. In 1908 Edith Wharton had published *A Motor-Flight through France*, a travel narrative of her European automotive journeys. The impact of the car on Wharton's life is clearly evidenced in the title of her autobiography, *A Backward Glance*, a reference to a quote from Walt Whitman: "A backward glance o'er travell'd roads." Books such as Ethellyn Gardner's *Letters of the Motor Girl* and Dorothy Levitt's *The Woman and the Car: A Chatty Little Handbook for All Women Who Motor or Who Want to Motor* (1909) publicized the increasing affinity between women and cars. Levitt contended that "Motoring is a pastime for women.... There are many pleasures in being whirled around the country by your friends and relatives, or in a car driven by your chauffeur; but the real, the intense pleasure, the actual realisation of the pastime comes only when you drive your own car" (15-16). An article in *Motor* from 1904 offered that a woman driver would gain "absolute confidence in herself" (Scharff 27). Automobile manufacturers, such as Oldsmobile, began advertising specifically for female customers. The Olds is the "ideal vehicle for shopping and calling," a 1903 ad proclaimed. The spirit of Claire and the new woman is clearly reflected in a famous 1923 automobile advertisement for the Jordan Playboy, an ad which captures the ever-changing image of a woman behind the wheel:

> Somewhere west of Laramie there's a broncho-busting, steer-roping girl who knows what I'm talking about. She can tell what a sassy pony, that's a cross between greased lightning and the place where it hits, can do with eleven hundred pounds of steel and action . . . . [T]he Playboy was built for her. . . . She loves the cross of the wild and the tame. (Anderson 293)

A Ford ad from 1924 states beneath the drawing of a businesswoman: "The car enables her to conserve minutes, to expedite her affairs, to widen the scope of her activities" (Stern 18). Ford even published a pamphlet, "The Woman and the Ford," asserting that the driving woman was "no longer a shut-in." She "reaches for an even wider sphere of action." The car "has broadened her horizon—increased her pleasures—given new vigor to her body . . . . It is a real weapon in the changing order" (Scharff 53-4).

A new catchword—the Automobile Girl—came into fashion. Songs and poems were written about these daring driving women. *Leslie's Weekly* versified the Automobile Girl as

> Like the breeze in its flight, or the passage of light,
> Or swift as the fall of a star,
> She comes and she goes in a nimbus of dust,
> A goddess enthroned on a car.
> The maid of the motor, behold her erect
> With muscles as steady as steel,
> Her hand on the lever and always in front,
> The girl in the automobile. (Anderson 198)

Though no Marianne Moore, the poet of "The Automobile Girl" describes the freedom and sense of responsibility the car afforded women of the day. It enabled them to get away from the confines of home, to widen their spheres of contact, and even to dress differently. As Levitt's book proclaims, "The all-important question is dress" (23). The formality and cumbersome nature of Victorian dress ill-suited the mud and dust of the open road; the corset proved poor attire for "getting out and under." Claire, though far from being a liberated woman in the now-current sense, nevertheless, used the automobile to loosen the corset of societal restraint and to facilitate her own freedom from cultural constraints.

The automobile culture of the 1910s was also marked by extreme contrast, as illustrated both in the automobile culture of the wealthy versus that of the general population and by the conditions of driving on the open road versus those of the urban street. Cars of the wealthy and those of the masses were clearly distinct, as envisioned in the differences between, for instance, a Duesenberg and a Model T. The power and wealth suggested by the Boltwood's fictional automobile, a Gomez-Deperdussin, clearly contrasts with the economy intimated by Milton's little Teal bug. Fine cars were assets of the wealthy. Marsh and Collett point out that "the image of the pioneer motorist consisted of two essential symbols: wealth and speed" (29). Boltwood owns two cars: one, a limousine, suggests wealth, and the other, the Gomez roadster, symbolizes speed and power. Money could even buy a motorist the appearance of ruggedness: "Open runabouts allowed the early motorists to present themselves as wild desperadoes. . . . [T]he man at the wheel was instantly recognized as a wealthy daredevil" (Marsh 30). Jeff Saxton, Claire's rich New York beau, serves as a good example of someone attempting to buy such an image. He drives a sporty runabout to suggest a daredevil attitude.

At one point in the novel, the Boltwoods encounter a real daredevil desperado who attempts to hijack their car. This desperado conforms well with the rugged, mud-filled roads of the West which the Boltwoods confront. These roads definitely contract to the accustomed "polite experience" (3) of the Boltwood's Long Island parkways and additionally illustrate the disparity between rural and urban driving. Outside of metropolitan areas, road conditions were often quite bad. Local farmers frequently contributed to poor road conditions by digging ruts and making mud holes in the roads adjacent to their property. By doing so they were able to prey on unsuspecting tourists who strayed into their traps and needed help getting out, help most often contracted at a ridiculous fee. When we first meet Milt, he springs the Boltwoods from the clutches of one such set of profiteers.

Not only does *Free Air* provide an excellent view of the place of automobility in the transforming culture of early twentieth-century society, the novel illustrates the role of the car in literature during the period as well. Lewis situates the automobile as a central figure in the novel, which indicates his sense of the literary merit of the car, and his characters read the poetry of Vachel Lindsay, a writer who exalted automobility even before Lewis. At one point in the novel, Milt reads from one of Lindsay's poems, "The Sante-Fe Trail," a "humoresque" which lauds the expansion of automobile consciousness in twentieth-century America. Lindsay's verse proclaims:

> Swiftly the brazen car comes on.
> It burns in the East as the sunrise burns.
> I see great flashes where the far trail turns.
> Its eyes are lamps like the eyes of dragons.
> It drinks gasoline from big red flagons. . . .
> It comes like hail, goes past roaring.
>
> . . . .
> While I sit by the milestone
> And watch the sky,
> The United States
> Goes by. (153, 155)

In Lindsay's poem, as in Lewis's novel, the development of the automobile as both a cultural icon and a literary device is clearly evident. In the poem, the automobile has replaced the horse on the Sante Fe trail. Just as the car has now entered into the myth of the American West, it is also associated with another legend—an Arthurian one. The car's headlights are like dragons, and it drinks from flagons. Those who drive automobiles are thus new knights of armor. In *Understanding Media* Marshall McLuhan explains how "the car gave to the democratic cavalier his horse and armor and haughty insolence in one package, transmogrifying the knight into a misguided missile" (223).

Though Milt may not be a "misguided missile," he nonetheless possesses virtues of the cavalier. His chivalric saving of the Boltwoods from the unscrupulous ditch diggers is but the first in a chain of ordeals undertaken in his quest for the exceptional Claire, and his actions illustrate the most common use for the automobile in the literature of the Teens—romance. Julian Pettifer and Nigel Turner comment on cinematic uses of this common device: "Time and again in early films, young men demonstrate their adaptability, virility, even superiority, by utilizing the motor car—the new technology—to capture the heart of beautiful heroines ..." (247). The automobile was changing the methodology of romance. *Free Air* reflects this trend, which surfaces in many fictional automobile romances of the period. Rudolph Anderson indicates that the earliest automobile romance in print may have been "How Cupid Stole An Auto," published in the August 1900 issue of *Automobile Magazine* (199). Nonetheless, the plots of all these stories resemble that of *Free Air*, which itself derives from even earlier automobile romance fiction, such as "The Wonderful Monster," a serial published by William Randolph Hearst in 1905, or Edward Field's *A Six-Cylinder Courtship* (1907), one of the earliest novels to feature cars. Field's novel has all the scenes of a contemporary Hollywood hit: a "follow-that-cab" chase, an encounter with the police, a fiery accident, and, of course, sexual attraction. The connections with movieland are not surprising to note considering the simultaneous emergence and rise of the motion picture and automobile industries, and early movies frequently located derring-do or romantic interludes in cars.[6]

A Six-Cylinder Courtship

A Six-Cylinder Courtship begins with William Snowden, Esq., mistaken for a driver by the beautiful Marian Standish, with whom he falls in love. Going by the name of Bill Snow, he serves as her driver until an incident with a stolen car reveals his true identity. Then, like Milt and Claire, after the appropriate squabbles, the couple embrace. From Snowden, the reader observes the culture's veneration of the automobile; however, one might wonder which Snowden venerates higher; car or lady?

> I tell you, it makes a fellow's blood tingle to look at a car like mine, and feel that it belongs to him; a car that will start on the direct drive, a car that will race a railroad train or jog contentedly behind a milk cart, a car that can make a steep hill ashamed of itself; a wild, dashing car that eats up the miles; a faithful, sweet-running car that purrs like a pussy-cat! To own such a car is to own a kingdom; the driver's seat is a throne, the steering-wheel a scepter, miles are your minions and distance your slave. (35-6)

Field's story of the woman who falls for her driver was fairly common, in actuality as well as in fiction. Professor Emil Dietrich declared after studying this phenomenon that a chauffeur "is so taciturn, so reckless, so skillful that the girl begins to admire him. He is a brief, daring, wooer.... He is so mysteriously masterful, so masterfully defiant of the law that he becomes a picturesque, romantic figure to a girl satiated with the ordinary man" (Anderson 201-02). The word *chauffeur* is derived from a French verb meaning "to heat" or "to stoke up." Colloquially, it is also used in the phrase "*chauffer une femme*"—"to make hot love to a woman" (Scharff 18). In *Automania* Pettifer and Turner add: "Chauffeurs were believed to be 'fast' and, because of the opportunities their job gave them to be intimately enclosed with ladies of higher social status, they became the heroes of a new range of romantic novels" (182). The *New York American* of 4 September 1910 carried the story, "Why Beautiful Heiresses Run Away with Humble Chauffeurs," and ostensibly the answer had to do with "the hypnotism of speed."

"Speed"

Automobile drivers heroically possessed speed. Some, such as Dreiser's real-life chauffeur in *A Hoosier Holiday*, are even named Speed. Others are fictional creations, such as the Speed Paxton of F. Scott Fitzgerald's story "A Night at the Fair" (1928). In 1919 Lewis penned a short story focusing on the romance of speed—the essence of automobility. Lewis's story, appropriately entitled "Speed," concerns the whirlwind romance (28 minutes) of auto-racer J. T. Buffum and Iowa girl Aurilla Rivers. J. T. and Aurilla first meet when Buffum's car breaks down in River's hometown, Apogee, while he is on his way to setting the cross-continental time record. "There aren't so many seventy-an-hour men in Apogee!" Aurilla comments (310), and Buffum is definitely a seventy-an-hour man: "The earth was shut off from him by a wall of roar and speed. He did not rouse to human feeling even when he boomed into Columbia Circle, the breaker of the record," writes Lewis (311-12). Buffum wishes to break the record just as Aurilla seeks to break free from her small-town life. She envies Buffum's lifestyle, telling him: "You infuriate me! You do things I've always wanted to—sweep across big distances, command men, have power" (308). Like Claire, Aurilla is captivated by a lifestyle embodied in the open road.[7]

Speed is comically presented in the story through the couple's impetuous romance, but the two also become a serious emblem of the new culture—the age of speed. Aurilla feels rooted in her New England aristocratic heritage, the heritage of the old America, but Buffum discovers on a trip to her ancestral home that Aurilla's father lied about his aristocratic progenitors and that she is not a descendant of this tradition at all. Upon learning this fact, Aurilla typifies the technological movement of twentieth-century American culture. She sheds her supposed cultural heritage, that of aristocratic, puritanical New England, and advocates a new cultural insignia, a crest for America's new age of speed: "She picked up a pencil, turned over the parchment, and drew a flying motor car. She turned and thrust the sketch at him, crying: 'There's the coat of arms of the family to come, the crest of a new aristocracy that knows how to work!'" (318). In fact, Aurilla echoes the creed of the Italian Futurists, who sought to make the car the coat of arms for the modern age.

Their leader, Filippo Tommaso Marinetti, published the Futurist *Manifesto* in the Paris *Le Figaro* 20 February 1909, declaring: "*Le temp et l'espace sont morts hier* . . . . *Une automobile rugisante qui a l'air de courir sur la mitraille est plus belle que la Victoire de Samothrace*" (Clough 41). [Time and space died yesterday . . . . A roaring automobile that races through the air like a hail of machine-gun fire is more beautiful than the Victory of Samothrace (author's translation).] Just as Aurilla casts off her New England heritage, Marinetti explicitly rejects the culture of the past in favor of the modern machine. The Winged Victory suggests the myth of flight, but the automobile truly embodies a victory over space and time. Riding in a motor car enabled the driver to put on the wings of flight. According to Marsh and Collett, the Futurists felt the automobile allowed us to clothe ourselves in the apparel of the machine age:

> Futurists saw the automobile establishing a new relationship between man and his handiwork. . . . Man and his transport had been joined together in a new symbiotic relationship. This was not the half-man, half-beast of mythology, but the half-man, half-machine of the modern age. Man and machine had become fused into a mechanomorphic centaur! (27, 142)

Rosa Clough agrees: "Marinetti and his disciples would convince us that the products of man can re-make their maker . . ." (39).[8]

Such a mechanomorphic centaur, a remade maker, is clearly seen in the mechanistic descriptions of Buffum, who does not rouse to human feeling, or of Field's William Snowden, who describes himself in terms of an automobile: "And when she asked me a question, I threw in my mental clutch so awkwardly that I seemed, for a moment, to have stripped my transmission-gear of speech.... Then she repeated her question, and I was conscious of being towed into Heaven by an angel at the rate of six thousand miles per minute" (8). Such comparisons between men and machines were quite common, perhaps nowhere more manifest than in the following "Efficiency Chart" published by the *Delaware Health News*:

Car	Man
Good gas	Good food
Clean spark plugs	Clean teeth
Clean headlights	Good eyes
Tuning and adjusting	Outdoor exercise
Full air pressure	Good posture
No carbon	No constipation
Keep clean and oiled	Frequent baths and plenty of sleep
Good mixture	Balanced ration . . .
Don't choke engine	Chew food thoroughly
Humming motor	Cheerfulness
Keep radiator filled	Drink plenty of water
Good brakes	Self control and self reliance
A hot spark	Ambition
Strong axles and frame	Stamina
Well balanced mechanism	Even temper
Rolls easy	Plays well
Good hill climber	Hard worker. . . .

(Berger 179)

In a similar fashion, a 1914 ad for Lexington and Howard cars begins, "There is a great similarity between men and motor cars," and then goes on to elaborate on these similarities, such as the error of judging car or man by their exteriors/paint-jobs alone, the notion that you pay for what you get in car or man, and the advantage of speed in both (Bowers 59). Snowden, the Lexington-and-Howard man, and Buffum illustrate half-man, half-car personifications of speed—ideals of the Futurists. Speed is their elixir of life. Buffum's rallying cry to Aurilla is a call to speed—"You better hurry—hurry—hurry!"—and so this couple whisks off to married life, incarnations of America's new age of speed.

Lewis's *Free Air* and "Speed" and a host of other like-natured works of the era clearly depict early twentieth-century America's positive sentiments toward the automobile. These good feelings are perhaps best expressed by James Doolittle, the first chronicler of the American automobile industry. In 1916 he proclaimed:

> The mission of the automobile is to serve mankind, by improving road transportation and through that improvement to foster knowledge, increase wealth, improve health, better living conditions, eliminate waste and add to the joy of living.
>
> The mission of the automobile is to increase personal efficiency; to make happier the lot of people who have led isolated lives in the country and congested lives in the city; to serve as an equalizer and a balance.
>
> Elegant in lines, powerful in action, wide in service, economical in operation, the modern automobile represents the incarnation of the transportation art—the silent, always-ready servant that has more strength than Aladdin's genii, and that already has accomplished vaster works for mankind's betterment than anything that has gone before. (441-42)

Automobile and America had romantically united and were honeymooning together so that by 1919 the car was genuinely ensconced into the American societal structure. But this honeymoon would not last for long. Already in Lewis's early works dichotomous forces can be seen at play. On one hand the car is seen as an embodiment of pastoralism, a move away from the industrial train; yet the same voice which lauds this virtue of the car upholds it as the epitome of speed, the foremost asset (and liability) of modern industrial output. In his next novel, as Lewis migrated into increasingly substantial cultural satire, these discordant forces would lead to a rapid deconstruction of his romantic view.

II

From Romantic To Rogue:
Satire and the Auto

I can stand those big things, but say, even the littlest squeak, why
say, it simply drives me crazy when I'm driving.

—Sinclair Lewis

Altering Our Ideals: *The Magnificent Ambersons*

Like Sinclair Lewis, novelist Booth Tarkington also realized the
powerful impact of automobility on American society, yet with a more
discriminating vision than that communicated by Lewis in either *Free
Air* or "Speed." In a *Saturday Evening Post* article from 1928,
Tarkington wrote that the automobile

> will obliterate the accepted distances that are part of our daily lives.
> It will alter our daily relations to time, and that is to say it will alter
> our lives. Perhaps everybody doesn't comprehend how profoundly
> we are affected by such a change; but what alters our lives alters our
> thoughts; what alters our thoughts alters our characters; what alters
> our characters alters our ideals; and what alters our ideals alters our
> morals. (Pettifer and Turner 83)

Like those of Lewis, Tarkington's earlier works, such as his play *The
Man from Home* (1908), romanticize the automobile, but with *The
Magnificent Ambersons* (1918) he begins to question, rather than
merely be caught up in, the achievements of the automobile age. *The
Magnificent Ambersons* marks a turn in the literary use of the car from

being chiefly a romantic device to being a signifier of societal tension and a vehicle for social satire.

The Magnificent Ambersons opens with a nostalgia for a lost age, one slower and quieter, one filled with horses and buggies, not horseless carriages. The last of the Ambersons, George Amberson Minafer, epitomizes this lost, genteel age and finds himself misaligned with the cultural changes of the early twentieth century. Eugene Morgan, George's mother Isabel's former suitor, serves as a foil to George and exemplifies the new age, particularly in his role as automobile manufacturer. Tarkington uses the automobile as the locus of contention between the two men and, hence, between the two ages. This tension manifests itself early in the novel when George rides with Morgan's daughter Lucy in a one-horse sleigh which overturns, leaving the couple to be rescued by Morgan and his companions riding behind in his latest automotive creation. Symbolically, the sleigh, an embodiment of the old aristocratic cultural order (the same society Aurilla Rivers rejects in "Speed"), is upset, literally leaving George out in the cold, a foreshadowing of events later in the novel.

Rather than bringing the young lovers together as it does in the great majority of romantic fiction, the automobile keeps George and Lucy apart and typifies the cultural clash between the fading aristocracy and the rising *nouveaux riches* industrialists. The conflict comes to a head at dinner one evening when George proclaims to Eugene, "Automobiles are a useless nuisance" (274). Eugene's pragmatic reply does not wholeheartedly contradict George's assertion, but rather it calls George's statement a moot point (while not surprisingly correlating with Tarkington's assessment of the car in his *Post* article written a decade later): "With all their speed forward they may be a step backward in civilization—that is, in spiritual civilization. . . . But automobiles have come, and they bring a greater change in our life than most of us suspect. . . . I think men's minds are going to be changed in subtle ways because of automobiles" (275).

Certainly the town in which the novel is set undergoes drastic changes. Tarkington writes that the new city planners "had one supreme theory: that the perfect beauty and happiness of cities and of human life was to be brought about by more factories; they had a mania for factories . . ." (389). The city expands rapidly on its outskirts as a result of the construction of these large factories (many of them automobile related) and the better roads and new housing developments which support them. This suburban expansion causes inner-city real-estate values to plummet, leaving the once-wealthy Ambersons destitute. Even their attempts to buy into the new wealth fail: they invest in an automobile headlight company that folds. The crowning blow comes when George, forced to earn a living as an explosives merchant, is run over and severely injured by a car.

Though Tarkington later ends the novel on a reconciliatory note, he clearly relinquishes the romantic view of automobility imbued in literature such as Lewis's early fiction. However, Lewis also soon followed suit and espoused a much less romantic role for automobiles in his own work.

The Car Comes to *Main Street*

Both *Free Air* and "Speed" appeared in 1919, a year called by Franklin Reck in his 1945 study of the social effects of the automobile on America,

> the beginning of the modern automobile age. It marked the passing of the linen duster, visored cap, and goggles. . . . The automobile came along and gave us something we had never completely possessed before. It gave us a sense of freedom, a feeling of independence, a means of escape from the monotony of our day-by-day surroundings. As engineers of our own craft, we found a new way of satisfying our love of motion. . . . It multiplied our power, expanded our horizons. (8)

In *Free Air* and "Speed" Lewis foregrounded the automobile as a catalyst of positive societal changes, as does Reck, but corresponding to the birth of the modern automobile age, Lewis parted with Reck and joined Tarkington to view these changes more discerningly. With his next novel, *Main Street* (1920), Lewis discarded the linen dusters and goggles of his earlier melodramatic romances to focus on a social satire of middle America. Coinciding with this change, he expanded his own horizons with regard to his perception of the automobile in society and correspondingly modified the presentation of automobiles in his work. From *Main Street* through *Babbitt* (1922) and finally to *Dodsworth* (1929), he increasingly orchestrated his use of automobiles to satirize the consumerist society which had exalted them to such preeminence.

Main Street

The first such orchestration comes in his prologue to *Main Street*, where Lewis sarcastically extols:

> Main Street is the climax of civilization. That this Ford car might stand in front of the Bon Ton Store, Hannibal invaded Rome and Erasmus wrote in Oxford cloisters. . . . Such is our comfortable tradition and sure faith. Would he not betray himself an alien cynic who should otherwise portray Main Street, or distress the citizens by speculating whether there may not be other faiths?

If they knew who Hannibal and Erasmus were, Lewis's Gopher Prairie residents would most assuredly think them predicators of the civilization of Ford, hyperbolic as it may seem, because the production and distribution of automobiles encapsulates the essence of Gopher Prairie's beloved capitalistic economy. Automobiles are thus of paramount importance in town life. Everyone in Gopher Prairie is quick to point out that the town's most famous native son is Bresnahan, the famed Velvet Motor Company auto manufacturer; and "the most energetic and vital place[s] in town" are "the Ford Garage and the Buick Garage, competent one-story brick and cement buildings opposite each other" (36). Furthermore, Gopher Prairie's esteemed citizen Dr. Kennicott, whose medical practice, like that of so many of his colleagues of the day, was greatly enhanced by the automobile, finds no greater pleasure than in the care, not of his patients, but of his car:[9]

> He nursed his two-year-old Buick even in winter, when it was stored in the stable-garage behind the house. . . . Winter noons he wandered out and stared owlishly at the car. . . . To him motoring was a faith not to be questioned, a high-church cult, with electric sparks for candles, and piston-rings possessing the sanctity of altar-vessels. His liturgy was composed of intoned and metrical road-comments: "They say there's a pretty good hike from Duluth to International Falls." (196)[10]

Lewis thus portrays the automobile religiously as an indubitably essential aspect of the "sure faith" of Gopher Prairiens, as it became to most other denizens of America's Main Streets.

This glorification of the car and other products of American industry is countered in the novel by the opinions of Kennicott's wife Carol, an "alien cynic" to whom the sacred car is just another non-aesthetic component of all small towns. She finds the residents of America's Gopher Prairies,

> A savorless people, gulping tasteless food, and sitting afterward, coatless and thoughtless, in rocking-chairs . . . listening to mechanical music, saying mechanical things about the excellence of Ford automobiles, and viewing themselves as the greatest race in the world. . . . Such a society functions admirably in the large production of cheap automobiles, dollar watches, and safety razors. But it is not satisfied until the entire world also admits that the need and joyous purpose of living is to ride in flivvers, to make advertising-pictures of dollar watches, and in the twilight to sit talking . . . of the convenience of safety razors. (265, 267)

In an elementary way, Carol espouses automobiles as icons of standardization which kindle the mass consumerism and uniformity characteristic of America under the grips of late capitalism.

Automobiles *have* manifested positive effects, as Dr. Kennicott articulates:

> The auto, the telephone, rural free delivery; they're bringing the farmers in closer touch with the town. Takes time, you know, to change a wilderness like this was fifty years ago. But already, why, they can hop into the Ford or the Overland and get in to the movies on Saturday evening quicker than you could get down to 'em by trolley in St. Paul. (22)

But, as Carol recognizes, automobiles have also overwhelmingly advanced the culture of consumption. Warren Susman's *Culture as History* chronicles the development of this culture of abundance. Susman corroborates Carol's recognition: "Everywhere there was a new emphasis on buying, spending, and consuming. Advertising became not only a new economic force essential in the regulation of prices but also a vision of the way the culture worked: the products of the culture became advertisements of the culture itself" (xxiv).

Later in the novel Carol voices an awareness that any one of us
who at one time or another has searched a strange town for the familiar
golden arches of McDonald's knows, i.e.—

The universal similarity—that is the physical expression of the
philosophy of dull safety. Nine-tenths of the American towns are so
alike that it is the completest boredom to wander from one to
another. . . . [T]here is the same lumber yard, the same railroad
station, the same Ford garage. . . . The new, more conscious houses
are alike in their very attempts at diversity. . . . The shops show the
same standardized, nationally advertized wares. (286)

Standardization, national advertising, franchising—though not created
by the automobile industry, these facets of American consumerist
culture were certainly facilitated by it; and Lewis's next novel, *Babbitt*,
set in the mythical mid-western city of Zenith, brings these traits to the
forefront.

Babbitt

"Standardization is excellent, *per se*," declares *Babbitt*'s Dr. Yavitch as
he argues with Seneca Doane, Zenith's liberal radical. Doane replies,
"No, what I fight in Zenith is standardization of thought . . ." (85). This
standardization of thought is ardently expressed in George Babbitt,
middle-class American Everyman, the ideal representative of the new
abundant class. At one point in the novel Babbitt addresses "the
specifications of the Standardized American Citizen" (151). High on
this list of specifications is the need to surround oneself with
"nationally advertised and quantitatively produced" (7) possessions
(like Carol Kennicott's dollar watches and safety razors), and chief
requisite is a stylish automobile complete with the latest accessories.

Babbitt, "a pious motorist" (7), embodies bourgeois American
society, a society in which the car is "an aspiration for knightly
rank. . . . [A] family's motor indicated its social rank as precisely as the
grades of the peerage determined the rank of an English family. . . .
Where Babbitt as a boy had aspired to the presidency, his son Ted [who
is "motor-mad" (184)] aspired to a Packard twin-six and an established
position in the motored gentry" (63). To Babbitt, the motor car
encapsulates all things noble: "poetry and tragedy, love and heroism"
(23). And what better symbol for a people on the go, always hustling,

always consuming. Babbitt realizes that hustling is his society's predominant occupation: "All about him the city was hustling, for hustling's sake. Men in motors were hustling to pass one another in the hustling traffic" (128).

Through the course of the novel, however, Babbitt undergoes a change in perception (as did Lewis in his own writing) and ascertains that his society's craze for motorization and standardization has led to an "incredibly mechanical" way of life: "Mechanical business . . . Mechanical religion . . . Mechanical golf and dinner-parties and bridge and conversation . . . mechanical friendships" (190). Productivity has outweighed passion to the point where even the Rev. Shaw's growing Presbyterian church is lauded not for its spirituality, but for its industrial efficiency and mass productivity. Still, in spite of his authentic realization, Babbitt cannot change his lifestyle. Though in an attempt to make his life less uniform, he boozes and carouses for a few weeks (once by taking a woman parking), he ultimately reverts to his imperturbably standardized existence, a life to which he has grown far too accustomed to abandon. In the long run, like Carol Kennicott, Babbitt is unable to transcend the ideals and standards of his society, and he remains inseparably controlled by a culture of consuming.

Dodsworth

What *Main Street* says about the standardized values of small-town Americans, *Babbitt* recapitulates about the suburban business class. In *Dodsworth*, his consummate story satirically employing the automobile, Lewis takes a product of the standardized culture of both *Main Street* and *Babbitt* and plunges him into the culture of Europe. That product is automobile manufacturer Sam Dodsworth, a character, according to Charles Sanford in his study, *Automobiles in American Life*, "modeled upon the best qualities of Ford and [Alfred] Sloan [of General Motors]" (4). As in *Main Street*, *Dodsworth* begins by ironically equating the rise of the automobile with the "climax of civilization." The status quo of the automobile industry does not satisfy Dodsworth, however; he seeks to unite aesthetics and machine by engineering "a new kind of beauty for autos. Kind of long straight lines" (4). In fact, Dodsworth, like other automotive designers of his day, advocates streamlining. Like Babbitt, Dodsworth's poetry truly lies in his cars, his sense of artistry inspired by the muses of the machine: "He dreamed of motors like thunderbolts, as poets less modern than himself might dream of stars and roses and nymphs by a pool" (11). Thus Dodsworth, automotive poet, sets out to market a new type of car, not for the rich but, in the tradition of Ford, for the masses; and he calls his company *Revelation*—seemingly positing his cars as eschatological fulfillments of automotive design possibility.

Dodsworth's company, however, is absorbed by the Unit Automotive Company (UAC), as part of the "booming industrial flood" overtaking America (16). The very name *Unit* suggests a monotonous uniformity like that bemoaned by Carol Kennicott but praised as beneficial standardization by Babbitt. In agreement with Babbitt, Kynance, President of UAC, sees standardization and uniformity as part of a grand universal scheme, and he posits a prophetic vision of automotive ascendancy:

> Do big things! Think of it; by making autos we're enabling half the civilized world to run into town from their pig-sties and see the movies, and the other half to get out of town and give Nature the once-over. Twenty million cars in America! And in twenty more years we'll have the bloomin' Tibetans and Abyssinians riding on cement roads on U.A.C. cars! Talk about Napoleon! Talk about Shakespeare! Why, we're pulling of the greatest miracle since the Lord created the world! (20-1)

More than Dodsworth even, Kynance sees automobiles as incarnate revelation, the Word made machine/flesh.

Dodsworth uses the profits from the sale of his company to travel with his wife Fran to Europe, "the last refuge, in this Fordized world, of personal dignity" (250). Like Carol Kennicott, Fran (a woman Dodsworth exalts as "brilliant," "an automobile's head-light") (228) finds herself dissatisfied with the mundanity of the American way of life, a lifestyle in which Dodsworth, like Babbitt, finds himself deeply entrenched. In Europe, away from his automotive position, Dodsworth feels isolated, of little worth. Adding to his sense of isolation is Fran's infatuation with Europe, and particularly its men. Additionally, Europeans like Lady Ouston roundly criticize commodities Dodsworth upholds as virtuous: standardization, mechanization, Yankee ingenuity. To entertain himself, Dodsworth takes to daydreaming of motorized creations, at one point prophesying the recreational vehicle vogue through his dream of making "a very masterwork of caravans [the Touricar perhaps?]: a tiny kitchen with electric stove, electric refrigerator; a tiny toilet with showerbath; a living-room which should become a bedroom by night—a living-room with radio, a real writing desk; and on one side of the caravan . . . a folding verandah" (21). (In fact, the first house trailer was produced in 1929, the year of *Dodsworth*'s publication.) It takes the sighting of one of his Revelation cars parked across from a church in Kent to reassure him once again he indeed is Somebody (76).

In fact, this connection between church and car leads Dodsworth to begin to see his role as creator of automobiles as a spiritual calling, divinely ordained. His experience at the cathedral of Notre Dame inspires this vision: "The whole cathedral expanded before his eyes; the work of human hands seemed to tower larger than the sky. He felt, dimly and disconnectedly, that he too had done things with his hands; that the motor car was no contemptible creation . . ." (141). A prescient structuralist, Dodsworth correlates automobile manufacturing and ecclesiastical architecture, predating by a generation Roland Barthes's assessment in *Mythologies*: "I think that cars today are almost the exact equivalent of the great Gothic cathedrals: I mean the supreme creations of an era, conceived with passion by unknown artists, and consumed in image if not in usage by a whole population which appropriated them as a purely magical object" (88).

Dodsworth's return to America, however, alters his newfound spiritual perception of his supreme creations. In contrast to the quiescence of Europe, he sees in America, "traffic jams and big movie theaters and radios yapping . . . and each family has to have not one car, by golly, but two or three—and all on the installment plan!" (163). America's mass consumption overtakes him in Grand Central Station, the hub of American mass transit. He envisions Grand Central as an American cathedral, but a temple of quite a different sort than Notre Dame:

> He fancied that this was veritably the temple of a new divinity, the God of Speed. Of its adherents it demanded . . . a belief that Going Somewhere, Going Quickly, Going Often, were in themselves holy and greatly to be striven for. . . . And with his motor cars Sam had contributed to the birth of this new religion. . . . He blasphemed against it now. . . . (164)

No longer is the new age of speed exalted as it was by J. T. and Aurilla in "Speed." Speed and sin are now brought together.[11] In this passage, as in *Main Street* and *Babbitt*, Lewis critiques the dangerous American equation of automobility and religious practice. Other writers have also commented on the parallels between automobility and religion. Marsh and Collett write that washing a car "might be seen as weekly worship, a motor show as a holy day" (5). Perhaps more than any other text, Lewis Mumford's anti-automobile treatise *The Highway and the City* reinforces the sense of automobility as an American religion. Mumford asserts that "the current American way of life is founded not just on motor transportation but on the religion of the motorcar, and the sacrifices that people are prepared to make for this religion stand outside the realm of rational criticism" (234). Like Henry James, who a generation earlier chronicled the incompatibility of European and American cultures and religions, Lewis in *Dodsworth* returns to this clash of cultural ideals by contrasting two "religions": one, the European deification of staid traditions of a noble past; the other, the American veneration of everything novel, fast, and plebeian, most decidedly represented in the worship of the car.

Dodsworth finds himself trapped between these two ideals. He cannot embrace European convention, yet his outmoded Yankee industrialism no longer satisfies him. Rather than renouncing automobility as vulgar, Dodsworth seeks to find cultural utility for it, but this dedication to a new order precipitates a series of laughable proposals. With religious zeal, he offers to become an automotive missionary, to "educate the South Americans to use more motors and especially to help them to build more through highways that would tap every square mile of the continent" (235). (Perhaps Dodsworth's concept of uniting ministry and automobility served as inspiration for Rev. Robert Schuller's drive-in Crystal Cathedral or Reverend Ike's collection of Rolls-Royces.) Should this plan fail, Dodsworth thinks he could become an automotive scholar: "Was it too infantile a fancy to think of himself becoming the first great historian of motors, historian of something which was, after all, more important in social evolution than twenty battles of Waterloo?" (267). He even dreams of uniting the best of American standardization with the best of European culture by creating Sans Souci Gardens, a European sub-division of houses: "French chateaux in a Henry Ford section!" (201).

His noble inspirations are squelched upon his return to Europe when Fran leaves him for a European nobleman. Dejected, he returns to England to take a motor tour, something Fran found too vulgar to do, and he travels along the old Roman roads. Here perhaps is the most representative image of Dodsworth: encased in his automobile, his only real friend, traveling along the highways of a society truly built at "the climax of a civilization." The juxtaposition of Dodsworth's automobile wandering along the *via* of Roman society, a society at the foundation of Western civilization, acutely conveys the sense of social irony Lewis aspires to in the work, particularly when we reflect back on the hyperbolic preface to *Main Street*: so that Sam Dodsworth might drive his car here, Hannibal invaded Rome.

In the end of the novel, Dodsworth locates a woman with whom he can recommence his life, Edith Cortright. She teaches him his greatest lesson: Edith says that the strength of Europe lies in its closeness to the earth, but America creates all sorts of inventions and buildings to "insulate it from the good vulgarity of earth!" (360). Confirming this observation in Lewis's own work, we can see that in ten years Lewis's fictional automobiles have been transformed from the tiny Teal bug of Milton Daggett, touring along the lonely prairie "so close to the earth," to the traffic jams caused by Sam Dodsworth's Revelation cars, from vehicles taking Henry Boltwood out into the healing powers of nature to those sealing American civilization away from "the good vulgarity of the earth." (And if we look as late in his career as the publication of *World So Wide* (1951), we see Lewis beginning his novel with a horrific car accident which kills Caprice, the wife of his protagonist, Hayden Chart.)

This shift in Lewis's work coincides with the shift in production of American automobiles from primarily exposed roadsters to enclosed sedans, further isolating and encasing the motorist/consumer. By 1929, the publication date of *Dodsworth*, approximately 90 percent of all passenger cars were closed sedans, as opposed to 1919, when *Free Air* was published and 90 percent of the automobiles manufactured were open roadsters (Cleveland 292-93).

Gatsby and "The Arrogance of Wealth"

As the move from roadster to sedan marks a revolution in automotive manufacturing, Lewis's shift from romancing the car to satirizing those who worship it marks a transition in American literature from the Edenic garden of early automobility to the discovery of a thorn. Images of pleasant drives and pastoral countryside so popularized in earlier writings about automobiles were being replaced with passages such as

this one describing an accident scene in an August 1935 article from
Reader's Digest:

> . . . the slack expression on the face of a man . . . staring at the Z-
> twist in his broken leg, the insane crumpled effect of a child's body
> after its bones are crushed inward, . . . an hysterical woman with her
> screaming mouth opening a hole in the bloody drip that fills her eyes
> and runs off her chin. . . . the raw ends of bones protruding through
> flesh in compound fractures, and the dark red, oozing surfaces where
> clothes and skin were flayed off at once. Maybe it will make you sick
> at your stomach, too. (Schneider, *Quotable* 86)

The honeymoon was over—signs of marital stress had set in. No longer
could American fiction writers embrace the automobile with simple
romantic innocence. Even as early as 1908, the British children's writer
Kenneth Grahame had written in *Wind in the Willows* about Mr. Toad,
"the terror, the traffic queller . . . before whom all must give way or be
smitten into nothingness and everlasting night." Mr. Toad wrecks
seven cars and is hospitalized three times. Clay McShane writes that to
Grahame, "the car symbolizes the evils associated with the idle rich"
(McShane 144-45). Concurrent with this changing ethos, America's
chronicler of the idle rich, F. Scott Fitzgerald, created in 1925 one of
American literature's most memorable automobiles, Jay Gatsby's
Rolls-Royce, an automobile which encapsulates the move from
automobile as romantic object to automobile as central icon of a
decadent culture. Fitzgerald's depiction of Gatsby's car substantiates
the pronouncement of no less than President Woodrow Wilson, who
regarded cars as "a picture of the arrogance of wealth, with all its
independence and carelessness" (Flower 41).

Lewis's works primarily characterize the effects of expanding
materialism on the culture of the middle class. Fitzgerald examines its
effects on the upper classes. As Luis Echevarria writes, "For Fitzgerald
—both in fiction and real life—the automobile was the ultimate status
symbol" (74). Jay Gatsby seemingly personifies the ultimate rags-to-
riches story, the self-made American male, but Fitzgerald exposes the
tarnish beneath the gleam of his apparent success. A clear social
symbol of Gatsby's prestige is his automobile. In the following
passage, Fitzgerald's narrator, Nick Carraway, describes the vehicle for
the first time:

> At nine o'clock, one morning in late July, Gatsby's gorgeous
> car lurched up the rocky drive to my door and gave out a burst of
> melody from its three-noted horn. . . . He was balancing himself on
> the running board of his car with that resourcefulness of movement
> that is so peculiarly American. . . . He saw me looking with
> admiration at his car.
> "It's pretty, isn't it, old sport!" He jumped off to give me a
> better view. "Haven't you ever seen it before?"
> I'd seen it. Everybody had seen it. It was a rich cream color,
> bright with nickel, swollen here and there in its monstrous length
> with triumphant hat-boxes and supper-boxes and tool-boxes, and
> terraced with a labyrinth of wind-shields that mirrored a dozen suns.
> (59-60)

Gatsby's (and his culture's) narcissism is clearly reflected in the
labyrinthine mirrors of his automobile. Like their owners, automobiles
such as Gatsby's and those of his cronies are beautiful objects to look
at, yet beneath their veneer lies the potential for death and destruction.

From the onset of the novel, Fitzgerald capitalizes on the potential
of the automobile to embody decay and dying. Though presented as a
hyperbole, Nick remarks to Daisy upon their reunion that in her
absence from Chicago, "All the cars have the left rear wheel painted
black as a mourning wreath" (14). Such images uniting the automobile
and death continue in Fitzgerald's description of the valley of ashes
presided over by the eyes of Dr. T. J. Eckleburg, where "occasionally a
line of gray cars crawls along an invisible track, gives out a ghastly
creak, and comes to rest" (25). These images continue in an ominous
foreshadowing of Daisy's accident occurring after Nick attends his first
Gatsby party: "a dozen headlights illuminated a bizarre and tumultuous
scene" as the departing guests come upon a wrecked car. Onlookers
gaze and horns from backed-up traffic sound as a man exits the
wreckage declaring, "I know nothing whatever about mechanics. . . . I
know very little about driving—next to nothing. It happened, and that's
all I know." We discover that this man is not the driver, who later
climbs out of the vehicle too dazed by alcohol and the accident to know
what has happened (51-53).

This scene of inebriated drivers out of control characterizes the
society of Fitzgerald's West Egg, of which Daisy and Tom Buchanan
are prime exemplars. Tom's automotive and moral recklessness is
exemplified by the scandal in Ventura when he ran off the road, ripping

a wheel of his car and breaking the arm of his female companion, a hotel chambermaid (71). Nick says of both Tom and Daisy: "They were careless people. . . . [T]hey smashed up things and creatures and then retreated back into their money or their vast carelessness, or whatever it was that kept them together, and let other people clean up the mess they had made . . ." (158). In his *Notebooks*, Fitzgerald uses a similar automotive metaphor to describe the reckless life as led by himself and his wife, Zelda:

> They rode through five years in open car with the sun on their foreheads and their hair flying. They waved to people they knew but seldom stopped to ask a direction or check on the fuel, for every morning there was a gorgeous new horizon . . . . They missed collisions by inches, wavered on the edge of precipices and skidded across tracks to the sound of the warning bell. Their friends tired of waiting for the smash . . . . One could almost name the day when the car began to sputter and slow up . . . . (Echevarria 75)

Such descriptions of the recklessness of Daisy and Tom and Scott and Zelda further the metaphor of automobility used by Fitzgerald to characterize his age. Jordan's final words to Nick continue the conceit: "You said a bad driver was only safe until she met another bad driver?" (156). Tom and Daisy are bad drivers, but so were Daisy and Gatsby, both literally and figuratively.

Fitzgerald punctuates the story of Daisy and Gatsby's relationship with the metaphor of automobility. Their affair both begins and ends with an automobile. According to Jordan (whose name recalls the Jordan Playboy, a car marketed specifically to women), her first recollection of Gatsby and Daisy came when Daisy's "white roadster was beside the curb, and she was sitting in it with a lieutenant I had never seen before" (69). The final connection between death and the automobile comes when Gatsby and Daisy return home from the city and Daisy accidentally runs over and kills Tom's lover Myrtle. "The 'death car' as the newspapers called it, didn't stop; it came out of the gathering darkness, wavered tragically for a moment, and then disappeared around the next bend," Fitzgerald writes (122). Gatsby pays for this accident (for which Daisy in reality is responsible) with his life when Myrtle's husband, George Wilson, murders him in revenge.

The business sign outside Wilson's garage proclaims: "*Repairs.* George B. Wilson. *Cars bought and sold*" (26). Like cars, people's lives in the novel are treated as commodities to be bought and sold. Money has corrupted Fitzgerald's society, and the grandest symbol of this financial opulence is Gatsby's car. Its "labyrinth of wind-shields" reflects not only the radiance of a dozen suns, it also mirrors the jaded values and false friendships of a society on the make and on the take, where lives and relationships are exchanged for new models and makes as easily as one trades for a new car, and where cosmetic alterations can mask realities as easily as automobile accessories terrace the chassis of a vehicle.[12]

The Great Gatsby, like Lewis's later works, presents an image of the automobile far removed from romantic portraits drawn only a decade earlier. Lewis and Fitzgerald were keenly aware of the conspicuous consumption practiced by their society and of the dubious effects of this obsession for things. The very lives and souls of people were becoming commodified, mass consumed, standardized. Within their own economic domain, a Babbitt and a Gatsby are interchangeable representations of a social type, assembled components in a growing American culture of consumption. At the root of interchangeability and standardization stood Henry Ford, and in the conception of Ford as both person and idea can be seen the evolving narrative of automobility in American writing.

III

An Intricate Relationship:
The Car as Complex Signifier

Civilization is like a Ford ... restless, aimless, but vital and
mobbing.

—Stuart Chase

Henry Ford is a watershed figure in the history of automobility. More
than any other person, he was responsible for the democratization of
the automobile, not only in this country, but around the globe. He
created a car (the Model T) and refined a process (the assembly line) of
which anyone even vaguely familiar with automobiles is aware.
"Someone should write an essay on the moral, physical, and esthetic
effect of the Model T Ford on the American nation," wrote John
Steinbeck in *Cannery Row* (1945). "Two generations of Americans
knew more about the Ford coil than the clitoris, about the planetary
system of gears than the solar system of stars" (69). Ford indeed single-
handedly changed the face of American automobility, so it is not
surprising that he would be a central figure in changing literary
representations of automobility as well. To codify Ford's effects on
literature, one has to move beyond simple labels such as romantic or
satiric and move into a new realm of metaphorical and contextual
sophistication. Thus, Ford himself proves an apt text for surveying the
development of automobility into an increasingly complex signifier
and structural tool.

"Discipline Perfectly Embroidered": Ford as Fiction

"Around this strange man have centered more worship, more hatred, more perplexity than around any private citizen in history," wrote Jonathan Leonard in 1932 (16). Three years later, humorist Will Rogers remarked: "It will take a hundred years to tell whether he helped us or hurt us, but he certainly didn't leave us where he found us" (Sears 277). As evidence of his renown, a poll of college students ranked him as the third most important figure of all time, behind Jesus and Napoleon (Nash 154). Finally, historian Warren Susman called him "a major architect of the new social order that came into being during the first two decades of the twentieth century" (132). The man, of course, is Henry Ford, and no one did more to disperse the fledgling automotive industry to the masses. Much has been said about him, both positive and negative, but regardless of what one thinks *about* Henry Ford, when the subject of automobiles is introduced, one must think *of* him.

In many ways, a book focusing on fictional representations of the automobile need not look for a fictional treatment of the man in a written text, one need only to look to Ford himself. To most of the public, Henry Ford was, and still is, a fictional text, a literary creation of Detroit. When it comes to Ford's life, separating reality from fiction proves a difficult task; only a few biographies compiled in recent years have fathomed the magnitude of the fictionalization. James Flink writes that "his extreme egocentrism deluded him into becoming the chief progenitor of a cult of personality based upon heroic myths" (*Culture* 74). Ford is mythic, and as with most American myths, writers have been unable to ignore him. From joke books entitled *Funny Stories about Ford* to Upton Sinclair's *The Flivver King* to E. L. Doctorow's *Ragtime,* Ford, both fictionally and factually, has been woven into the fabric of American writing and, particularly, American satire.

Thousands of myths and apocryphal stories have evolved around Ford, some created by Ford owners, others by journalists or pulp fiction writers, and even some by Ford and his compatriots themselves. Stories are told that Ford once offered to run over a man who killed a robin, that he refused to plow over a patch of land on his farm because he lost the hand of his watch there and hoped to find it one day, and that he returned to the government his $29 million in profits from World War I (as to the latter, Andrew Mellon, upon checking the Treasury Department files, said there was no record of such a deposit)

(Wik 43). An example of the genesis of such myths lies in the following story. While traveling by car to Detroit, Ford resolved the problem of creating a satisfactory rear axle for his tractors, the *Detroit Times* reported. Later, the *Detroit Free Press* reported an embellished version of the story: Ford suddenly stood up in the car shouting, "Stop a minute." For forty minutes no one said anything, and then Ford declared, "Drive ahead. I've got it." By the time the story reached the *Baltimore Evening Sun*, Ford was reported to have stood on the hill of his estate one day, examining the farmlands spread out before him, wondering how to develop a rear axle for his tractor. Then one day shortly after, while riding in a car with his son, he shouted, "Stop!" For forty-five minutes he scribbled notes furiously until finally exclaiming, "I've got it!" (Wik 45-46).

On another occasion, after driving his open-seater into his factory just before a thunderstorm broke, Ford remarked that he had been only a gas tank ahead of the storm all the way from home. His publicity agent, E. LeRoy Pelletier, quickly dispatched a story that Ford had raced an oncoming storm from Dearborn to Detroit, all the time driving in bright sunshine. Upon arrival, Ford himself was completely dry, but the rear end of the car was filled with enormous hailstones. Papers around the world ran the story (Anderson 180-81). Some myths—that Ford invented the automobile, that he was the first to make an inexpensive car, that he put together the first assembly line—are still accepted by great numbers. In short, Ford was, and still is, read by most people like a piece of fiction, the Paul Bunyon of transportation.

Though a great deal of the mythologizing of Ford was comic in nature, some of it had quite serious intent. In 1932 Jonathan Leonard published *The Tragedy of Henry Ford*. Leonard avows that he wanted to fashion a muckraking exposition of the man and his company, but the facts lent themselves much more to tragedy. Like Lear or Oedipus, Ford at age 69 was vaulted by Leonard into the realm of heroes and gods, given status as a protagonist replete with *hamartia* and full of *hubris*. Indeed, I find it surprising that none of America's theatrical tragedians of the common man have turned to Ford as a subject for their work. He is, after all, the archetypal salesman, inventor, rags-to-riches, Puritan-work-ethic American, a populist peach ripe for dramatic picking. Perhaps, however, because Ford is so difficult to decipher, so enmeshed in contradictions and myths, both external and internal, dramatists have feared approaching him.

To see Ford as a tragic text, one must know the plot of the play; therefore, allow me to present a brief synopsis of the acts of this bio-drama followed by an interpretive gloss.

Act I

Born to a poor rural family, Henry Ford migrated to the city for work, much to his father's chagrin. A natural inventor, he began working in his spare time to perfect a horseless carriage. In 1896 he finished his first car. He formed one automobile company, but dissatisfied with the direction of his fellow stock-holders, he pulled out to form and control another, the Ford Motor Company. Ford did not want to build fancy cars for the wealthy; his goal was to create an inexpensive car for the masses, and in 1908, he introduced what was to become the greatest selling automobile for decades—the Model T (which remained number one in sales for eighty years until the Volkswagen Beetle overtook it). Henry Ford, creator of the ultimate car of the folk, became a populist hero.

Ford's essential desire was to build a car the masses could afford to purchase and drive, and when he brought the Model T out for $825, his goal was realized. "I will build a motor car for the great multitude," said Ford, "so low in price that no man making a good salary will be unable to own one—and enjoy with his family the blessings of hours of pleasure in God's great open spaces" (Wik 233). Ford viewed his creation as a machine in the garden, a way for the average American to get back to nature by using the machine. But foremost, the Model T was a car for the masses. Flink argues that "the Model T symbolized a victory of the people, who looked upon automobility as a major social reform, over a shortsighted group of budding monopoly capitalists who put short-term higher unit profits ahead of the mass automobility denied by the average person" (*Culture* 55).

Act II

Ford wanted to make his automobiles cheaper and to produce more of them, so he perfected the concept of assembly-line mass production (coining the term in a 1926 *Encyclopedia Britannica* entry) and offered his workers an unheard-of five dollars a day (if they met certain social criteria—did not drink, took good care of their families, and so forth). Fascinated Americans made the display of Ford's assembly line the most attended exhibit at the San Francisco exhibition of 1915 (Wik 37). Sales of the car and popularity of the man soared.

The opening of the Highland Park plant in 1910 led to price reductions and an eventual low cost of $290 for the Model T, and by 1916 over 738,000 were being built each year (Flink, *Age* 37-38). If the coupling of the inexpensive price of the Model T with the additional good press from his announcement of the five-dollar, eight-hour work day in 1914 were not enough to earn his respect among middle and lower classes, the Selden Patent case, in which he took on a powerful group of automobile manufacturers seeking to monopolize the trade, cemented the public's perception of him as a defender of the small man, a battler for the underdog.

All over the world Ford became known as the champion of the masses. His autobiographical *My Life and Work* became a best-seller in Berlin in 1925. The Germans praised what they called *Fordismus*. In Spain a Barcelona newspaper declared in 1924, "Henry Ford is the superman" (Wik 4). Russian parents named their children Fordson after his popular-selling tractor. In an article for *Outlook* (1927) entitled "Ford Conquers Russia," Maurice Hindus wrote that next to Lenin and Trotsky, Ford was probably the most widely known person in the Soviet Union. According to Leonard, "On the steppes of Russia the peasants have placed his picture in the icon corner of their hovels beside the picture of Lenin" (15-16). The Soviets saw him as a great revolutionary of the working class, "the symbol of competence, efficiency, achievement" (Leonard 282). All across Russia the slogan, "Do it the Ford way," reverberated.

Act III

Mass production began to show its negative side. The repetition and drudgery of the assembly line coupled with many lay-offs and poor plant conditions led to labor unrest. Ford responded by trying to break the unions. Labor conditions on the assembly line, in spite of seemingly good pay, were not ideal. Worker turnover and unrest ran high. Flink attests that "conditions on the assembly line were grudgingly accepted only by workers accustomed to even more repressive systems of labor or whose opportunities for employment elsewhere at a living wage were almost nil" (*Age* 118). Upon leaving Ford, Walter Cunningham published a pamphlet entitled *J8*, his work number at the plant. He wrote: "In exchange for the identity numbers

and our wages . . . we also surrendered our individuality . . ."
(Batchelor 53). Ford's attempts to control his workers through union
bashing and scare tactics led to his being dubbed "the Mussolini of
Detroit" by the *New York Times*, 8 January 1928 (Flink, *Age* 125).
Among the general public, the perception of Ford began to be
tarnished.

Act IV

Competition and growing customer dissatisfaction over style combined
with the obsolescence of the Model T led to declining sales and
eventually to the discontinuation of the line in 1927. Meanwhile, Ford
became even more distrustful of both the public and big business.

The collapse of the Model T and the onslaught of the Depression
did little to improve Ford's image. Stephen Sears elaborates:

> During the Roaring Twenties Henry Ford had been an almost
> mythical figure to millions of Americans. He was *the* symbol of the
> age of mass production; single-handedly he had liberated the farmer,
> raised the quality of everyday life, made the benefits of the auto
> culture available to all. As the Depression deepened, however, the
> common man's faith was shaken . . . so ingrained was his image as
> the Messiah of Dearborn that the disillusionment was
> widespread. . . . Certainly Ford did not enhance his image with such
> thoughtless statements as . . . "If you lost your money, don't let it
> bother you. Charge it up to experience." (235-36)

Act V

In the depths of the Depression Ford began to look for scapegoats and
found them in the Jews, publishing the anti-Semitic treatise *The
International Jew: The World's Problem* in installments in his paper,
the *Dearborn Independent*. Later he publicly disclaimed these
publications. By the time of the U.S. entry into World War II, Ford
paranoically perceived the war as an effort to take his company away
from him. His son Edsel, who had been endlessly tormented by his
father, died, and finally, at the urging of his wife and the U.S.
Administration, Ford resigned and allowed his grandson to take over as
president of the company. Two years later, Ford died.

Ford's economic problems were complicated by his social and
political activities, including a failed Senate race and the publication of

the anti-Semitic *Independent.* "By late 1933 the Nazis had published some twenty-nine German editions of *The International Jew*, with Ford's name on the title page and a preface praising Ford for the 'great service' his anti-Semitism had done the world." At the Nuremberg trials, von Schirach testified he learned his anti-Semitism at seventeen from reading Ford. Hitler himself awarded Ford the Grand Cross of the Supreme Order of the German Eagle in 1938 (Flink, *Age* 113). The Fuhrer, anxious to build his own *VolksWagen*, highly esteemed Ford, telling one friend: "I am a great admirer of his. . . . I shall do my best to put his theories into practice in Germany. . . . I have come to the conclusion that the motor car, instead of being a class-dividing element, can be the instrument for uniting the different classes, just as it has done in America, thanks to Mr. Ford's genius" (Nevins 95).

The End

What becomes apparent from this brief examination of Ford's dramatic life are the numerous conflicts and contradictions all present within one source. Since Ford did so much for the common people, one would think he upheld them and their ideals, but Flink contends: "Ford viewed the common man with a cynical, elitist paternalism, fundamentally at odds with the egalitarian populist philosophy he supposedly represented. 'We have to recognize the unevenness in human mental equipment,' wrote Ford" (*Age* 114). Concerning Thomas Jefferson, Ford stated: "There can be no greater absurdity and no greater disservice to humanity than to insist that men are created equal" (Cohn 165). Concerning the repetitiveness of assembly-line work, Ford wrote that it is "a terrifying prospect to a certain turn of mind": "I could not possibly do the same thing day in and day out." Yet he firmly believed that the average person "wants a job in which he does not have to think" (Batchelor 52). Another internal conflict revolves around the fact that although Ford embraced technological achievement and reportedly declared that history is bunk, he spent a great deal of his life collecting historical artifacts for his museums and reconstructing historical sights, such as the Wayside Inn and the Stephen Foster home.[13]

Perhaps nowhere is the dichotomy of his beliefs so evident as in his attitude towards farming. Roderick Nash claims that the tension in Henry Ford's thought between old and new, between a belief in progress and a tendency to nostalgia, is dramatically illustrated in his attitude toward farming and farmers.... [H]e believed farm life to be a ceaseless round of inefficient drudgery.... Ford addressed himself to the problem of industrializing agriculture. The farmer, in Ford's opinion, should become a technician and a businessman.... Mechanization would make it possible to produce in twenty-five working days what formerly required an entire year. (157)

Ford even spent thousands of dollars trying to develop a mechanical cow because he found the real one inefficient and nasty.

The Flivver King

In Ford's life the basic binary opposition in American culture between machine and garden is dramatically played out. His own life is a prime text illustrating what writers would come to see as an essential tension which exists between the automobile and American tradition. Whether viewed as a tragedy or not, Ford's life has been surprisingly ignored by non-fiction writers. The first novelist to approach the subject of Ford at full length was Upton Sinclair. In 1919 Sinclair met Ford, and during their interview Ford declared: "I am going to tell the people what they need to know. I am going to tell them who makes war, and how the game of rotten politics is worked.... Above all else, I am going to tell the young men to find useful things to do, because that is the way to be happy in this world" (Jardim 140). One would think the politically leftist Sinclair would agree with Ford, and he did at that time. However, by 1937 a great change had come over Ford, and in *The Flivver King*, his fictionalized biography of Ford, Sinclair chronicles this transformation as he shows through Ford the effects of the capitalist system on an individual trying to effect social change.

 The Flivver King parallels the story of Ford with that of Abner Schutt, a poor youth living in the same Detroit neighborhood as Ford, who is attempting to perfect his horseless carriage. Abner's father tells his son of the American Dream: how men can rise from poverty by producing useful things that raise the standard of living. Ford tells Abner he is making such a thing, an automobile, not for the rich, but for everyone. Eventually Ford builds his car and starts a company, and Abner gets a job on the assembly line screwing on spindle-nuts, becoming "a cog in a machine which had been conceived in the brain of Henry Ford" (33). Through Abner's work experiences, Sinclair demonstrates how assembly-line manufacturing demeans the worker, particularly a good worker like Schutt, who sees his job as a duty and responsibility. Like many Ford workers, Abner wanted enough money to buy the product he was manufacturing. However, Sinclair relates how Ford's five-dollar days perpetuated a system of consumer exploitation: now that the workers made more money, capitalists indoctrinated them into believing they needed to buy more things, cars in particular. A 1924 advertisement for Chevrolet accentuates the perpetuation of the concept that owning a car bettered the life of a worker. The ad proclaims: "The once poor laborer and mechanic now drives to the building operation or construction job in his own car. He is now a capitalist . . ." (Stern 21).

As in the case of Leonard's book, *The Flivver King* also underscores the tragic nature of Ford's life. Leonard professes, "In the United States a record of commercial success makes a man an authority on every subject" (241). Sinclair focuses on how this dictum changed Ford. In the novel, Ford's pragmatism and simplicity gradually evolve into protectionism and paranoia. He becomes a pawn to all those who tell him what he wants to hear. Sinclair's version of Ford's connections to the famed "peace ship" is a good example. Desiring peace and American non-intervention in the Great War raging in Europe, Ford is convinced by pacifists to sail to Europe as an American anti-war advocate, but Ford becomes sick and disillusioned with the trip, returning home ultimately to oversee the manufacturing of countless instruments of destruction used in the war. This event is the first of many in the novel that sour Ford's social zeal. The more money Ford makes, the more he uses his wealth to isolate and insulate himself from all that he dislikes. "'What shall I do?' asked the Flivver King; and the billion dollars was at his ear, whispering like Mephistopheles into the ear of Faust," writes Sinclair (234). Corresponding to this insulation, the less Ford cares for the average worker.

Later in Ford's life, he turns to collecting pieces of Americana for his museums, seemingly in an effort to recapture a past he has been greatly responsible for reconfiguring. As Robert Lacey maintains, the Flivver King

> looked back to an age of pastoral content and plenty . . . the vanished world which Henry Ford, later in life, was to seek to recapture—

although he more than anyone else was instrumental in its destruction. As wealth gave the great carmaker the means to give shape to his beliefs, those beliefs turned out to be very much those of a late nineteenth century Michigan farmer: temperance, an odd familiarity with currency theories, mistrust of the eastern establishment, and a particular mistrust of Wall Street, moneylenders, and the Jews. (29)

Ford "had thought that men could have the machinery and comforts of a new world, while keeping the ideas of the old," but he was wrong, writes Sinclair (138).

In Sinclair's view, Ford, in essence, becomes a feudal lord over his goods and factories. He has "two hundred thousand slaves making themselves parts of machines—pick-up, push-in, turn, reverse, pickuppushinturnreverse, pickuppushinturnreverse" (Sinclair 146). Rather than promote goodwill among his workers, he spies on them. His so-called intelligence bureau develops into a mafia of informants and union busters, led by one Harry Bennett. As Sinclair says, the promotion of Bennett, who replaced Rev. Samuel Marquis as Ford's closest advisor, was akin to "casting out Christ and putting Caesar in his place" (183). The story of Abner Schutt continues as one of his sons, Henry Ford Schutt, becomes a henchman for Bennett's security force.

Ultimately, Abner is broken by Ford's feudalism. Frequently impoverished by lay-offs and poor worker treatment, he is discarded and replaced on the assembly line by someone younger and faster. In *Middletown*, Robert and Helen Lynd reflect thus on this phenomenon: "In modern machine production it is speed and endurance that are a premium. A boy of nineteen may, after a few weeks of experience on a machine, turn out an amount of work greater than that of his father of forty-five" (31-32). Ford's own writings also reflect this premium on youth and the expendability of experience in favor of quantitative production: "A business is men and machines united in the production of a commodity and both the men and the machines need repairs and replacements. . . . Machinery wears out and needs to be restored. Men grow uppish, lazy, or careless . . ." (Rothschild 34). This view corresponds perfectly with Ford's desire to make the parts of all things interchangeable and uniform, whether they be inanimate or human.

Abner's youngest son, Tom, becomes a labor activist campaigning to redress the injustices of the exploitational factory system. As such,

Tom deplores how his own family, particularly his oldest brother, who becomes an engineer for Ford, "had become ravenous for success; worshipping the Ford machine and everybody in it with such fervor that they were intolerable . . ." (218). The conclusion of the novel contrasts proletarian Tom being attacked and beaten by Ford's henchmen for organizing a labor rally while Ford, oblivious to the life of his oppressed workers, dines at a party on a huge cake made in the shape of a V-8 engine.

Like many of Sinclair's works, *The Flivver King* exposes the evils of a worker-exploiting system and calls for action from the proletariat. Yet Ford, the man, is not presented solely as a diabolical promoter of this corrupt system, but rather as a person, like Abner Schutt, caught in its clutches. The system destroys Ford as much as it does Schutt, though Ford's decimation in the novel is spiritual, not economic or physical. Like Leonard, Sinclair was apparently unable to write a muckraking attack on Henry Ford; Sinclair also greatly pities Ford as if he were the hero of a Greek tragedy. In fact, his book ennobles Ford as a king—a Flivver king—an ironic rank if ever one were so titled.[14] Sinclair's subtitle, *A Story of Ford-America*, also intimates that Ford's story is exemplary of the exploitations of the American capitalistic system.

Ragtime

Nearly forty years after *The Flivver King*, E. L. Doctorow once more treated the subject of Henry Ford in *Ragtime* (1975), a novel of American life in the decade of the 1910s. Automobility comprises an integral part of this novel. Critic Geoffrey Harpham has suggested that the novel was "produced by a narratological assembly line" as if it were a car (Gentry 111), while Marshall Gentry has gone so far as to say that "this novel is itself an automobile" (106). The central conflict of the book arises when the Model T of African-American Coalhouse Walker is destroyed by a racist fire chief and Walker seeks retaliation for this crime. The book opens and closes with scenes involving automobiles. At the onset, Harry Houdini literally drives into the lives of central characters Father and Mother when his Pope-Toledo Runabout hits a telephone pole outside their house. And at the book's conclusion, Mother, now divorced from Father, motors through upstate New York in her Packard touring car.[15]

With so much attention focused on automobiles, it is not surprising that Ford plays a role in the novel. Like Sinclair, Doctorow also captures the sense of paradox in Ford himself, particularly in his juxtaposition to the high-society J. P. Morgan, with whom Ford dines. Ford is still a man who wears "good comfortable shoes" from L. L. Bean (173), and he projects a seemingly simple attitude about him, though Doctorow finds it to be a manufactured aura: "Part of his genius consisted of seeming to his executives and competitors not as quick-witted as they" (154-55). Morgan exalts Ford, not as a Flivver King, but as a pharaoh, a literal reincarnation of Seti I, father of Ramses. At a private dinner in Ford's honor, Morgan, the economic pharaoh of the decade, asks Ford, the industrial one: "Has it occurred to you that your assembly line is not merely a stroke of industrial genius but a projection of organic truth?" (168). "I could look at something and tell you how it worked and probably show you how to make it better," Ford tells Morgan in response (174). Ford's philosophy of interchangeability is thus seen as his attempt to better society by making it machine-efficient: "Ford established the final proposition of the theory of industrial manufacture—not only that the parts of the finished product be interchangeable, but that the men who build the products be themselves interchangeable parts" (155). Doctorow's words echo those of Sinclair concerning the worker's reduction to a cog in the industrial machine, and his description of Ford's reaction to his discovery of the assembly line solidifies both the sense of Ford's own pragmatic world view and his feelings toward the work force: "Now he [Ford] experienced an ecstasy greater and more intense than that vouchsafed to any American before him. . . . He had caused a machine to replicate itself endlessly. He allotted sixty seconds on his pocket watch for a display of sentiment. Then he sent everyone back to work . . ." (155).

Assembly and interchangeability, central concepts to Ford, are also central to the novel's theme and structure. Barbara Estrin elaborates:

> *Ragtime* examines the philosophy of interchangeable parts as an economic and psychological construct. The book's central thesis turns human beings into cogs on the wheel of time. . . . As interchangeable parts, famous, near-famous, and infamous personalities of the period cross paths. . . . And, as interchangeable parts, the three central and separate families of the novel not only meet but merge, become . . . proof positive that America is a melting

> pot. . . . This melting represents the great American idea as the
> narrator views it. The genius of the twentieth century is, by
> industrialization and by assimilation, to produce more of the
> same. . . . History becomes a cycle of . . . 'interchangeable parts'. . . .
> (21-22)

Hence, the organic truth of Ford's industrial philosophy becomes the
organic truth of America and of the construction of the novel itself.
Like Ford turning his workers into parts of the machine whole,
Doctorow turns his characters into interchangeable parts on the
assembly line of history. As Marshall Gentry concludes, "[T]he society
of the ragtime era appeared to value automobiles more highly than
people . . ." (105).

John Dos Passos

This literary use of the assembly-line process is perhaps most lucidly
illustrated in the works of John Dos Passos, particularly his *U.S.A.*
trilogy. In fact, John L. Grigsby argues that the automobile is "the
central vehicle by which Dos Passos simultaneously presents and
satirizes American life in the 1920s," finding particularly in *The Big
Money* that "the automobile is the central symbol of industrial
society's, of the 'big money's' power run amok, technological and
automotive power which is satirically presented as corrupting the
characters' values, controlling their individual choices, and often
violently and prematurely ending their lives" (36).

Similar to Sinclair's treatment of Ford in *The Flivver King*, Dos
Passos's biography of Ford in *The Big Money* accentuates the tragedy
of Ford's rags-to-riches story and condemns Ford's treatment of
assembly-line workers. The excerpt below resembles the rapid structure
of Sinclair's "pickuppushinturnreverse" passage in which the prose
mimics the speedup of the assembly line. Here, Dos Passos lambastes
the oppression of Ford's system:

> At Ford's production was improving all the time; less waste, more
> spotters, strawbosses, stoolpigeons (fifteen minutes for lunch, three
> minutes to go to the toilet, the Taylorized speedup everywhere,
> reachunder, adjustwasher, screwdown bolt, reachunderadjustscrew-
> downreachunderadjust, until every ounce of life was sucked off into

production and at night the workmen went home gray shaking husks). (59)

Even the title of Dos Passos's book reflects Ford's realization of the profitability of his system of mass assembly: "*The big money* was in economical quantity production, quick turnover, cheap interchangeable easilyreplaced standardized parts" (Dos Passos 54). Thus Dos Passos, like Sinclair and Doctorow, satirically comments on the consequences of interchangeability and assembly.

More interesting than Dos Passos's thematic treatment of Ford however, is his structural utilization of Ford's methodology in the assemblage of his novels. Though, like Sinclair, Dos Passos condemns Ford's system for its abuses, like Doctorow, he makes use of it in the composition of his own fiction. As early as 1942 Alfred Kazin said of *U.S.A.*: "The book lives by its narrative style, the wonderfully concrete yet elliptical prose which bears along and winds around the life stories in the book like a conveyor belt carrying Americans through some vast Ford plant of the human spirit" (353). Dos Passos's style is that of the literary assembly-line worker, putting together component stories and texts within the structure of his four basic units of the trilogy: the Newsreel, the Camera Eye, the Biography, and the main narrative. An anonymous review in *Time* (10 August 1936) purported that Dos Passos "never talks about creation in connection with his work. His job, he feels, is simply to arrange the materials" ("Private" 52). Cecelia Tichi adds:

> Dos Passos's numerous characters are presented as human components integrated in a large-scale, dynamic system conceived on the model of machine and structural technology. In this sense the characters function virtually as parts interchangeable throughout the American scene. . . . Dos Passos severely criticizes a world in which people are so vulnerable to sociocultural forces that drive them apart; his novels, however, are marvels of integrated structure. He is America's engineer-novelist. (202)

Indeed, Dos Passos himself would seem to agree with Tichi, entitling his address before the 1935 Congress of American Writers "The Writer as Technician."

Though few fiction writers have made Ford the principal character of a work, his paradoxical figure nevertheless holds a central role in American fiction. To most Americans, Ford is a fictional conception, a rags-to-riches archetype, a populist hero. Like the Russian peasants, we too have placed Ford on our icon shelf. When fiction writers approach Ford, their works generally capture the sense of tragedy in the life of this once simple man who became entangled in the complex web of American capitalistic success. Beyond his personal biography, Ford perhaps influenced American fiction even more in his advocacy of interchangeability and assembly manufacturing, concepts which have been adopted as integral structural tools in modern American fiction. Dos Passos's *U.S.A.* and Doctorow's *Ragtime* clearly make use of these concepts. Other works, such as Norman Mailer's *The Naked and the Dead*, also demonstrate how component parts and characters of a novel can be assembled into a coherent fictional creation, much as the component parts of a Model T were put together.

In *Ragtime* Doctorow sees all of history through Fordized glasses, viewing it as a cycle of interchangeable parts—an interesting conception to be connected to a man famed for the observation that "history is bunk." Nonetheless, the impact of *Fordismus* on American history and writing is not bunk, a fact which has led to dis-ease in more than one writer. Writing in a 1923 issue of *Broom*, Matthew Josephson expressed this sense unswervingly when he called Ford, "not a human creature. He is a principle, or better a relentless process. . . . Let Ford be president. Let him *assemble* us all into his machine" (Silk 100). And perhaps he did. As British writer Aldous Huxley saw it, maybe in our brave new world we do live in "the year of our Ford." In *Flesh of Steel* Thomas West asserts that "when Henry Ford invented his automotive assembly line, he established not only a method of manufacture but a kind of intellectual and literary convention. For the assembly line has come to represent the machine process itself, . . . it is Discipline perfectly embroidered" (ix).

"The Inescapable Destiny": Cars and Rural America

Ford wanted to build automobiles for the masses, to create a great nation of auto-mobile citizens, and examining contemporary American culture would lead one to conclude that Ford's dream has been realized for the most part. Because Ford cars were readily available even to the poorest workers, the alliance between cars and American culture increased at all levels. Winthrop Scarrett expressed this deepening affiliation in Harper's as early as 1907: "Yesterday it [the automobile] was the plaything of the few, to-day it is the servant of many, to-morrow it will be the necessity of humanity" (Schneider, Autokind 29).

On the literary scene, few writers before the 1930s concentrated on the "servant of many"; hence, the majority of automobiles presented in American literature belonged to the middle and upper classes. With Erskine Caldwell, John Steinbeck, and William Faulkner, however, this fact changed. Their works illustrate how automobility transformed America's rural poor, becoming the "necessity of humanity" by creating new possibilities for them, yet simultaneously entrapping them in a new cultural order.

Erskine Caldwell

Focusing on the lives of poor Southerners, Erskine Caldwell's novels establish the growing role of automobility in rural America during the late Twenties and early Thirties. Both *God's Little Acre* (1932) and *Tobacco Road* (1933) portray how the automobile altered rural life by expanding rural and urban contact; by increasing mobility, thereby allowing farmers to get away from the country to pursue other forms of employment, particularly mill work; and by restructuring the lives of poor farmers by diminishing the importance of the extended family and increasing their material desires.

The title of *Tobacco Road* harkens to an era already rapidly diminishing by the 1930s. Dirt tobacco roads once led back off main highways to farms and shanties representative of the old South, but the pace of life found on tobacco roads was no match for the speed of the new highways on which motorists "raced over the hot concrete at seventy miles an hour" on their way to larger towns and cities (*God's* 65). These highways paved the way to economic opportunities beyond the farm: for example, Jim Leslie in *God's Little Acre* and Lov in *Tobacco Road* have both left the farm to secure non-agricultural work. However, Caldwell does not present a rosy picture of the life to which these highways lead.[16]

The society of automobility was also the society of exploitational factory work and alienating city life, particular concerns of Caldwell's socialistic mission. To former country dwellers, urban life also presented added temptations, such as whores who "came down to the street and dragged men out of their cars" (*God's* 99). Caldwell's rural characters have difficulty adapting to urban culture, as exemplified by Ty Ty's comment in *God's Little Acre*: "You know good and well I can't drive an automobile in the big city" (93). Urban economics required a rejection of the soil not viable for an individual rooted to the land. As Lov, the mill worker, eulogizes Jeeter in *Tobacco Road*:

> He was a man who liked to grow things in the ground. The mills ain't no place for a human who's got that in his bones. The mills is sort of like automobiles—they're all right to fool around in and have a good time in, but they don't offer no love like the ground does. . . . When people . . . walk around on hard streets, the ground sort of loses interest in the human. (169)

Lov's comments reinvoke those of Lewis's Edith Cortright, who warns Dodsworth about the dangers of life detached from contact with the good earth.

The breakdown of the division between rural and urban society also led to an increased desire for material culture among rural inhabitants. Quite often this desire was for an automobile, a visible symbol of upward mobility. Though the car was not new to this generation of Southerners, the previous generation held the object in a different light. To them it was essentially a beast of burden, a farm tool. For example, Pa Jeeter owns a dilapidated rusty car and has no desire for a new one; however, unlike his father, Jeeter's son Dude clamors for a fancy new vehicle to keep him on the go: "'When is you going to buy yourself an automobile, Lov?' Dude asked. 'You make a heap of a lot of money at the chute—you ought to buy yourself a great big car, like the ones the rich people in Augusta has got'" (34). To Dude, the automobile is the ultimate representation of material culture, the object which all city people should work to possess. Dude marries Sister Bessie, an older woman, solely because she offers to buy him a new car. He even expresses his concern over Bessie's fidelity in terms of the car: "You ain't going to let nobody else drive it, is you?" Dude asks (96). Writing on John Ford's version of *Tobacco Road*, Kenneth Hey addresses the difference between Jeeter's and Dude's generations in their assessment of automobility. Hey argues that the dilapidation of Jeeter's car matches his "indifference to efficiency, progress, and increased productivity," the essence of modernism. Jeeter's view therefore directly contradicts that of Dude, who desires these things. This contrast leads to direct conflict between old and new generations, as exemplified when Dude pushes Jeeter's old car into a ditch. Tranquility, nature, and the family are thus disrupted by the vehicle (195-97).

Indeed, the automobile disrupts and even destroys family life in Caldwell's novels. Not only does the car lead to the breakup of the extended family as a result of increased mobility for the children, the car also leads in both *God's Little Acre* and *Tobacco Road* to the death of one family member at the hands (wheels) of another. In *God's Little Acre* Jim Leslie becomes fatally attracted to Buck's wife Griselda when she visits him on an automobile trip to Augusta. Later he drives to the country to steal her away and in an ensuing brawl with Buck is shot and killed. Significantly, Buck shoots Jim Leslie in front of his automobile. The narrator writes that Jim Leslie could have stepped behind the vehicle and used it for protection from the gun blast, but the car did him no good (181).

The automobile is even more directly related to a family death in *Tobacco Road*. At one point, Ada, the mother, is nearly run over in the attempt by Jeeter, Bessie, and Dude to run off to Augusta without her. This event foreshadows the manslaughter of Grandmother Lester near the end of the book. After a family argument, Dude and Bessie run down the old woman and then back over her in their escape: "The automobile had struck her with such force that she did not know what had hit her. Both of the left wheels had rolled over her, one of them across her back and the other on her head" (153). Mother Lester's death graphically illustrates the automobile's contribution to the destruction of family order.

Not all events connected to the automobile are as dark as Mother Lester's accident, though. Some are quite humorous, but the humor in these situations ultimately points to the rural poor's misguided attempts to appropriate the culture of urban consumption. Darling Jill in *God's Little Acre* is inept at automotive upkeep: she speeds along in a car with a flat tire, thereby ruining both tire and inner-tube. Dude and Bessie are just as incompetent. This passage from *Tobacco Road* sarcastically describes Dude's driving ability and signifies how out of control these people's lives are:

> Dude was a good driver, all right; he swung out of the tracks just at
> the right moment every time he met another automobile. Only two or

three times did he almost run head-on into other cars. He was so busy blowing the horn that he forgot to drive on the right hand side of the road until the last minute. Most of the cars they met gave them plenty of road when they heard the horn blowing. (126)

As further indication of their inability to operate the vehicle, almost as soon as they purchase their new car, Bessie and Dude run all the oil out of the engine, spring the front axle, crack the windshield, scar the paint job, tear holes in the upholstery, sell the spare tire, and run over a Negro. Furthermore, they consider these events "nothing more than the ordinary hazards of driving a car" (142).

Bessie is particularly dumfounded over her bad luck with the car, particularly since she said a prayer to bless the vehicle upon its purchase:

> Dear God, we poor sinners kneel down in this garage to pray for a blessing on this new automobile. . . . This new automobile is for me and Dude to ride around in and do the work You want done for You in this sinful country. You ought to make us not have wrecks with it, so we won't get hurt none. . . . And these two men here who sold the new car to us need your blessing, too. . . . You ought to bless their work and show them how to sell people new automobiles for the best good, just like You would do if You was down here selling automobiles Yourself. . . . (85-86)

In this comic passage the infusion of the automobile into religious practices leads to an ironic juxtaposition. In fact, the automobile led to numerous changes in the practice of rural religion. Though many pastors attacked the "devil wagon" for decimating Sabbath worship attendance, others praised it for "permitting the church to reach out to a wider field and thus increase the area of its influence" (Berger 131 ff.). Of greater concern to many religious moralists was the automobile's role in promoting immoral behavior in youth, particularly in the area of sexual ethics. Bessie, however, appears not to be concerned with the negative aspects of automobility but with the opportunities the car will afford for spreading the Gospel. Yet as the novel progresses, we become increasingly aware of the dubious nature of her "mission." The consecration of her automobile thus seems to have been a hollow sacrament.

Tom Wolfe suggests that in the South "the automobile represented not only liberation from what was still pretty much a land-bound form of social organization but also a great leap forward into twentieth-century glamour" (132-33). Finding much twentieth-century glamour in Caldwell's works proves a difficult task. Instead, Caldwell's novels present a sometimes comic, but invariably acute historical picture of the metamorphosis of rural culture during the automobile age. His observations are supported by those of historians such as Michael Berger, whose *The Devil Wagon in God's Country: The Automobile and Social Change in Rural America, 1893-1929* echoes analogous nationwide changes in rural family and community life, leisure, religion, education, and labor to those seen in the portrayal of the South in *God's Little Acre* and *Tobacco Road*. Other historians such as Joseph Interrante chronicle still another shift in agrarian America due largely to automobiles: "During the 1920s farm labor changed from an all-male occupation organized around the social milieu of rail-riding and hobo camps to one composed of poor families who used automobiles for travel" (96). This type of change directly underlies the circumstances of Steinbeck's *The Grapes of Wrath* (1939).

John Steinbeck

In *The Automobile Age* James Flink argues that "mass motorization played a key role in creating the most important necessary conditions underlying the Depression" (189). Admitting that obviously the Depression cannot simply be reduced to a single cause, Flink then elaborates how the new-car market saturation of the late Twenties and technological stagnation in the automobile industry were significant contributors to the nation's economic decline. The steep decrease in spending prior to the stock market collapse "resulted from economic dislocations that were an essential ingredient of the automobile boom, and from the inevitable drying up of that boom" (189).

Probably no work of fiction depicts this Depression era as vividly and powerfully as Steinbeck's *The Grapes of Wrath*; and given Flink's hypothesis, it is not surprising to find the automobile at the heart of Steinbeck's novel. Nevertheless, on the surface Steinbeck places no obvious blame on the automobile for the conditions of the displaced Joads and thousands of similarly disenfranchised families. One might even suggest that the automobile could be seen as their only tool of empowerment, a machine allowing them to escape the crushing forces of the dust bowl and to migrate to and within California in search of work. As described by Interrante, the Joads represent a new kind of American poverty, a mobile one made possible by the car, and, according to Flink and others, possibly even caused by the automobile. Two factors contribute to the family's being supplanted from their Oklahoma farm: the "Dust Bowl" drought, and the mechanization of the farm, with the latter signifying replacement of sharecropping and small-farm ownership by technologized agri-business. The same type of internal-combustion engine powering the vehicle of the Joads' migration to California also powers the tractors which replace sharecroppers like them, and it powers the vehicles of the wealthy and powerful who turn them off their land. Thus, though motorized vehicles suggest possible redemption for families like the Joads by enabling them to travel to more prosperous parts of the country in search of work (even when such prosperity proves illusive), they simultaneously displace families and embody images of the corporate structure which exploits the plight of these workers. In fact, within the framework of the novel the automobile becomes a compound signifier representing a myriad of interpretive possibilities as complex as the causes of the Depression itself.

When the film version of the novel premiered in Europe in 1940, lower-class workers could not understand the plight of the Joads. After all, how could a family rich enough to own and travel about in an automobile be considered destitute? This inability to empathize with the Joads' condition clearly dramatizes the unique situation of homeless Depression-era Americans within the context of more global perceptions of poverty. Though the Joads are homeless in the sense that they do not have a permanent house in which to live, they nevertheless have shelter, if not in government or workers' camp houses, a boxcar, or a barn, then in the automobile, which, in essence, becomes a mobile home for them. Thus, to the poor of Europe, the Joads had it made. In their sequel to *Middletown, Middletown in Transition* (1937), the Lynds report that car ownership

> was one of the most depression-proof elements of the city's life in the years following 1929—far less vulnerable, apparently, than marriages, divorces, new babies, clothing, jewelry, and most other measurable things. . . . All of which suggests that, since about 1920, the automobile has come increasingly to occupy a place among Middletown's "musts" close to food, clothing, and shelter. (267)

Simeon Strunsky's 1939 book on contemporary civilization, *The Living Tradition*, supports the Lynds' assessment: "When the great depression struck we had in the country twenty-six million automobiles against eighteen million telephones and less than twenty-five million consumers of electric light" (174). European film audiences were unable to realize what the Lynds and Strunsky had concluded: the car had become a "must" in America—an inextricable symbiosis existed between an American and a car, a bond as strong as family ties in some cases.

In a passage from the novel which occurs immediately after the Joads have packed for their departure from Oklahoma, the focal importance of the vehicle in these people's lives is made prominent: "The family met at *the most important place*, near the truck. The house was dead, and the fields were dead; but this truck was *the active thing, the living principle*. The ancient Hudson, with bent and scarred radiator screen ... was the new hearth*, the living center of the family* ..." (136—emphases added). This Hudson Super-Six with its top cut off and a truck bed fitted on becomes the crux of family life. Cynthia Dettelbach asserts that "Steinbeck distills the vast range of human experience" into the vehicle: "The young children sleep, the men talk and reminisce, and Connie and Rosasharn make love under the stars. A couple of feet away from the young couple, grandma lies dying and ma ... keeps the vigil alone and in silence through the night" (74). Indeed, family and vehicle are symbiotic, as evidenced when Steinbeck writes that Al Joad "had become the soul of the car" (167). With the Joads, car and American family are unquestionably spiritually united.[17] The new adjective *motorcentric* appeared in the early Thirties; originally applied to architecture, it nevertheless accurately describes the focus of the Joads' lives—they center on the car.[18]

In the late Thirties countless thousands of Americans packed their vehicles and joined the Joads on the road in search of opportunity. The Joads are emblematic not only of these families, forced to relocate during the Depression, but of a general drive among the populace to move in search of new possibilities. Steinbeck himself outfitted an old bakery truck to travel among migrant workers while doing research for the book (Benson 332), and thirty years after writing *The Grapes of Wrath* he traveled across the country with his dog in another half-breed vehicle, a truck camper, collecting his observations for *Travels with Charley*: "I was to see over and over in every part of the nation—a burning desire to go, to move, to get under way, anyplace, away from any Here. . . . Nearly every American hungers to move" (*Travels* 10). Later in the book Steinbeck continues: "Could it be that Americans are a restless people, a mobile people, never satisfied with where they are as a matter of selection? The pioneers, the immigrants who peopled the continent, were the restless ones in Europe. . . . [E]very one of us, except the Negroes forced here as slaves, are descended from the restless ones . . ." (93).

Steinbeck embraces this spirit of movement in his own cross-country circuit, but in spite of his apparent appreciation for his vehicle, which allows him to travel freely, he condemns the technological apparatus which makes automobility readily accessible to the masses. He attacks both the driving force of automotive marketing, "planned obsolescence" (*Travels* 41), and the premier method of automotive manufacturing, the assembly line, by exalting the story of "a humble man who didn't care for mass production" (53) and declaiming: "I protest the assembly-line production of our food, our songs, our language, and eventually our souls . . ." (97). Steinbeck's personal observations exude similar duplex responses to automobility that are expressed in his story of the Joads and America in the late 1930s: on one hand the car delivers these people, yet on the other it is responsible for their plight.

The Joads, however, see their car only in a positive light. It carries them to the promised land of California, and to get them there they give it their every attention. They even take on the responsibility of upkeep for another family's car, the Wilsons', nursing it to health when it breaks down. Attention to human needs does not fare nearly so well as assistance to vehicles: for instance, Grandma dies sacrificially in the back of the vehicle while the car continues on its safe passage through the desert in the cool night air. To the Joads the car is priority one. Tom is shocked to learn there are families without cars: "Ain't you got no car?" he asks his vehicleless co-workers at the government camp, astonished to discover people are able to work in spite of a lack of wheels (400).

To impoverished Americans like the Joads, the car represented hope for a new place and a better life, and a better life meant partaking not of *The Grapes of Wrath*, but of the fruits of conspicuous consumption. A good example of this desire is seen in Rosasharn's husband Connie, who wants a car of his own, a house for him and Rosasharn, and lots of "things": "Connie says all new stuff" (224). Throughout America the highways were filled with families heading west, heading hopefully for the "new stuff" Connie desires so much. They traveled to California on Highway 66, "the main migrant road":

> 66—the lone concrete path across the country, waving gently up and down the map, from the Mississippi to Bakersfield. . . . 66 is the path of a people in flight, refugees from dust and shrinking land, from the thunder of tractors and shrinking ownership, from the desert's slow northward invasion. . . . From all these are the people in flight, and they will come into 66 from the tributary side roads, from the wagon tracks and the rutted country roads. 66 is the mother road, the road of flight. (160)

Route 66 replaced the Mississippi as the primary arterial system of American movement. In the novel, one diner along the route houses all types of people on the move: truck drivers, Okies, wealthy Easterners. The waitress there wipes the counter, "And her eyes were on the highway, where life whizzed by" (220). On this highway thousands headed toward what they hoped would be new and better opportunities.

Like vultures, some were quick to prey on this hopeful exodus. "People are wandering in, bewildered, needing a car" (87), Steinbeck writes as he depicts how unscrupulous salesmen capitalized on the need of these Americans for cars:

> In the towns, on the edges of the towns, in fields, in vacant lots, the used-car yards, the wrecker' yards, the garages with blazoned signs—Used Cars, Good Used Cars. Cheap transportation, three trailers, '27 Ford, clean. Checked cars, guaranteed cars. Free radio. Car with 100 gallons of gas free. Come in and look. Used cars. No overhead. . . . Salesmen, neat, deadly, small intent eyes watching for weaknesses. Watch the woman's face. If the woman likes it we can screw the old man. . . . Flags, red and white, white and blue—all along the curb. Used cars. Good Used Cars. (83-84)

The unscrupulous practices of these car lots bode of other ills to befall the migrating hoards. The worn lives of these individuals are much like the used cars they buy. As one character notes, "You're not buying only junk, you're buying junked lives" (118).

As is evidenced by these unscrupulous salesmen, the highway and automobility, in spite of seemingly teeming with life and possibility, conceal malevolence. As in Caldwell's works, automobiles also embody death. The car can take families to promised opportunities, but like a bad used car, many of these supposed opportunities turn out to be illusions, death-traps. That the car contains both possibilities is first suggested in Chapter Three in the story of a turtle crossing the road. The slow turtle is certainly no match for the powerful speeding vehicles storming down the highway. It has good luck when the driver of the first vehicle that approaches swerves to miss it, nearly causing the car to wreck; however, the driver of the second vehicle, a transfer truck, runs over the turtle on purpose and leaves it fatally wounded. Death from the automobile is further suggested when a car runs over the family dog outside a service station, an event which foreshadows the deaths of both grandparents, which also take place on the road. And no differently than the family dog, Grandpa is buried by the side of the highway.

Not only are people dying as a result of the automobile, ways of life are dying as well. The service station at which the family first stops suffers from the same automobile-related factors which dislocate the Joads. Tom says prophetically to the station attendant: "'Pretty soon you'll be on the road yourse'f. And it ain't tractors'll put you there. It's them pretty yellow stations in town. Folks is movin','' he said ashamedly. 'An' you'll be movin', mister'" (174). Tom recognizes the technological forces leading to the family's displacement, and he identifies tractors and the pretty yellow service stations in town, both emblems of the mass production and standardization characteristic of big business, as two of those forces.

Tractors, products of the same technology as car manufacturing, also led to the replacement of the small farmer. As one character notes in Chapter Five: one tractor can take the place of twelve to fourteen families. Tractors revolutionized farm life, dispossessing not only farmers but farm animals as well. A car salesman pronounces: "Mules! Hey, Joe, hear this? This guy wants to trade mules. Didn't nobody tell you this is the machine age? They don't use mules for anything but glue no more" (87). Still, in spite of the tractor's taking the farmer out of contact with land and animals, thereby removing agriculture's humanistic element, some farmers were nonetheless captivated by the machine:

> He could admire the tractor—its machined surfaces, its surge of power, the roar of its detonating cylinders.... Behind the tractor rolled the shining disks, cutting the earth with blades—not plowing

but surgery. . . . The driver sat in his iron seat and he was proud of
. . . the tractor he did not own or love, proud of the power he could
not control. (48-9)

Like Al, who becomes the soul of the Joads' Hudson, this farmer
becomes one with the machine, riding along like countless other farm
workers unable to control the changes overpowering them.

These changes were financed chiefly through wealthy industrialists
and landowners. The hegemony of this class and its exploitation of
other classes are central concerns in Steinbeck's work. At the core of
Steinbeck's novel is the division of America into two opposing camps:
land owners and laborers, the haves and the have-nots. It has already
been demonstrated how the huge landowners replaced sharecroppers
with machines like the tractor; moreover, these members of the landed
class quite often in the novel are connected to another machine—their
cars. While migrant workers like the Joads are also attached to their
vehicles, the cars of the poor are usually comically depicted, never
described as imbued with the menacing quality which Steinbeck infers
from the vehicles of those in the power structure. In Chapter Five
Steinbeck relates the story of landowners who drive big roadsters and
come to dispossess sharecroppers. These men never exit their
expensive cars, and they talk to the farmers through rolled-down
windows, their faces concealed behind headlights. The same is true of
the police and bosses who patrol the Hoovervilles in California.
Standing in the shadows of their automobiles, they too are empowered
by their intimidating and piercing headlamps.

The sentiments of the empowered toward the disenfranchised are
clearly seen in the inhumane treatment of the less fortunate. The
fortunate seek to hide away all signs of the poor, as evidenced by the
greeting the Joads receive upon arriving in California: "The whole
United States . . . ain't big enough. There ain't room enough for you
an' me, for your kind an' my kind, for rich and poor together all in one
country. . . . Whyn't you go back where you come from?" (163). This
attitude is clearly reflected in American society's changing perceptions
of automobile camping. As noted in an earlier chapter, in the Teens and
Twenties wealthy Easterners headed west on the highways, spending
the night in tourist camps or by the side of the road. The rapid growth
of tourism originated in this travel movement. By the middle of the
Depression, however, communities no longer accepted this
vagabondage. Terms like "auto gypsy" and "motor vagabond" now

took on negative connotations (Belasco, *Americans* 114). When the lower classes took to the road, spending the night by the highways or on the edge of town, the local people began to worry about the respectability of their communities. An Iowa mayor writing in the periodical *American Municipalities* (October 1924) charged:

> Ten years ago ... the average tourist was the person who was traveling for pleasure and was a desirable visitor. Today many of the tourists are people with no means whatever. If a tenant on a farm fails to make good, ... he immediately loads his family in a jitney and starts traveling.... This type of tourist is no value to any community.... (Belasco, *Americans* 110)

The Joads are warned that California has laws against vagrants sleeping by the roadside. No less than FBI Director J. Edgar Hoover warned about automobile tourist camps in the February 1940 *American Magazine*, calling these places, "a new home of crime in America, a new home of disease, bribery, corruption, crookedness, rape, white slavery, thievery, and murder." "KEEP CLOSE WATCH ON TOURIST CAMPS!" he exclaimed (14). Established Americans grew to distrust the new mobile poor, especially since they had appropriated the transportation machinery of the middle and upper classes.

The conclusion of the novel places a final emphasis on the complex combination of the car and the rural family. In the end of the book, as the family hangs on in desperation, its members scattered, a flood approaching, the car which has served them so faithfully is torn apart to provide materials to build a platform to raise the family to safety above the rising flood waters. Parallel to this ultimate sacrifice comes the death of Rosasharn's baby, Al's departure, and Tom's self-imposed exile. Seemingly as the car is torn apart, so is the family. Finally, the family leaves the flooded automobile and for the first time sets out on foot in their search for higher ground. We are left wondering as to their chances of survival now that they, like the men Tom met in the government camp, are carless, truly destitute.

In *The Grapes of Wrath* the automobile as signifier moves into a new realm in American fiction. Never before had the symbiosis between Americans and an automobile been so visibly portrayed. David Laird writes of the history of machines in America:

Machines promise power, mobility, freedom, even a 'poetic' space that beckons from beyond the too familiar course of things, from beyond the rush of time and time's sad waste. But . . . something like the special rule about machines begins to take effect. We sense its operation in the eventual discovery of unforeseen liabilities and losses. (244)

The Twenties marked the transition in literature from writers viewing the car romantically to those seeing and exposing its liabilities and losses. With Steinbeck, however, no longer is the automobile presented in an either/or fashion, but rather it is seen in all its cultural complexity. By the late Thirties the automobile was inexorably entrenched in the American way of life, for all its good and bad, and with *The Grapes of Wrath* we see one writer who predates what for most Americans was a post-1950s realization about the evils of motorized transport: that in spite of the negative realities of the automobile, it had achieved a condition of symbiosis with Americans and American life. Like a metastasized cancer, its effects had grown so deep that its excision would perhaps lead to social and economic fatality. The question thus became—how to live with the beast? Ignore the bad? Accentuate the good? The fact remained that the answer was not a simple yes or no. Steinbeck was perhaps the first writer to capture in one text the extensive variety of complex and conflicting messages conveyed by automobility, which by the late Thirties had truly become an inescapable phenomenon.

William Faulkner

Though Steinbeck captured these complexities in one text, William Faulkner, perhaps better than any other writer, detailed throughout his works the impact of automobility on rural Americans, specifically those living in the South.[19] It is also fitting to place Faulkner as a bridge between pre- and post-World War II literary representations of the automobile because his writings span five decades, and Faulkner employs automobiles in his works from the sketch "Country Mice," written in 1925, up to his last novel, *The Reivers*, published in 1962, the year of his death. Not surprisingly, because of the breadth of Faulkner's career, many previously employed and herein discussed literary manifestations of automobility also appear in his works. In many ways then, Faulkner's writings can be viewed as a summation of representations of automobility in American literature prior to World War II and as both a precursor to and a contemporary of many post-war significations of the car.

Throughout his career Faulkner was a prescient observer and critic of automobility. Like Boss Priest in *The Reivers*, Faulkner beheld a "vision of our nation's vast and boundless future in which the basic unit of its economy and prosperity would be a small mass-produced cubicle containing four wheels and an engine" (24). In previous works he had already attested to and ridiculed the quintessential nature of the car to the average American. "The American really loves nothing but his automobile: not his wife his child nor his country nor even his bank-account first . . . but his motorcar," he wrote in *Intruder in the Dust* (1948) (238). And in *Requiem for a Nun* (1951) he declared that soon "all America, after cutting down all the trees and levelling the hills and mountains with bulldozers, would have to move underground to make room for, get out of the way of, the motor cars" (248).

As early as 1925, in one of his earliest works, "Country Mice," Faulkner makes significant use of a motor car. Randall Waldron has insightfully pointed out how the source of this early sketch probably lies in *The Great Gatsby*, published earlier the same year. Structurally the description of the bootlegger's automobile in "Country Mice" virtually parallels Fitzgerald's description of another bootlegger's car, Jay Gatsby's Rolls-Royce; and in both works the car is used to satirize its owner. Waldron suggests that though wryly comic, Faulkner's work carries an undercurrent intimating the dark, violent power latent in the automobile. Though he does not move beyond a discussion of "Country Mice," Waldron briefly and insightfully summarizes perceptions of automobiles located throughout Faulkner's fiction:

> Faulkner viewed automobiles . . . with a mixture of good-humored affection, aesthetic admiration, and emotional—even psycho-sexual—exhilaration on the one hand, and on the other, ridicule, abhorrence and dread—as symbols of social and moral decadence, disrupters of the natural order, and instruments of violence and death. (284)

Exhilaration versus ridicule, romance versus satire—Faulkner's dichotomous representations of the automobile echo the classic opposing perceptions of the car in earlier American literature, yet not by any means with simplification. I wish to expand on Waldron's summation by examining in greater detail these manifold and tension-ridden significations of automobility in Faulkner's novels.

Somewhat surprisingly, at first glance, Faulkner's last work, not an earlier one, presents the car with more good-humored affection and in its most romanticized light. Perhaps the automotive exhilaration of *The Reivers: A Reminiscence* seems more akin to the rebellious spirit of youth characterized in the 1950s through *On the Road* than to the romances of the 1910s such as *Free Air*; nevertheless, the story of eleven-year-old Lucius Priest nostalgically waxes as it paints a picture of the rugged and adventurous nature of early automobiling, a portrait more akin to *Free Air* than *The Grapes of Wrath*. Lucius, now a grandfather himself, reminisces (as the novel's subtitle suggests) about his adventures of stealing away to Memphis with two family retainers in his grandfather's Winton Flyer (the same model as the first car to be driven across the continent).

As in *Free Air*, the threesome endures many automotive ordeals, most noteworthy their muddy crossing of a quagmire at Hell Creek. For Lucius, this experience is a rite of passage into manhood, and how fitting that the car should be a major part of it since the car would eventually become central to the maturation rites of most American youngsters. Psychologist Jean Rosenbaum attests that in the U.S., "learning to drive, getting a driver's license, and getting an automobile are the equivalent of primitive puberty rites" (10), and Lucius was born into the first generation of adolescents for whom this passage took place. Not only does learning to drive the car and his adventures with the vehicle alter Lucius, the narrative also indicates how automobility changed the life of Lucius's family by addressing the transformation of his father's livery business into the Priest Motor Company. Through the story of Lucius, *The Reivers* clearly illustrates David Laird's assertion that "cars furnish the stuff of raw sensation and exhilaration; they are vehicles of initiation into the riddles and perplexities which await the self in relation to the world it seeks to enter, and they are tokens to spend again in nostalgic reflection and celebration" (247). In the thinly disguised autobiography of this novel, Faulkner nostalgically reflects and celebrates the place of the motor car in his own youth and in the adolescence of the twentieth century, a "fabulous and legendary time when there was still no paradox between an automobile and mirth" (*The Town* 13).

In addition to embodying an emotional exhilaration, the car foments a psycho-sexual one as well. As Rosenbaum points out: "the automobile is the most common sex symbol in our modern society" (9). Gavin Stevens illustrates and corroborates the same in Faulkner's *Intruder in the Dust*:

> The automobile has become our national sex symbol. . . . We have to divorce our wife today in order to remove from our mistress the odium of mistress in order to divorce our wife tomorrow in order to remove from our mistress and so on. As a result of which the American woman has become cold and undersexed; she has projected her libido onto the automobile not only because its glitter and gadgets and mobility pander to her vanity and incapacity . . . to walk but because it will maul her and tousle her, get her all sweaty and disarranged. So in order to capture and master anything at all of her anymore the American man has got to make that car his own. Which is why let him live in a rented rathole though he must he will not only own one but renew it each year in pristine virginity, lending it to no one, . . . spending all Sunday morning washing and polishing and waxing it because in doing that he is caressing the body of the woman who has long since now denied him her bed. (238-9)[20]

Perhaps Stevens draws these conclusions from his own sexual experiences in automobiles. *The Mansion* relates the story of his and Linda Kohl's "fumbling and panting in a parked automobile like they were seventeen years old" (213), and Rosenbaum affirms that such sexual contacts are very common in our society, a fact which seems self-evident to most of us.

In *The Reivers* Boon sees the car as an object of his own lust: "Boon found his soul's lily maid, the virgin's love of his rough and innocent heart. It was a Winton Flyer" (24).[21] Marshall McLuhan asserts in *The Mechanical Bride* "that there is a widespread acceptance of the car as a womb symbol" (84). Both Stevens and Boon foster a concept of the car as mistress, a concept proffered by McLuhan and Rosenbaum, and by John Keats, who appraises the automotive marketing postulation that men buying cars are looking for a mistress. He posits that Detroit operates on the theory "that Americans don't buy automobiles, but instead buy dreams of sex, speed, power and wealth" (71-73). As early as "The Wonderful Monster," a serial published in 1905, Lady Dorothy Beeston thought of her car and "wanted to feel the throb of its quickening pulses; to lay her hand on lever and handle and thrill with the sense of mastery" (Scharff 21). Even as early as *The*

Sound and the Fury (1929) Faulkner had depicted the car as an instrument of sexuality and power through Quentin, who sneaks out to go riding (and parking) with a carnival worker, and through Caddy, who is last seen pictured beside the chromium-trimmed sports car of her lover, a German general.

Caddy's association with the German general points to another facet of this psycho-sexual alliance—it is not always exhilarating; it also incorporates a dark side. Rosenbaum asserts that automobile accidents are frequently associated with suppressed rape fantasies, particularly in young women (24). The story of Temple Drake best exemplifies this baseness. In *Sanctuary* (1931) we first see Temple associated with cars in her date with Gowan Stevens or when we learn she was once caught slipping off the college grounds to go driving, both fairly innocent connections. But as Gavin Stevens states in *Intruder*, the car can maul and tousle a woman; and with Temple, the car does just that. Her innocent experiences turn nightmarish when the drunken Gowan runs his car into a tree near a bootlegger's farm. Taken into the home of the bootlegger, Lee Goodwin, she encounters the evil Popeye, who brutally rapes her with a corn cob and murders a man who tries to protect her. Popeye then kidnaps the young woman and takes her to a Memphis brothel. Goodwin's wife last sees the transformed Temple in the front seat of Popeye's "powerful car":

> Sitting beside him, braced against jolts that had already given way to a smooth increasing hiss of gravel, Temple gazed dully forward as the road she had traversed yesterday began to flee backward under the wheels as onto a spool, feeling her blood seeping slowly inside her loins. She sat limp in the corner of the seat, watching the steady backward rush of the land . . . . (133)

Like the powerful car, the powerful evil of Popeye adulterates her, carrying her into diabolic dimensions as she dissociates herself from the road of innocence her life has previously traveled. When Horace Benbow, a lawyer defending the wrongly accused Goodwin, discovers her in the brothel only a few weeks later, he finds that she, like Popeye, has become carlike—cold, mechanical, possessing no soul. Her coldness chills to evil proportions when she returns to purger her story in court, accusing Goodwin of the crime, an act which leads to his lynching.

In the story of Temple Drake the potential for violence and death concealed in the automobile manifests itself. Even in "Country Mice" this potential is made clear when the narrator confesses he is convinced that on its first opportunity the bootlegger's car "is going to retaliate by quite viciously obliterating him" (193). This view of the machine also appears in Gavin Stevens's conviction that "man's machines had at last effaced and obliterated him from the earth" (*Intruder in the Dust* 65). These depictions of mechanization echo the pronouncements of Vanderbilt professor Andrew Nelson Lytle, who wrote in *I'll Take My Stand: The South and the Agrarian Tradition* (1930): "Since a power machine is ultimately dependent upon human control, the issue presents an awful spectacle: men, run mad by their inventions, supplanting themselves with inanimate objects. This is, to follow the matter to its conclusion, a moral and spiritual suicide, foretelling an actual physical destruction" (202). David Laird addresses this perception of machines and technology in Faulkner's work as follows: "In Faulkner's harsh chronology, the ends men seek to serve are not those they do serve; ends are mastered and transformed, emptied of meaning, by the means employed to reach them" (246). Thus machines, the automobile included, do not serve their intended purposes, but rather turn the tables on their creators, possessing and overruling them.

This belief is clearly illustrated in *Sartoris* (1929). In this novel, young Bayard Sartoris returns home to America in 1919 despairing over the death of his brother John, whose plane was shot down in the war. To assuage his melancholy, Bayard buys a fast car, in spite of the protests of his grandfather and namesake Bayard, a banker who refuses even to lend his customers money to purchase motor vehicles. Through the speed of the car, perhaps Bayard feels he can flirt with violence and even death, as he and his brother did as pilots in the war. The novel documents a series of worsening accidents Bayard endures because of his daredevil flirtations with speed. Even without the car, he is thrown from a horse he rides at full gallop; with the car, he drives off the side of a bridge, declaring of the wrecked vehicle: "Hope I didn't hurt her guts any" (212). To encourage safer driving, his grandfather takes to riding in the car with him despite doctor's orders to the contrary because of the condition of the old man's heart. The next accident occurs when a Ford runs the two Bayards off the road and down an embankment above the cemetery where John is buried, the elder Bayard dying of heart failure induced by the wreck.

The young Bayard finds himself unable to return to the life of the past, the way things were before his brother's demise; and after his grandfather's death, his attempts to do so prove even more futile. He next strives to recapture the past by abandoning his automobile and cavalierly riding his horse in a fox hunt, but the adage of getting back on the horse after falling off is no longer applicable—he cannot put his soul at ease. He thus runs away, eventually dying in the crash of a test-plane he pilots. Perhaps Bayard's obsession for speed stems from a desire to overtake time itself or from a yearning to stray as close as he possibly can to the edge of death, which has claimed both his brother and grandfather.[22] Nonetheless, Bayard finds that neither time nor death can be overcome by an automobile.

In addition to illustrating the car's capacity for violence and death, *Sartoris* also highlights what perhaps is the foremost use of the motor car in Faulkner's novels: as an incarnation of the New South, the supplanting of the ways and means of an agrarian society with that of a modernized, mechanized, mercantile class. Time and again the car is associated with this new society. In *The Mansion* Faulkner writes that the rural South had to be brought "abreast of the mental condition which accepted, could accept, the automobile as a definite ineradicable part of not only the culture but the economy also" (364). In concert with Erskine Caldwell's observations, the automobile in Faulkner's novels represents the complex transition from Old South to New South, from cavalier tradition to aggressive consumption. This vehicle of the new order actually kills Colonel Sartoris, who stood in its opposition. The progress of the new order thus appears to be ineradicable and calamitous to all those who get in its path. Southerners are left with no choice but to get on the bandwagon of progress (or the motor wagon, as the case may be) despite tradition or their obeisance to the old order.

Colonel Sartoris's reappearance in *The Reivers* further illustrates this point. Faulkner writes that Lucius's Grandfather, Boss, president of the oldest bank in Jefferson (and thus another representative of the Old South), would not even have purchased a car had it not been for Colonel Sartoris's attempts to outlaw automobiles in the town limits. He thus purchases one to stand in opposition to his arch competitor and to serve as a symbol of new wealth and power:

> Despite his life-long ramrod-stiff and unyielding opposition to, refusal even to acknowledge, the machine age, Grandfather had been vouchsafed somewhere in the beginning a sort of—to him—

> nightmare vision of our nation's vast and boundless future in which
> the basic unit of its economy and prosperity would be a small mass-
> produced cubicle containing four wheels and an engine. (24)

Boss publicly avows "that the motor vehicle was an insolvent phenomenon like last night's toadstool and, like the fungus, would vanish with tomorrow's sun," yet privately he realizes it to be a symbol of a new age which has arrived (22). Richard Milum asserts that characters like the willful old Sartoris "in their instinctive refusal to acknowledge or accept the new machine, display simply one more instance of an unwillingness to accept the inevitability of change—a notion which more than one observer has pointed to as a major cause for the failure of the old aristocratic order" (163).

Central to Faulkner's work is his analysis of the failure and replacement of this aristocratic order, and this transformation is often depicted in his fiction through the relationship between the Sartoris and Snopes families as two opposing sides of the transition. The car often represents the sterile and mechanical world of the Snopeses, which is supplanting the old traditions of the Sartorises. Cynthia Dettelbach addresses how this signification of the automobile functions in *The Town* (1957), the second of three novels chronicling the history of the Snopeses. She maintains that in the novel, "Snopes' vehicle is all business; it represents the powerful, inexorable forces of modernity which the author himself views with increasing ambivalence and distrust" (69). The Snopeses, once stricken in poverty, are becoming part of the new standardized middle class superseding the aristocracy. In *Sanctuary* a Snopes has become a state senator, though his standards are brought into question because of, among other incidents, a broken nose he supposedly attributes to his getting hit by a car in Jackson (258). This standardized class of merchants and consumers does not drive an "expensive car: jest a good one, jest the right noticeable size, of a good polite unnoticeable black color" (*The Town* 352). Perhaps they drive the ultimate standardized black car, a Ford Model T, which, significantly, was responsible for running the Sartorises off the road and causing the elder Bayard's death. In *The Sound and the Fury* Jason Compson, himself a scion of the dying aristocracy, derides the "mass market" classes like the Snopeses when he declares: "I think too much of my car; I'm not going to hammer it to pieces like it was a ford" (297).

Some characters, like Manfred de Spain of *The Town*, try to mix the best of both worlds by driving a new vehicle which reincarnates characteristics of the old age, such as chivalry and romance. The narrator of *The Town* goes so far as to call De Spain's vehicle "debonair" (14). This red E.M.F. roadster, the first manufactured car to come to Jefferson, Mississippi, challenges Sartoris's edict against automobiles in the town. (Representationally, De Spain's supposed purchase of the E.M.F. in 1904 would have been impossible because the first E.M.F. was not built until June 1908). De Spain's successful challenge leads to his being elected mayor of the town: "The new age had entered Jefferson; he was merely its champion, the Godfrey de Bouillon, the Tancred, the Jefferson Richard Lion-heart of the twentieth century" (12-13). However, his mediating position as romantic motorist does not endure. Snopes ultimately replaces De Spain as bank president, and his "unnoticeable" sedan displaces the flamboyant roadster.

The South's movement into the automobile age is prevalent in a majority of Faulkner's novels in both subtle and blatant expressions. *Light in August* (1932) subtly parallels Lena Grove's maturation with that of Southern mobility through her entrance in the novel hitching a ride in the back of a wagon and her exit riding off in the back of a pick-up truck. A humorous example of subtle change can also be found in the story of Jabbo Gatewood in *The Town*. Once a drunken blacksmith frequently arrested for his bacchanalian behavior, he now no longer remains in jail for long because he is the best mechanic in the county and "somebody with an automobile always needed him enough to pay his fine by morning" (68).

More blatant expressions of change come in the perception of the car's usefulness. As observed in Caldwell's writings, the automobile was first viewed in the South as a farm tool serving a utilitarian function. Boss Priest expresses this attitude in *The Reivers* when he first inspects his new automobile: "[He] walked slowly around the car, looking at it exactly as he would have examined the plow or reaper or wagon" (26). However, a utilitarian perception of the car proves substantially groundless, Faulkner argues in *Pylon* (1935) when he writes that the automobile is

> a machine expensive, complex, delicate and intrinsically useless, created for some obscure psychic need of the species if not the race, from the virgin resources of a continent, to be the individual muscles,

> bones, and flesh of a new and legless kind . . . its displacement and
> the sum of money it represented concentrated and reduced to a single
> suavely illuminated dial on which numerals without significance
> increased steadily towards some yet unrevealed crescendo of ultimate
> triumph. . . . (64)

Perhaps there is no more blatant discussion of the automobile's effects on the country than in *The Reivers*, which is logical considering that by 1962 Faulkner had witnessed this transformation first-hand for sixty-five years. The novel's narrator assesses the transformations which have transpired because of the car, particularly in the shrinking gap between civilization and wilderness, and he prognosticates of more changes to come:

> [I]n 1905 the wilderness had retreated only twenty more miles. . . .
> Though by 1925 we could already see the doom. . . . [T]heir
> inheritors [Boon and De Spain's] switched off their automobile
> engines to the sound of axes and saws where a year ago there had
> been only the voices of the running hounds. . . . [B]y 1980 the
> automobile will be as obsolete to reach wilderness with as the
> automobile will have made the wilderness it seeks. (19)

Ultimately the novel concludes that the changes wrought by automobility are inescapable: "We passed each other, commingling our dust into one giant cloud like a pillar, a sign-post raised and set to cover the land with the adumbration of the future; the antlike to and fro, the incurable down-payment itch-foot; the mechanised, the mobilised, the inescapable destiny of America" (71).

Faulkner makes one additional use of automobiles in his work that merits comment. In conjunction with his continuing experimentation with fictional style and structure, automobiles are often used for aesthetic purposes, essentially as cinematographic sources for descriptive viewpoints. A good example of this practice occurs in the previously quoted passage from *Sanctuary* where Popeye flees with Temple or in this section from *Pylon*: "The cab moved on. Through the back window Shumann saw the reporter standing at the kerb in the glare of the two unmistakable pariah-green globes on either side of the entrance, still, gaunt. . . . As though having chosen that one spot out of the entire sprawled and myriad city he stood there without impatience or design" (133-34).

An even better example can be seen in this lengthy but nonetheless illustrative passage from *Intruder in the Dust*:

> They were going quite fast now . . . out the long road where he had ridden last night on the horse . . . ; now he could see the white bursts of dogwood in the hedgerows marking the old section-line surveys . . . and bands of greening woods and the pink and white of peach and pear . . . and always beyond and around them the enduring land—the fields geometric with furrows . . . the farmhouses from which no smoke rose . . . the paintless Negro cabins . . . and as the car flashed past the blank and vacant doors he would catch one faint gleam of fire on hearth . . . in monotonous repetition the land's living symbol—a formal group of ritual almost mystic significance identical and monotonous as milestones tying the county-seat to the county's ultimate rim as milestones would: the beast and the plow and the man integrated . . . immobile like groups of wrestling statuary set against the land's immensity . . . the car flashing past and on while he leaned first out the open window to look back through the rear window, watching them still in their rapid unblurred diminishment. . . . (146-48)

In these highly cinematic scenes, Faulkner was perhaps drawing on his experience as a Hollywood scriptwriter. In attesting to the relevance of Faulkner's automotive tableaus, Chester Liebs proposes that twentieth-century society constantly practices "windshield perception," noting that the windshield of any car can "be transformed into a proscenium arch framing one of the most fascinating movies of all—the landscape played at high speed" (4). He goes on to point out the conjunction between cinema and car: "Gazing at moving images through the windshield of a car, along with moviegoing and watching television, has become one of the primary visual experiences of twentieth-century life" (6). Throughout his fiction, Faulkner experiments with this visual experience.

"People will pay any price for motion. They will even work for it. . . . We dont know why," Faulkner posits in *The Reivers* (34); and throughout his works he examines the ever-elusive *why* in regards to the automobile. Like most rural Southerners, Faulkner acknowledged the importance of the automobile in his own life. Writing in a letter to Malcolm Cowley, Faulkner attested: "I imagine I would have been in the livery stable yet if it hadn't been for motor cars" (*Selected Letters*

212). Needless to say, he realized that the debt the South owed to automobility was not all gratitude and that automobility had exacted a high price in the order of Southern society. In *Sartoris* Miss Jenny says of the automobile, "Why, it's as comfortable as a rocking-chair" (77); and like a rocking-chair, the automobile oscillates in Faulkner's work from being an emblem of nostalgia and exhilaration to being an object of ridicule and a violent disrupter of tradition and order. As with Steinbeck and Caldwell, Faulkner too saw the automobile as a complex signifier, but perhaps most importantly as an embodiment of the radical transition from Old South to New South, from cavalier tradition to aggressive consumption. In 1939 Simeon Strunsky noted that the term *revolution*

> is a sadly overworked word in describing social change, but the Automobile Revolution would not be too strong a phrase to describe the changes brought about in America by the motorcar in the space of less than a generation. . . . [It gives man] command over time and space. It gives him the exhilaration of speed and the exhilaration of dominating a carrier, in this case a machine; but primarily it is a space that counts in the psychological aggregate. (172, 177)

Thus, at the onset of World War II the automobile had already become as Steinbeck saw it: "the active thing, the living principle" in American culture. As exemplified in Ford and various literary manifestations of *Fordismus* and in the works of Caldwell, Steinbeck, and Faulkner, its signification had moved beyond simplicity. No longer an object of romantic admiration nor simply an instrument of satire, the car in its literary manifestations of automobility had taken on an active, living role as complex as the role of the automobile within the culture. The post-war culture extended this imbroglio even further.

IV

Permanent Union/Impossible Escape: Post-War Literature and Automobility

> The fun is gone.
> —Edward Cole, GM Chair (1974)

From 9 February 1942 to 6 July 1945, commercial automotive production in the United States came to a virtual standstill: raw goods necessary to produce passenger cars were redirected for military purposes; gasoline, tires, and spare parts were rationed; the speed limit was lowered to 35 m.p.h. to conserve fuel; and non-essential driving was banned in seventeen eastern states (Cleveland 298). Automobility came thus to a state of suspended animation as consumers were denied the substance of their addiction. But when cars became readily available after the war, users went on a buying frenzy unparalleled in the history of the American automotive industry. By the late 1950s this overwhelming mass consumption came to be known as automania.

Automania reigned in post-war America. General Motors' profits leaped from $87 million in 1946 to $656 million in 1949, to over $1 billion in 1955. By 1949 the industry was producing a record six million cars a year. The automaniacal Fifties became the decade of the car culture, and the car was perceived as a coveted instrument of change in social status, living habits, and recreation, and most of all, as a vehicle of youth (Cleveland 299-300, Sears 278-91). The union between car and American seemed immutable.

In the Fifties cars became bigger and more grotesque, looking like amalgamations of chrome idols and fighter planes, complete with tail fins and rocket boosters. By the mid-Sixties the number of make and model choices had reached astounding proportions—luxury car, family car, intermediate car, small car, sports car. Here is Vladimir Nabokov's description of such automotive multiplicity in *Lolita* (1955):

> He seemed to patronize at first the Chevrolet genus, beginning with a Campus Cream convertible, then going on to a small Horizon Blue sedan, and thenceforth fading into Surf Gray and Driftwood Gray. Then he turned to other makes and passed through a pale dull rainbow of paint shades, and one day I found myself attempting to cope with the subtle distinction between our own Dream Blue Melmoth and the Crest Blue Oldsmobile he had rented; grays, however, remained his favorite cryptochromism, and, in agonizing nightmares, I tried in vain to sort out properly such ghosts as Chrysler's Shell Gray, Chevrolet's Thistle Gray, Dodge's French Gray. . . . (239-30)

These baroque excesses had to end somewhere, and they did in the new automotive consciousness of the 1960s. In spite of extraordinary variety, most cars were unsafe, as Ralph Nader roared in *Unsafe at Any Speed: The Designed-In Dangers of the American Automobile* (1965). Not only physical safety, but environmental safety, as well, came under attack. *Pollution*, *smog*, and *carbon monoxide* became household words, and the byproducts of automobility fell into disfavor. Consider the conclusions drawn by this pamphlet entitled "Kill the Car": "Let us reiterate our desire to rid ourselves, once and for all, of that most representative creation of capitalism and everything that is most foul, imbecilic, and corrupt about it, most thoroughly destructive of the possibilities for genuine ecological and social harmony. Down with the Car Culture! Kill the Car!" Clearly this text offers a very different message from the "speed, glorious speed" of Lewis's early writings.

The straw that seemingly broke the camel's back of America's love affair with the auto came in the form of the Arab oil crises of the 1970s. America was held at mercy over its dependence on foreign oil to run its cars. Did America then abandon its precious vehicles? No. Automotive engineers worked on ways to curb pollution, increase safety, and improve gasoline efficiency, yet the dependence on oil continues. The Persian Gulf War demonstrated again a nation still willing (and ready) to fight rather than switch.

In spite of outrage over the negative aspects of the automobile, Americans still do not seem ready to abandon their devotion. Like a quarreling lover, the American tosses his/her automobile in and out of the doghouse because of unfulfilled promises and failed escapes, yet despite indications of a possible divorce, automobiles are repeatedly reconciled into the home, into an ever-increasingly labyrinthine coexistence. This convoluted entanglement is clearly reflected in the works of the authors of post-war literature to follow. Faulkner's later novels function as an apt introduction to the hard-to-define status of automobility in contemporary literature. Faulkner's fellow Southerner, Flannery O'Connor, serves as ample witness to the manifold stylistic and thematic uses of the automobile in one post-war writer's *oeuvre*. She employs the automobile in the creation of her fiction perhaps more than any other female writer. From O'Connor, we can progress to the quintessential American automobile book—Jack Kerouac's *On The Road*. No one can ignore the huge impact of the Beats and particularly Kerouac on a generation of younger Americans. *On the Road* and like-minded works encapsulated the sense of movement and speed characteristic of the automobility of an emerging generation coming to the fore in the 1950s.

When it comes to mobility and contemporary culture, John Updike's Rabbit quartet clearly illustrates the desire to go found throughout four decades in the life of one middle-class white American male. To complement the discussion of automobility and middle-class whites, Updike is followed with an examination of the automobile in the literature of the African-American experience, particularly the works of Ralph Ellison, Arna Bontemps, and Richard Wright. The works of these writers and non-African Americans who have chronicled the black experience, such as E. L. Doctorow, paint very different pictures of the impact of automobility on a culture that has been economically and socially disenfranchised from the American power structure, a structure often represented by the power of automobility.

First, though, an examination of textual vehicles in the short stories of O'Connor reveals a post-war Southern writer continuing and expanding upon uses of automobility as communicated in both Caldwell and Faulkner.

Driving Miss Flannery

"I have the notion that a symbol is sort of like the engine in a story and I usually discover as I write something in the story that is taking on

more and more meaning so that as I go along, before long, that
something is turning or working the story," Flannery O'Connor
avowed ("Recent" 73). The automobile is the metaphorical engine
driving many of her short stories. Readers like Joel Wells have noticed
the vehicular congestion on O'Connor's fictional freeways, as he
humorously recounts in the story of driving O'Connor from Chicago to
South Bend, Indiana, for a conference at Notre Dame University: "I
told her I had illogical but real misgivings about driving with her since
so many terrible things seem always to happen to people in her stories
while they are out driving. She assured me that such things only
happen in the South."

J. O. Tate's seminal study of autos and O'Connor, "The Essential
Essex," addresses in detail Hazel Motes's Essex automobile in *Wise
Blood* (1952) but does not go beyond this novel in its treatment. Tate's
conclusions, however, can be transferred to several of O'Connor's
shorter works of fiction, but the roles of the automobiles in her short
stories extend far beyond the uses in this, her first, novel. Motes buys a
nearly worthless Essex and preaches the gospel of his new church from
it. He virtually lives in the vehicle and develops an enormous
attachment to it. When a police officer pushes the junky vehicle off an
embankment, Motes blinds himself in an act of repentance. According
to Tate, Motes's Essex is his "place to be"; it represents freedom,
mobility, sex, and his movement against the sacred. O'Connor
recognized the car as "a symbol of every exploitation associated with
industrialism, corporate capitalism, and the New." It is thus used as a
"vehicle" in "O'Connor's mordant satire of secularity" (Tate 53).

Tate asserts that in Motes's Essex O'Connor found the perfect
symbol for her novel; moreover, I would assert that O'Connor
discovered in the automobile the appropriate metaphorical vehicle for
use in all of her fiction. Brian Ragen believes that "what attracted
O'Connor to the automobile was the abundance of meanings that have
become associated with it in the American mind" (55). As evidence of
O'Connor's use of the automobile, one will find that every short story
written after *Wise Blood* contains a car used in some fashion, while her
works prior to the novel contain scarcely a reference to a vehicle. The
automobile is thus the compelling force driving several of her stories:
for example, "A Good Man Is Hard to Find" and "The Life You Save
May Be Your Own." In other stories, such as "Parker's Back," "The
Displaced Person," "Greenleaf," and "A View of the Woods," the car is
a lesser, yet still vital force which transports both its fictional occupants

and the readers of the story. Evidently, O'Connor experienced some sort of "catalytic conversion" during the composition of *Wise Blood*. She recognized the significance of the automobile as a shaping factor in contemporary Southern culture and the metaphorical possibilities inherent in using it to address concerns central to her work. Examining these stories gives us a clearer picture of the extensive utility of the automobile in O'Connor's fiction.[23]

In "The Life You Save May Be Your Own" one-armed Shiftlet arrives on Mrs. Crater's farm and converses with her, the entire time focusing his eyes on her rusty car, which he judges to be a '28 or '29 Ford. Shiftlet's name suggests both the modifier *shifty* and the physical act of shifting gears, and Shiftlet attempts to change gears in his own life by appropriating Mrs. Crater's Ford through shifty means.[24] The car is, significantly, a '28 or '29, the first production years of Ford's Model A, a model created to replace the long-standing Model T and to keep up with the stylistic advances of General Motors. Shiftlet also seeks a make-over, much like the one Ford gave his car during these model years. He declares to Mrs. Crater that this car "had been built in the days when cars were really built. You take now, he said, one man puts in one bolt and another man puts in another bolt so that it's a man for a bolt" (150; all quotations of O'Connor taken from *The Complete Stories*). Like Mrs. Crater when she reflects back to the days when the car ran and her husband was alive, Shiftlet idealizes the past. This past never really existed, however, because we know that the very car he alleges as one built the old way was indeed a product of the company of Henry Ford—the champion of assembly-line mass production. Shiftlet, however, does not want to be a product of mass production; he seeks a means whereby he can be distinguished from the mass of humanity.

This means is the auto, and possession of it obsesses him. He tells Mrs. Crater that "a man had to escape," and he sees the car as providing this possibility (148). As does the Essex to Motes, the Ford represents for Shiftlet the possibilities of place, freedom, and mobility. When Mrs. Crater offers the car to him as a place to sleep in return for work, he accepts, telling her, "the monks of old slept in their coffins!" (149). And in reality, the car becomes his sanctuary, his cloister. Like a monk on the hard cot of his cell, "Mr. Shiftlet slept on the hard narrow back seat of the car with his feet out the side window. He had his razor and a can of water on a crate that served him as a bedside table and he put up a piece of mirror against the back glass and kept his coat neatly on a hanger that he hung over one of the windows" (150). Shiftlet offers with religious zeal to fix the car, and when he gets it to run, he has "an expression of serious modesty on his face as if he had just raised the dead" (151).

In agreement with both Lewis Mumford and Sam Dodsworth, O'Connor notes how Americans look upon their automobiles with religious fanaticism, and certainly no object has led more to fanatic consumerism than the car. Unlike Shiftlet, Mrs. Crater is not consumed with desire for an automobile, but she is in a buyer's market: she wishes to purchase Shiftlet as a husband for her retarded daughter, Lucynell. Her actions are thus as reproachable as his. Mrs. Crater proposes a simple exchange: he can have the car and have it painted in return for a marriage contract. Though Shiftlet accepts, he tries to warn Mrs. Crater of his potential harm to Lucynell when he says: "Lady, a man is divided into two parts, body and spirit. . . . The body, lady, is like a house: it don't go anywhere; but the spirit, lady, is like a automobile: always on the move. . . . [A] man's spirit means more to him than anything else" (152-53). This division between body and spirit manifests itself to Shiftlet particularly in his awareness of his own physically imperfect body. He thus sees the car as a way to make him whole and to make him mobile.

This Manichaean duality becomes most evident after the wedding. Though Shiftlet, like the car, has metaphorically gotten a new coat of paint, he still has the same rusted interior. With great pride about his new ownership, he drives his new wife towards Mobile (a city chosen for the obvious denotation of its name); yet in spite of having the auto, he becomes depressed on account of the bride, who represents responsibility as opposed to the freeing spirit of the car. He leaves her in a diner, but he is still depressed. While driving away, he becomes more aware of his interconnectedness to all humanity: "He felt that a man with a car had a responsibility to others"; however, he is drawn back to selfishness by the road signs which read, "Drive carefully. The life you save may be your own" (155). He picks up a hitchhiker out of his sense of obligation, but the youth's verbal attack on his mother and on Shiftlet's false, cliché-filled defense of motherhood leaves him in shock, suddenly fully aware of the depravity of the human condition: "A cloud had descended over the sun, and another, worse looking, crouched behind the car. Mr. Shiftlet felt that the rottenness of the world was about to engulf him" (156). Rain begins to fall in heavy drops, but instead of returning to Lucynell in an act of repentance for his own moral state, he flees: "He stepped on the gas and with his stump sticking out the window he raced the galloping shower into Mobile" (156).

For Shiftlet, the automobile is the locus for transformative possibility, the answer to his prayer for a means of escape. It is a profane object, a thing, but it gives him momentary insight into the world of the sacred: in this case, his epiphanic realization of the depravity of the human condition. Melvin J. Friedman has addressed O'Connor's reliance upon a "literature of Things," placing it within the concept of hierophany (the manifestation of the sacred) as expressed in Mircea Eliade's *The Sacred and the Profane* (Friedman 197). Eliade states concerning hierophany:

> By manifesting the sacred, any object becomes *something else*, yet it continues to remain *itself*, for it continues to participate in its surrounding cosmic milieu. A *sacred* stone remains a *stone*; . . . nothing distinguishes it from all other stones. But for those to whom a stone reveals itself as sacred, its immediate reality is transmuted into a supernatural reality. (12)

The automobile is clearly a hierophanic object in "The Life You Save." While it remains profane in its natural setting, it is transmuted to the prospect of the sacred by Shiftlet, who has the spiritual vision to see it so. While undoubtedly bushes still burn in the recesses of the Deep South, O'Connor seldom chooses such classic hierophanic objects for her fiction. As Eliade points out, "Man's reactions to nature are often conditioned by his culture and hence, finally, by history" (16). Therefore, O'Connor instead chooses an object more akin to her age and locale: the automobile.

In "Parker's Back" a vehicle again becomes hierophanic, and as in "The Life You Save," O'Connor confronts Manichaean duality in this story. The story opens with Obadiah Elihue Parker's wife, Sarah Ruth, watching the road: "At intervals a car would shoot past below and his wife's eyes would swerve suspiciously after the sound of it. . . . One of the things she did not approve of was automobiles. In addition to her other bad qualities, she was forever sniffing up sin" (510). To Sarah Ruth, the automobile represents carnality. She rejects the body and things of it as sinful; hence, she rejects Parker's tattoos. Not surprisingly, Parker is thus likened to a vehicle: "[T]his old woman looked at him the same way she looked at her old tractor" (511); and on another occasion, we are told during his stint in the navy he "seemed a natural part of the gray mechanical ship" (514). The tractor's collision into a tree and an ensuing fire lead Parker to an epiphany: the burning tractor becomes Parker's burning bush, his hierophany. Like Shiftlet, Parker flees, driving off in his truck to express his newfound revelation. He receives a tattoo of the Christ, an attempt to give substance to his spiritual kindling, and returns in his truck to Sarah. However, her Manichaeism will not allow her to receive Parker's offering, so she rejects him, unable to see his tattoo as hierophanic. Parker's sacred is profane to her; thus she leaves Obadiah, and the new prophet weeps, rejected in his own country.

With much darker vision, O'Connor presents the epiphanic moment in "A Good Man Is Hard to Find" as a result of the chance encounter of two automobiles. In the beginning of the story the car of the vacationing family is a microcosm in which we see the family members' personalities and conflicts unfolding.[25] O'Connor focuses on the grandmother, who dresses neatly so that "[i]n case of an accident, anyone seeing her dead on the highway would know at once that she was a lady" (118). O'Connor describes the woman, an incessant meddler, in terms of a well-known metaphor—the back-seat driver. The grandmother tries to control her son and his family, as evidenced by her back-seat chatter: "She said she thought it was going to be a good day for driving, . . . and she cautioned Bailey that the speed limit was fifty-five miles an hour and that the patrolmen hid themselves behind billboards and small clumps of trees and sped out after you before you had a chance to slow down" (118-19). The grandmother constantly measures people and experiences, as when she seeks to measure change in terms of the odometer reading: "[T]hey left Atlanta at eight forty-five with the mileage on the car at 55890. The grandmother wrote this down because she thought it would be interesting to see how many miles they had been when they got back" (118). Like Shiftlet, the grandmother also recounts the past, to which she clings so faithfully, through the evolution of automotive transportation: "The grandmother recalled the times when there were no paved roads and thirty miles was a day's journey" (124).

As the family travels, they experience the locale detached, not as part of the environment but as an invisible presence in it. David Laird has written how cars "furnish protection and containment, distancing their occupants from the pressures and influences that impinge upon them" (247). This method of perception is perfect for the grandmother, who, like many O'Connor characters, views the world aloofly, prejudging people and experiences. She lets prejudice direct her like the road signs direct the family to The Tower, a diner. There they meet Red Sammy, who also measures people, often in terms of their autos: "'Two fellars came in here last week,' Red Sammy said, 'driving a Chrysler. It was a beat-up car but it was a good one and these boys looked all right to me'" (122).[26]

The lives of the family are irreparably altered when their car is involved in an accident. In her ensuing plea for help after the wreck, the mother optimistically asserts, "Maybe a car will come along" (125), seemingly indicating that their redemption will come from the vehicle itself, not through the aid of its occupants. Indeed, a car does come along, but it does not bring the hoped-for deliverance. The narrator describes its arrival loomingly:

> [T]hey saw a car some distance away on top of a hill, coming slowly as if the occupants were watching them. The grandmother stood up and waved both arms dramatically to attract their attention. The car continued to come slowly, disappeared around a bend and appeared again, moving even slower, on top of the hill they had gone over. It was a big black battered hearse-like automobile [a description O'Connor once applied to her own automobile in a letter (*Habit* 294)] . . . . It came to a stop just over them and for some minutes, the driver looked down with a steady expressionless gaze to where they were sitting, and didn't speak. (125-26)

From the hearse-like vehicle, the Misfit descends. In the desacralized age of O'Connor's fiction, the prophets no longer descend from the clouds nor ride on fiery chariots; they must arrive like the Misfit, through more vulgar means.[27] The Misfit and his men show great concern over the condition of the vehicle, yet they massacre the family without mercy. He shoots the grandmother, but before her death she realizes her kinship to him. Like the Misfit, she possesses a stubborn willfulness; and she realizes that, like him, she is depraved in the body of humanity. Had she recognized this fact sooner, she might not have been "a back-seat driver." As the Misfit says, she might have been a good woman "if it had been somebody there to shoot her every minute of her life" (133).

Though not evil himself, Mr. Guizac, the title character of "The Displaced Person," first appears like the Misfit, exiting an automobile, but his arrival leads to evil and misfortune.[28] The immigrant Guizac arrives on Mrs. McIntyre's farm in a black car driven by a black-suited priest, his presence a reminder of the black cloud of Nazism hanging over Europe. While he brings his family to America for freedom and liberty, what instead greets him is the "black thunder cloud" of "dark suspicion" promulgated particularly by Mrs. Shortley (204). Parallel to the main theme, which focuses on the displacement of millions because of the evils of Nazism and how displacement occurs even in the supposedly free atmosphere of the American climate, runs an undercurrent centering on the displacement of human labor through mechanization, a theme which O'Connor shares with Steinbeck.

Motorized vehicles provide the dominant images of this form of displacement. While Mrs. Shortley fears that Guizac's hard work will lead to her husband's replacement, in fact, all forms of human labor are being rapidly replaced through agricultural industrialization. O'Connor writes:

> The tractor, the cutter, the wagon passed, rattling and rumbling and grinding before them. "Think how long that would have taken with men and mules to do it," Mrs. McIntyre shouted. "We'll get this whole bottom cut within two days at this rate."
>
> "Maybe," Mrs. Shortley muttered, "if don't no terrible accident occur." She thought how the tractor had made mules worthless. (205)

Mrs. Shortley's reply ironically foreshadows her own death, resulting from her displacement, and that of Guizac, which results from a machine and the inaction of his fellows.

Mrs. McIntyre becomes obsessed with mechanization, and in her zeal loses her disposition towards humanity. She wants her farm to be more "efficient," so she buys "a new drag harrow and a tractor with a power lift because . . . she had someone who could handle machinery" (207). Ultimately though, her possessions outweigh her sense of community: "the figure on the tractor was no larger than a grasshopper in her widened view" (224). In the end of the story, she, Shortley, and the Negro collude in Guizac's death by a machine: the large tractor which rolls over him. An automobile then brings his story full circle: as Guizac was carried onto the farm in the back of the priest's black car, he is carried out in the back of an ambulance.

Ironically, Mrs. McIntyre fears most on her farm the desire of her hired help to possess a machine—the automobile. She tells the priest how she has hung on to the farm in spite of "people who came from nowhere and were going nowhere, who didn't want anything but an automobile" (229) and how Guizac will "work at the mill and buy a car . . . all they want is a car" (231). In this sense, automobiles represent the desire for freedom from the oppression of the farm or, on a more metaphorical level, freedom from the type of oppression experienced by Guizac and his fellow Poles. But this symbol is paradoxical. The priest reminds Mrs. McIntyre of other "cars," the boxcars which take prisoners to concentration camps. American embodiments of such cars are depicted in the story when the Shortley's (reminiscent of Steinbeck's Joads) pack all their belongings on their "square black automobile": "They tied the two iron beds to the top of the car and the two rocking chairs inside the beds and rolled the two mattresses up between the rocking chairs. On top of this they tied a crate of chickens" (212). The Shortleys have the look of exiles escaping with all their goods on their backs, and like so many European exiles who died in the cars, Mrs. Shortley does not survive the trek. She dies in her car, and the vehicle of her escape becomes her coffin.

Connections between the car and other forms of mechanization and the loss which comes from the depersonalizing effects of technology continue in "Greenleaf."[29] Mr. Greenleaf, a caretaker, arrives on Mrs. May's farm "in a pieced-together truck, his wife and five daughters sitting on the floor in back, himself and the two boys in the cab" (319). Both the names *May* and *Greenleaf* suggest the renewal and rebirth of spring, yet only Greenleaf is potent, as indicated by his large family and his association with a bull. Though Mrs. May has given birth to two sons, both are fruitless (Wesley's impotency is suggested by the flat tire of his automobile); and despite her owning a farm, she has no connection to the fecundity of nature. We are repeatedly shown her dependence, not on natural objects, but rather on machines, the automobile being the chief emblem of such. For instance, Mrs. May is more dependent on her wheels rather than her legs to get around: she drives to the house of Greenleaf's sons, O. T. and E. T.; she drives to their barn; she drives Greenleaf in the car to kill the bull. In fact, Mrs. May's cold, mechanical automobile directly opposes Greenleaf's vital, living bull, who "don't like cars and trucks" (322). The animal brandishes his prowess by advancing on the house using the same avenue as Mrs. May's car; Mrs. May sees the bull and its "jutting hips and long light horns, ambling down the dirt road that ran in front of the house" (323). In the end of the story, she chases the bull with the car, but the automobile and Mrs. May prove to be no match for the masculine brute as it impales her on the car's bumper.

Mrs. May finds herself literally crushed between the force of nature and that of the machine. Grandfather Fortune in "A View of the Woods" is placed in a similar position. Fortune's materialism and cold, mechanistic behavior are characterized by his close alliance with his automobile and other machines. Every morning he drives his granddaughter in his "battered mulberry-colored Cadillac" to a construction site on his former pasture. The machines there overwhelm the child, Mary Fortune Pitts; she sits, "watching the big disembodied gullet gorge itself on the clay, then, with the sound of a deep sustained nausea and a slow mechanical revulsion, turn and spit it up" (335). While watching the machine do its work, man and child unite with the automobile: "He sat on the bumper and Mary Fortune straddled the hood and they watched, sometimes for hours ..." (335). On one occasion, "She reached the car and climbed back onto the hood ... and put her feet back on his shoulders ... as if he were no more than a part of the automobile" (339).[30]

"He wanted to see a paved highway in front of his house with plenty of new-model cars on it," so Fortune decides to supplant the woods in front of the home with Tilman's new gas station and store (337). O'Connor's description of Tilman's is as indicting as that of the construction machinery: the place is desolate, dumpy, death-like, "bordered on either side by a field of old used-car bodies, a kind of ward for incurable automobiles. He also sold ... tombstones and monuments" (345). Fortune has chosen this "field of sinking automobiles" to replace his view of the woods (346). Because of the granddaughter's violent emotional outbursts concerning this decision, Fortune decides to teach her a lesson by beating her like her father does. Furious with the child, he is again likened to a vehicle: "His heart felt as if it were the size of the car and was racing forward carrying him to some inevitable destination faster than he had ever been carried before. . . . [He] sped forward as if he were being driven inside his own fury" (353). When they get out of the car, the child, whose "feet mechanically battered" Fortune, fights with the old man mercilessly (355). He silences the child by crushing her skull against a rock, like one of the construction vehicles might obliterate an object in its path. In the story's conclusion, Fortune is dying, and he can find help only in one of his machines of progress, "one huge yellow monster which sat to the side, as stationary as he was, gorging itself on clay" (356).

After "A View of the Woods" O'Connor continued to use automobiles in her short stories, though not with the same prominence as in the works discussed above. For example, "The Comforts of Home" contains a humorous passage concerning the automobile as a place for sexual misconduct, a situation O'Connor also uses in other stories: in *Wise Blood*, in "A Temple of the Holy Ghost" when the young girls are warned about what to do in case a young man should "behave in an ungentlemanly manner with them in the back of an automobile" (238), and in "Good Country People" when Glynese's chiropractor beau says he can cure her sty if she will get in the back seat: "just lay yourself down acrost the seat of that car and I'll show you" (281). Autos are also used as structural devices: "The Partridge Festival" opens with Calhoun arriving at his aunts' house in his "pod-shaped car"; he sees a hearse, which leads him into the central action of the story; and the story ends as he and Mary Elizabeth escape from an asylum at full speed in his car.

Following *Wise Blood*, O'Connor continually used the automobile as a convention in her fiction. Though she learned to drive only late in her life (Ragen 55) and failed her first driver's test (*Habit* 288), she learned early in her writing career the value of the automobile as a fictional tool. The automobile is the engine under the hood of many of her short stories and a significant accessory in most of the rest. In O'Connor's works the automobile is a place to be, a hierophanic object, a vehicle for escape, an embodiment of the new, an object of materialism, an emblem of the duality of the body and the spirit, a symbol of the depersonalization of humanity through mechanization, a locus for transformation, a structural device, a metaphor for characterization, a microcosm for society, a symbol of isolation and insulation, a deliverer of prophecy, and a place for sex. In short, O'Connor's works embody the diverse connections between people and cars that existed in the mid-century South. She could have found no better symbol. "Symbols are big things that knock you in the face," O'Connor once declared (Fugin 59); and to borrow her metaphor, we must certainly see the automobile as one of the biggest punches in all her short stories.

On New Year's Day 1954, O'Connor wrote: "I can't drive myself. I am waiting until it's all automatic, and you sit there and it goes" (*Habit* 65). Though she could not drive herself, her works demonstrate an overwhelming understanding of the prominence automobility was attaining in the post-war culture, particularly in the South. Her style and themes are seemingly far removed from those of another 1950s' writer, Jack Kerouac, yet in his works Kerouac, too, elevates automobiles to a new prominence while dealing with the impact of automobility on another facet of post-war society. O'Connor may have been waiting until you could "sit there and it goes," but for Kerouac the place to be was off and going.

The Road as Life

Jack Kerouac

"The road is life" (175), Jack Kerouac pronounces in *On the Road* (1957), his semi-autobiographical account of numerous cross-country automobile trips and other exploits made between 1946-50 with his cronies: Neal Cassady (Dean Moriarty in the novel[31]), Allen Ginsberg (Carlo Marx), William Burroughs (Old Bull Lee), and John Clellon Holmes (Tom Saybrook), among others. These writers formed the nucleus of the Beats, a generation of post-World War II Americans not unlike World War I's own Lost Generation; however, the Beats, rather than expatriating themselves in Europe, practiced a form of domestic expatriation, attempting to become lost in the speed and vastness of America. Central to their experience was the verb *go*, the title of Holmes's autobiographical novel about the group. A group on the move, the Beats found the car essential to their circumstances. In her biography of Kerouac, Ann Charters avows, "No book has ever caught the feel of speeding down the broad highway in a new car, the mindless joyousness of 'joyriding' like *On the Road*" (104). Indeed, in *On the Road* Kerouac caught a novel feeling, putting his finger on the pulse of a new post-war American heartbeat of restlessness, discontent, juvenility, and, most importantly, movement. While the Beats did not look to the future with utopian vision, they nonetheless agreed on the road as the site for transformation.

More than anything else, *On the Road* is about being on the go. Many writers before Kerouac (Steinbeck, for one) had already asserted that the basic impulse of America is to move, to go west, young man. Kerouac listened to his forbearers, doing just that—moving, again and again. Like Huck Finn, Sal Paradise (Kerouac) "lit out" for the territory; he then returned east, then lit out west again, then east again, then south, then to Mexico, and finally back east—the ultimate restless

American. Sal cannot find Paradise because he finds the American Edenic myth just that, a myth—there is no Shangri-La. Therefore, since Paradise cannot be found in a place, Paradise must become movement itself, and the car thus became a method of nirvanic transport to the Beats.

On the road, the Beats experienced American life at its fullest. Not tied to an established position, they enacted the classic American fantasy of freedom adrift from social constraint. Sal sees himself aligned with this anti-establishment tradition, associating himself with America's frontier spirit and charting his connection to the rest of America: "I'd been pouring over maps of the United States in Paterson for months, even reading books about the pioneers . . ." (12). In *The Open Road: A Celebration of the American Highway*, Phil Patton holds that "the automobile and its highways froze the values of the frontier by making movement a permanent state of mind, turning migration into circulation" (13). Thus in their circulatory migrations, the Beats supplanted the westward-moving pioneer in a Conestoga wagon, the adolescent drifting on a raft down the Mississippi, and the lone rider atop a horse on the prairie, replacing these images with one of the driver behind his wheel speeding in isolation through the vast openness of the West.[32]

In his travel narrative *Blue Highways*, William Least Heat Moon has this to say about driving in the West:

> The true West differs from the East in one great, pervasive, influential, and awesome way: space. The vast openness changes the roads, towns, houses, farms, crops, machinery, politics, economics, and, naturally, ways of thinking. . . . [T]he terrible distances eat up speed. . . . Still, drivers race along; but when you get down to it, they are people uneasy about space. (136)

Like archetypal Americans preceding them—frontiersmen, explorers, river men, cowboys—Kerouac and company were uneasy about space, uncomfortable with established conventions and decorum. Brian Ragen concludes it was inevitable that this tradition of "heroes in space" would come to the automobile (56). Charters agrees that Kerouac's vision of Dean Moriarty "centered in one of the most vital fantasies of America, the dream of the cowboy, free and footloose, become a drifter with the crowding and commercialization of modern life" (289), in search of pastoral felicity.

In many ways, *On the Road* resembles a pastoral romance, not unlike Lewis's *Free Air*. Leo Marx argues that the pastoral romance often takes the form of a quest, contending in his discussion of the pastoral quest in Twain's *Huck Finn* that

> Jim and Huck on the raft enjoy pastoral felicity: the absence of social constraint; the recovery of an easy, flowing tempo of life; the pleasures afforded by the sensory experience of nature, and especially the beauty of the landscape; the creation of a virtually self-contained economy whose purpose it is not to achieve wealth or power, but material sufficiency; the relative independence of mind. (*Pilot* 193)

Do not Sal and Dean in their car also enjoy the absence of social constraint and create a new economy, replacing the Mississippi with the cross-country highway? ("What is the Mississippi River?—a washed clod in a rainy night," Sal remarks) (130.)

Dean and Sal *are* on a romantic quest, but by the 1950s a significant change has occurred in the quest motif—in 1950s' America, the quest itself overrides the object of the quest in importance. Sal and Dean do not stop to enjoy the beauty of the landscape—they consume it at the highest speed possible: "The state of Illinois unfolded before my eyes in one vast movement that lasted a matter of hours as Dean balled straight across at the same speed," Sal recounts (194). Like mystics who walk with bare feet over heated coals, the drivers have a focus beyond what lies beneath them and towards what lies ahead—yet when they reach a destination, they still do not reach the end of the road. Charters writes of Dean/Neal: "Driving the Cadillac as fast as he could push it, he saw no end to the trip, telling Jack, '. . . we'd dig the whole world with a car like this because, man, the road must eventually lead to the whole world. Ain't nowhere else it can go—right?'" (115-16). "The call of the open road is to movement pure and simple, not to any place down the highway" (Ragen 60). Such a concept of the endless road is reflected in this Ford ad from 1951:

> Today the American Road has no end; the road that went nowhere now goes everywhere. . . . The wheels move on endlessly, always moving, always forward—and always lengthening the American Road. On that road the nation is steadily traveling beyond the

troubles of this century, constantly heading toward finer tomorrows. The American Road is paved with hope. (Stern)[33]

Going for going's sake—in the 1950s, American culture fostered such a position, exalting "the purity of the road" (*On the Road* 111) or, as Kerouac calls it in his introduction to Robert Frank's *The Americans*, the "madroad driving men ahead" (iv). Eisenhower's Secretary of the Treasury, George M. Humphrey, proclaimed in 1955: "America lives on wheels, and we have . . . to keep America living on wheels and keep the kind and form of life that we want" (M. Rose 69). The Beats capitalized on this advocacy. To the Beat generation, the trip became all important. Leo Marx asserts that the language of the drug culture, who also "took trips," ultimately emanates from a desire for movement (*Pilot* 202); and whether through drugs or automobiles, the Beats attempted to be somewhere else. Kerouac professes their mission: "We were leaving confusion and nonsense behind and performing our one and noble function of the time, *move*. And we moved!" (*On the Road* 111).

The car thus became an exalted machine because it could move—and move fast. Like Hemingway enamored by the bullfighter's mastery of the entanglement with death, Sal/Jack admires anyone who can control the car, who is a master of transport. Sal admits he personally is "fearful of the wheel": "I hated to drive and drove carefully" (100), so he thus becomes an *aficionado* of Dean/Neal's skill as a driver.[34] In his job as parking-lot attendant, Dean can "back a car forty miles an hour into a tight squeeze and stop at the wall, jump out, race among fenders, leap into another car, circle it fifty miles an hour in a narrow space, back swiftly into a tight spot, *hump*, snap the car with the emergency break so that you see it bounce as he flies out; then clear to the ticket shack . . ." (10). Dean loves cars for the sake of themselves. The sight of a '49 Hudson makes him squander all his money and forget about his wife and child. In fact, the real-life Neal Cassady discovered cars at the age of fourteen, frequently stealing them and taking them on joyrides in the mountains. "Neal had no intention of destroying the cars or selling their parts or doing anything in them more illegal than driving without a license. . . . By his own account he took 500 cars between 1940 and 1944 and was caught by the police only three times" (Charters 69).

In the economy of the establishment, however, Neal is a mere parking-lot attendant; his responsibilities do not extend to the highway.

It takes the open road to gratify Dean's ability and enervate his spirit. The road gives you a great feeling of power, Sal tells Dean, recounting how as a child riding down the highway in a car, "I used to imagine I held a big scythe in my hand and cut down all the trees and posts and even sliced every hill that zoomed past the window" (170). Dean enlarges the power of the vehicle, asserting that his scythe could "curve over distant mountains, slicing off their tops, and reach another level to get at further mountains" (171). Most of all, the car provides a feeling of comfort and community for both Sal and Dean. Dean says, "'As we roll along this way I am positive beyond doubt that everything will be taken care of for us—that even you, as you drive, fearful of the wheel' (I hated to drive and drove carefully)—'the thing will go along of itself and you won't go off the road and I can sleep'" (100). As anyone who has taken a long automobile trip knows, a camaraderie develops out of the confinement of the vehicle, or as Chris Challis puts it in *Quest for Kerouac*: "isolation and self-sufficiency grows up in the community inside a moving car" (66).

Through their common search for speed and their Whitmanesque exaltation of America's greatness, the Beats developed a countercultural sense of community disenfranchised from the mainstream. The car made possible an extension of their experience beyond Whitman's by breaking down distance and space. The frequency of cross-continental excursions in *On the Road* bears ample testimony to this fact. The America of the late '40s and early '50s, however, differed greatly from Whitman's. As Dean notes, it had become a nation of standardization. What Sinclair Lewis had realized was happening in the 1920s had now been fully realized. Ironically, despite his penchant for individualism, Dean finds this consistency oddly comforting: "[W]e know America, we're at home; I can go anywhere in America and get what I want because it's the same in every corner . . ." (100). Kerouac depicts this America deftly in the following passage from *Visions of Cody*, another novel focusing on Neal Cassady. Significant to note in this panorama is the degree to which the culture of automobility has created the image of an archetypal American roadside corner:

> A Great American intersection . . . with a White Tower on one
> corner, diner . . . opposite, small beat white Mobilgas station another
> corner (topped by red neoned flying redhorse, becluttered, white
> curbs soiled, car for sale, sign says *Complete wheel alignment service*

and *Brakes relined*, tires for sale, used, including one vast graypainted truck tire), outdoor vegetable and fruit stand on the other (*ice cold watermelon, red like fire, we plug 'em*). Traffic lights shuttle this wild restless travel, cars nudging around impatiently and even hitting dips near sewers to do so, panel trucks, taxis, big trucks all mixed with cars, a four-direction confusion and anger and also buses, tooting, wheeling, jumping by, sending up fumes, buses growling, squeeking [*sic*] to stop, massing, surging, occasional sad pedestrians completely lost. (37-38)

Yet in the phrase, "Sad pedestrians completely lost," we detect that the vision of the open road is not all idyllic.

As seen in Steinbeck and Faulkner, the automobile in the work of the Beats, while encompassing possibility, also embodies a negative side. One can see in *On the Road* a gradual festering disillusionment with road culture and automobility, a disenchantment prevalent in Sal's growing awareness of Dean's instability, coming to a climax in his description of the Mexico trip near the novel's conclusion. In this section of the novel, Mexican Indians come to greet them in their big American car, but Sal warns that what these unassuming people think they will be receiving from the Americans is a two-edged sword. True, American technology and industry have made Sal and Dean's automobile journey to the heart of Mexico possible, but Sal expresses remorse over what his culture has to offer to reciprocate the Indians' enthusiastic reception. He thinks:

They had come down from the back mountains and higher places to hold forth their hands for something they thought civilization could offer, and they never dreamed the sadness and the poor broken delusion of it. They didn't know a bomb had come that could crack all our bridges and roads and reduce them to jumbles, and we would be as poor as they someday, and stretching our hands in the same, same way. Our broken Ford, old thirties upgoing America Ford, rattled through them and vanished in dust. (246)

The destruction evident in technology, whether in the form of the bomb or an "old thirties upgoing America Ford," reappears in other works of the Beats. That Allen Ginsberg placed his poem, "Car Crash," at the center of *The Fall of America* doubtlessly illustrates this perception;

and Gregory Corso's poem, "Last Night I Drove a Car," from the aptly titled *Gasoline* (1958), provides an even better example:

> Last night I drove a car
>   not knowing how to drive
>   not owning a car
> I drove and knocked down
>   people I loved. . . .

In these works, the car is obviously perceived as a destructive force.

In *On the Road* the key to relating this perception of technology to the automobile rests clearest in Sal's own assertion that he hates to drive. Not in the driver's seat, he is unable to control America, which is speeding by. He practices "windshield perception," observing Illinois fly by at 120 m.p.h., but doing nothing to claim it, change it, or even interact with it: "What is that feeling when you're driving away from people and they recede on the plain till you see their specks dispersing?" Sal asks (130). In the novel's conclusion, the car and the system of possibility it represents recede and fail him. Kingsley Widmer agrees, assessing that Kerouac's travels in *On the Road* "end in a tired acceptance of an unchanged self and society" (314). Can the road protect, comfort, and make known, as Dean suggests? Will the road protect them as God protects the lilies of the field? Sal concludes no—"nobody, nobody knows what's going to happen . . ." (254).

In his poem "Poesy LA-Albuquerque-Texas-Wichita" Ginsberg declares: "up up and away! / we're off, Thru America" (14), and so the "hiway poesy" of the Beats resounded through the 1950s. The Beats became the rallying voice for a generation of young people captivated by the idea of movement and change. Probably the most influential adolescent novel of the decade, Henry Felsen's *Hot Rod* (1950), and his follow-up books—*Street Rod* (1953), *Rag Top* (1954), and *Crash Club* (1958)—also spoke to this generation consumed by automobility. *Hot Rod* tells the story of Bud—teenage mechanic, hot-rod builder, road racer. Like the characters in Lewis's "Speed," he is mechanomorphic: "Bud's car . . . was like Bud himself. In a way he had built a mechanical representation of his life, and its oddly assorted parts could be likened to his patch-work past. . . . From the wreckage of normal cars Bud had salvaged a part here and there, and assembled them, and modified them so they would fit" (17). Bud has clearly been assembled from the romantic car culture of America's past; and like the

Beats, he is most at home on the road: "behind the wheel, he could think. Give him the road and speed, the roar and rock of motion . . ." (44). Yet as in *On the Road*, a series of incidents, including a violent automobile accident which kills all his friends but one, lead him to view the automobile as a failed means of salvation:

> Nothing had happened. He had driven blindly, crazily, he would have killed anyone had he met them on the road. He had given himself up to speed to take or leave, and it had left him. He had found nothing at the peak but fear, he felt nothing now but frustration, confusion and loss. . . . Whatever the wheel had been to him in the past, it meant nothing now. . . . Driving had lost its thrill, its charm, its challenge and its peculiar rewards. (148-49)

In the end of the novel, Bud disassembles his hot rod, takes a drivers' education course to learn safe driving skills, and heads off to college with an engineering scholarship.

On the Road may not end with Sal Paradise enrolling at MIT, but as in *Hot Rod*, there is a concluding realization that the road cannot resolve the growing sense of disillusionment felt by America's youth. Even so, with both the book and the highway, a generation found the trip more captivating than the destination. Ann Charters maintains that youth responding to *On the Road*

> read it not as 'literature' but as an adventure, recognized that Kerouac was on their side, the side of youth and freedom, riding with Cassady over American highways chasing after the great American adventure—freedom and open spaces, the chance to be yourself, to be free. Kerouac hadn't offered any real alternative to the conformity of twentieth-century industrial America. . . . He offered instead a vision of freedom, a return to the solipsistic world of childhood. . . . (291)

In spite of lacking any real alternatives, this generation, measuring their conformed nonconformity in terms of hot rods and cool cars, represented a fundamental shift towards youth in American society. Historian Gilman Ostrander argues that products, especially automobiles, came to be more important than landed property in fixing a man's position in society.... When manufactured products instead of land and improvements on land came to determine social status, the newness of one's property came to be prized, whereas formerly its age had commanded respect. In fact, when the natural environment was replaced by the technological environment, there occurred a comprehensive reorientation—from a patriarchal faith in the wisdom of age and experience to a filiarchal faith in the promise of youth and innovation and in technologically oriented and therefore continually changing values. (9-10)

Coinciding with the growth of this generation of changing values came an automotive explosion. The Decade of Detroit saw vehicles grow in size and ornamentation until they resembled rocketships designed more for space travel than highway transport. But had the Beats not already acclaimed "space travel"—the displacement of space through trips and the road? The road for them was certainly far more akin to the mystic adventures of outer space than the terrestrial realm of main street.

Nearly as soon as the Beats' voice ascended, however, a new road began to develop in America—the Interstate Highway. In fact, a decade after *On the Road* in Kerouac's novel *Big Sur*, the drunken Jack Duluoz returns to San Francisco and notices that all the cars are now family cars and the highways are now all lined with homes (Hipkiss 20). Dennis McNally asserts that even as *On The Road* was being published, America was beginning to calcify: "Modern concrete superhighways, like the just-opened New Jersey Turnpike, were starting to replace the cracked-tar two-laners that Jack had known" (154).[35] These controlled-access highways, promoted originally for military purposes, exemplified a type of road far different than that extolled by the Beats. Kerouac's short-lived age was over.

Vladimir Nabokov

The idea of "road as life" is captured adroitly in another automobile travelogue novel of the 1950s: Vladimir Nabokov's *Lolita* (1955). Kingsley Widmer writes that in *Lolita* Nabokov "finds his most precise moments of grotesque comic vision and of character revelation and penance in the prolonged journey down the culture of the American highway" (315). Humbert Humbert, aware of the impropriety of his actions, tries to escape with the adolescent Lolita on the vastness of the highway and to become absorbed into the uniformity of the American climate. Like the Beats, Humbert acts outside the social norm yet seeks consolation in the measurelessness of America.

Though his perception of sexual propriety seems exceedingly contemporary, Humbert nevertheless embodies classic European ideals of beauty and tradition. In this sense he represents an idyllic tradition, yet ironically he finds his pastoral ideals in icons of automobile-age consumerism, such as motels. Consider this "pastoral" description of motels, "clean, neat, safe nooks, ideal places for sleep, argument, reconciliation":

> We came to know ... the stone cottages under enormous Chateaubriandesque trees, the brick unit, the adobe unit, the stucco court, on what the Tour Book of the Automobile Association describes as 'shaded' or 'spacious' or 'landscaped' grounds ... the would-be enticements of their repetitious names—all those Sunset Motels, U-Beam Cottages, Hillcrest Courts, Pine View Courts, Mountain View Courts, Skyline Courts, Park Plaza Courts, Green Acres, Mac's Courts. (147-48)

The ultimate embodiment of this consumerism is Lolita herself. Emblematic of youth, Lolita is consumed by the elder Humbert.

W. T. Lhamon reads *Lolita* as an allegory of the growth of American consumption and consumerism in the Fifties: "Lolita's tastes are less for this ex-French teacher, this bundle of European *partis pris* and psychoses, than for the immediate gratification her era permits" (17). Lolita abandons connections to the historical past (such as Humbert, who speaks romance languages) and instead pronounces the language of immediacy. She is a classically consumptive American, whom Humbert calls, "the ideal consumer." Having strayed into the fast lane, "Lolita's life coincides with the fulcrum years of the country's tip from pre- to full-consumption economy ..." (Lhamon 17).

No object embodies this consumerist economy as well as the 1950s' car; thus, not surprisingly, the automobile is a prime propellant of insatiable consumption in the novel. Even though Nabokov never learned to drive (Patton 241), he captures perfectly the spurious sense of movement and consumption the automobile offers. But like Sal Paradise, Humbert ultimately realizes that automotive consumption is mechanical, not natural, and that the car, like a drug, only simulates real motion. Humbert proclaims of his attempts to consume Lolita:

> By putting the geography of the United States into motion, I did my best for hours on end to give her the impression of 'going places,' of rolling on to some definite destination, to some unusual delight. I have never seen such smooth amiable roads as those that now radiated before us, across the crazy quilt of forty-eight states. Voraciously we consumed those long highways, in rapt silence we glided over their glossy black dance floors. (154)

At the time, their consumings please him, but he grows to become distrustful of the road. Humbert's conscience shadows him, first in the form of an Aztec Red Convertible which follows them; but then this vehicle becomes every-vehicle, changing and altering its form: "A veritable Proteus of the highway, with bewildering ease he switched from one vehicle to another. This technique implied the existence of garages specializing in 'stage-automobile' operations, but I never could discover the remises he used" (239-30).

The remises of morality tail him, and finally Humbert abandons his idyllic conception of the highway and tosses aside the law of the road, his last bastion of refuge:

> [I]t occurred to me—not by way of protest, not as symbol, or anything like that, but merely as novel experience—that since I had disregarded all laws of humanity, I might as well disregard the rules of traffic. So I crossed to the left side of the highway and checked the feeling, and the feeling was good. It was a pleasant diaphragmal melting, with elements of diffused tactility, all this enhanced by the thought that nothing would be nearer to the elimination of basic physical laws than deliberately driving on the wrong side of the road. (308)

Humbert has now become the true consumer—disregarding reason for the experience of momentary gratification. But had he not already made such a choice in regard to Lolita? Indeed, Humbert is "driving on the wrong side of the road" with his life. Now, no place is left where he has not violated the natural order. Like Kerouac, however, Humbert discovers in the end that the experience of the road does not lead to fulfillment. Both the youth of Lolita and the movement of the road are fleeting and illusory.

Something happened in the 1950s. As Tom Wolfe observes, "Things have been going on in the development of the kids' formal attitude toward cars since 1945, things of great sophistication . . ." (79). The idea of "go," the quest for youth, ultimate consumption—all came to the forefront in post-war culture. Yet these ideals were ultimately unfulfilling. Mary Catanzaro writes that the automobile in *Lolita* proved to be "the vehicle that asserts that human beings are trapped in a psychological and spiritual dilemma that offers no solution" (91). The car—the foremost incarnation of youth, movement, and consumption— thus fails to convey lasting salvation. Perhaps better than any other, one character in particular, John Updike's Rabbit Angstrom, defines this place of automobility in the traffic of post-war American culture. Reared in the Fifties, he carries with him throughout the next three decades the influence of these developments.

Rabbit in Traffic

In his "frictional theory" of vehicular movement Miller McClintock describes four types of "frictions" created by automobiles in traffic: internal-stream, the friction from passing other vehicles moving in the same direction; marginal, the friction from encountering parked cars, pedestrians, or fixed objects; intersectional, the friction from angular interception (crossroads); and medial, the friction from opposing directions of travel (Meikle 206-07). This paradigm proves helpful in approaching one of America's most interesting fictional creations, a character whose traffic jams, collisions, and bang-ups span four decades of American history. That character, of course, is Updike's Harry "Rabbit" Angstrom, who, from the Fifties of *Rabbit, Run* to the Eighties of *Rabbit at Rest*, has driven and been driven through the radical changes which have shaped contemporary American culture.

Rabbit is caught in the traffic of American society, a society which, to him, has evolved from the simple two-lane joyride of the 1950s to the complex plurality of the freeway traffic jam called contemporary America. Traffic is the perfect metaphor to describe Rabbit's existence because the automobile and automobility are central to the dynamism of his psyche. Rabbit is the quintessential American male, possessor of and possessed by his automobiles. As Dilvo Ristoff notes, in Updike's America "the car is omnipresent" (68). From the opening chapters of *Rabbit, Run*, in which Rabbit tries unsuccessfully to drive south in a night flight from his marital woes, to his flag-bearing Falcon in *Rabbit Redux*, to his successful Toyota franchise in *Rabbit Is Rich*, and finally to the collapse of his auto empire and subsequent renewed escape south in *Rabbit at Rest*, Rabbit's world is an auto-world: a world focused both on his own self and on his means of transport—the car. As a driver (and as driven), he is constantly a part of the friction stemming from various "traffics" contiguous to him.

Though frictions of all sorts do occur in each novel, one can read each work as a focused exposition of one of McClintock's frictional types of traffic. *Rabbit, Run* focuses on the internal-stream friction emanating from Rabbit's primary traffic jammer—his own self. Marginal friction abounds in *Rabbit Redux* in Rabbit's abutment to then-present conditions: Vietnam, drugs, race relations, the counterculture. Especially prevalent in *Rabbit Is Rich* is the intersectional friction arising from conflicting goals and desires in his family relationships. Finally, in *Rabbit at Rest* medial friction comes from a head-on collision of the ultimate binary opposites—life and death—as seen in Rabbit's own struggle to survive. Throughout all four novels Rabbit constantly gets himself into traffic, ensnared in a briar patch of confusion and contusion in which he seemingly thrives. Indeed, the Rabbit tetralogy can be read as one huge traffic jam of ideas, relationships, and accidents driven through by one Brer Rabbit American male tossed by Updike into a thistled thirty-five years of American existence.

The most telling picture of Rabbit in *Rabbit, Run* (1960) comes at the novel's onset. There, Rabbit seeks auto-mobility—the movement of self without external control. The external control prohibiting his full range of motion is his wife, Janice, and their disintegrating relationship. The medial friction resulting from their repeated head-on collisions leads Rabbit to attempt escape by car, an escape emblematic of the generation of the Fifties, a decade on the road with Kerouac and Dean behind the wheels of their chrome dreams. Rabbit searches for signs of direction for his life; but though he encounters numerous STOP signs on his race away from home, he nevertheless accelerates in his quest south for the Gulf of Mexico, where he hopes to be baptized into soothing warm waters. At his first gas stop he asks the attendant for maps. "Son, where do you want to go?" "Where are you headed?"

the attendant asks; Rabbit replies: "I don't know exactly" (26). This exchange highlights the motivating determinant of Rabbit's life: the quest for an unknown somewhere. Like the Beats, Rabbit privileges the trip over the destination.

Though Rabbit does not know where he wants to go, he knows he wants to get there. He also realizes he does not have a map to guide him. Writing in the same year as the publication of *Rabbit, Run*, historian John Hicks remarked that automotive psychology had characterized American society in that "American people, like the drivers of many cars, were relentlessly on their way, but not quite sure where they were going, or why" (169). Rabbit's sense of wandering parallels that expressed by Hicks and by Nathan Asch, who wrote in his travel narrative *The Road*:

> I began to see the entire country with its maze of road, twining, twisting, entering everywhere. I saw the million automobiles, and trains, and buses, and people walking on the road, all trying to get somewhere. I suddenly saw the map of America . . . with scarlet roads extending through the states, across mountains, by the sides of rivers, through the cities, and never getting back anywhere but into itself. (141)

In many ways, Rabbit has discovered the same atlas of America as Asch—a map with all roads leading to each other, none leading to someplace else.

Harry does not know where he is driving to, but motivated by a nostalgia for the heroic era of his life when he was a high-school basketball star, he does know something to which he is trying to return. Corresponding to this backward shift, the music on his car radio changes from "rock and roll for kids" to "old standards and show tunes and comforting songs from the Forties." Compounding the tensions between old and new music, Rabbit senses a friction with the world now surrounding him: his is the only out-of-state license plate parked outside a cafe where he senses "he is unlike the other customers." This friction extends beyond the cafe to the entire nation: "He had thought, he had read, that from shore to shore all America was the same. He wonders, Is it just these people I'm outside, or is it all America?" (31).

Rabbit is in conflict with the motion of his own life. This internal-stream friction most frequently leads him to run; like a jack rabbit in an open field, Rabbit darts from all difficult encounters. But in the middle of nowhere on this particular jaunt, his road of escape suddenly ends: "It meets at right angles a smooth broad highway overhung by the dark cloud of a mountain ridge. One car zips north. Another zips south. There are no signs. Rabbit puts the shift in neutral . . . and turns on the roof light and studies his map" (33). Here, Rabbit finds no signs as he encounters the existential intersection, the crossroads of life. "Two roads diverged in a wood," but Rabbit does not take the one less traveled. He decides to return home, wondering "why there are so many signs coming back and so few going down" (36).

Home, however, does not include Janice. Rather than contain the emotional damage within one relationship, Rabbit creates an even larger pile-up by moving in with Ruth Leonard, whom he later discards. Also involved in the pile-up is Rev. Jack Eccles, who urges Harry to soul-search. Eccles—part psychologist, part social worker, part existentialist philosopher—seeks to prepare a way for Harry in the wilderness of his existence. Yet Eccles is no John the Baptist, though he would like to be. At one point in the novel we see ironically that Eccles's "head across the top of the car looks like a head on a platter" (108). In this allusion, Salome's silver platter has been replaced by a car, an excellent substitution, because the car has been a sort of silver platter to Rabbit: it served as bedroom for him and Janice when they were dating; it precipitates his escape; it gives him work when Janice's father offers him a sales job in his used-car lot as a means to restore some responsibility to his wayward son-in-law. Interestingly, in spite of his many screw-ups, Harry seems most repentant in the course of the novel for turning back the odometers of used cars at the lot, an action for which he feels compelled to ask forgiveness (196). But Harry cannot turn back his own odometer. He must own up to the mileage he has driven and face the dents he has incurred. However, this internal-stream friction created from confronting his own actions proves too much for Rabbit in the end of the novel, and he exits the book as he enters it: running alone—auto-mobile.

Rabbit Redux (1971) returns to Angstrom's life at the end of the 1960s, a time tormented by the friction of Vietnam, race riots, drugs, the youth counterculture. Behind *Rabbit, Run* stood the organization-man mentality of the Eisenhower regime (an administration whose defense secretary was once president of General Motors, Charles "What's good for GM is good for the country, and vice versa" Wilson). Now, this era has been replaced by one of confrontation between revolutionaries and reactionaries, hawks versus doves. Cities have become battle zones, no man's lands, and Updike uses the metaphor of the parking lot to describe this decimation: "The city . . . has torn away blocks of buildings to create parking lots, so that a desolate openness, weedy and rubbled, spills through the once-parked streets . . ." (13). Yet in the midst of chaos, Harry Angstrom plays the good citizen. To exhibit his patriotism Rabbit proudly displays a flag decal on his Ford Falcon (not quite an Eagle, but as close as one could get in 1969); however, the various cultural movements around him soon upset his status quo: Janice embraces the sexual revolution; Skeeter promotes African-American and anti-war causes; Jill embodies the counterculture; and as a background to his new discoveries on planet earth, the Apollo mission delivers Americans to the moon. It is a time of upheaval, of marginal friction from all directions.

This time, Rabbit does not run. He cannot, because when Janice moves out to live with Charlie Stavros, she takes his car. While all about him cars are "hurrying faster home to get out again" (98), Harry stays at home, a home which becomes the traffic exchange for the revolutionary Skeeter and the drugged Jill. His house becomes a microcosm of the cultural frictions tearing at the nation. Skeeter, shattered by Vietnam, lectures Harry about the end of culture as white men know it, about the destruction soon to overcome the establishment. Harry does not agree, however, asking Skeeter if this revolution is to be so, "Why do so few American Negroes want to give up their Cadillacs and . . . go back to Africa?" (203).

Harry is torn as to how he should respond to this invasion of his home. At one point he beats up Skeeter; on other occasions he is overwhelmed, doing nothing while Skeeter abuses Jill sexually and destroys her with drugs. Meanwhile, his son Nelson surveys the friction first-hand. Like America, Nelson grows up amidst the new confusion. Jill tells Harry about allowing Nelson to drive her car: "I used to stay in the driver's seat and let him just steer but that's more dangerous than giving him control" (145). Rabbit himself is not mature enough to take control, much less Nelson. In point of fact, no one is in the driver's seat; as Updike says, "The table has taken a turn down a road Rabbit didn't choose. He and Nelson have taken a back seat" (45).

Like the nation, Harry's home is out of control—full of friction. Things are moving too rapidly, and Harry, like many Americans of the time, would like it all to stop. Updike parallels this sense of society's moving too quickly to control with Jill's driving of her Porsche: "Jill drives urgently, rapidly, with the arrogance of the young; Rabbit keeps slapping his foot on the floor, where there is no brake" (233). Rabbit cannot stop Jill's car nor the torrential social forces swirling around him, which, like the engine of Jill's car, eventually blow up. Jill burns to death in a fire at Harry's home, yet even before the fire starts, she, like the car's engine, is burned out, a victim of social upheaval. After the fire, Harry drives Skeeter out of town in a borrowed Mustang, leaving him at a crossroads. Once again Harry finds himself at an intersection in life, and again he returns home, this time reuniting with Janice. He tells her, "I'm not sure I still know how to drive" (343); nevertheless, he takes his place behind the wheel. Unlike Harry's escape at the beginning of *Rabbit, Run*, this time he and Janice both get away from the city. "It is easy in a car," Rabbit feels as they drive to the Safe Haven Motel (an appropriate, yet ironic, name), where they make love and sleep (345). "O.K.?" the novel questions in the end (352). We are unsure, as both, like the rest of the nation, attempt to heal from ulcerations created by the abrasive marginal frictions of the decade.

If *Rabbit Redux* shows America at the height of entropy, *Rabbit Is Rich* (1981) shows it at lowest energy. In this new age, "THE ERA OF COROLLA" (403), motorscape continues to replace landscape: "Route 111 is buzzing with shoppers pillaging the malls hacked from former fields of corn, rye, tomatoes, cabbages, and strawberries" (4). Godlike Exxon and Mobil signs tower above the freeways, looking down on loyal devotees, but these signs are empty signifiers, for there is no gas: "Running out of gas, Rabbit Angstrom thinks as he stands behind the summer-dusty windows of the Springer Motors display room watching the traffic go by on Route 111, traffic somehow thin and scared compared to what it used to be. The fucking world is running out of gas" (1). *Rabbit Is Rich* opens amidst a new crisis—the gas shortage of the late 1970s. Americans are again at war, this time with each other in an attempt to fill their precious tanks. One woman's legs are crushed in an accident at the pumps, but instead of helping, others in line use the distraction to fill their vehicles and drive off. "Oh, what a feeling." "You asked for it, we got it," Toyota commercials declare. America demanded her driving machines and now proceeded to run out of gas for them.

Rabbit, however, profits from the fuel shortage. He has become half-owner of Springer Motors, car salesman extraordinaire, consummate capitalist. A veritable consumer reporter, he knows what America needs—a new car, one that gets better mileage: "This particular car has four-speed synchromesh transmission, fully transistorized ignition system, power-assisted front disc brakes, vinyl reclining bucket seats, a locking gas cap. That last feature's getting to be pretty important" (12). And Rabbit has such a car: "[T]here isn't a piece of junk on the road gets better mileage than his Toyotas, with lower service costs. Read *Consumer Reports*, April issue" (1). Amidst the energy crisis Angstrom holds firm to his course, a one-way street named sell:

> Car sales peak in June: for a three-hundred-car-a-year dealer like Harry this means an upwards of twenty-five units, with twenty-one accounted for already and six selling days to go. Average eight hundred gross profit times twenty-five equals twenty grand minus the twenty-five per cent they estimate for salesmen's compensation both salary and incentives leaves fifteen grand minus between eight and ten for other salaries . . . . (25)

In this stream-of-capitalism passage, Updike highlights Rabbit's newfound place among the haves. He is no longer a wanna-be; his garage runneth over, giving him "a strange consciousness of having not one child now but two" (35).

Rabbit finds it difficult to savor his newfound fortunes, however, because, like his garage, his house also runneth over. A crowded intersection of family friction, Rabbit's home is shared with his wife, his mother-in-law (who, in fact, owns the home), and his son Nelson, who, confused about the direction of his life (and looking much like Rabbit himself at an earlier age), returns home with first one woman, then another, the second pregnant. Nelson subsequently quits college and deserts his laboring wife. Whereas Rabbit took the car and ran to escape his youthful dilemmas, Nelson takes the car and runs into things, wrecking successively the Toyota Corona, the Chrysler, and the Mustang convertible (not to mention his wife Prudence's and Harry's peace of mind). Nelson's life is truly a wreck. And the cars which Nelson wrecks affect Harry personally. When Harry sees the dented Corona, "He feels his own side has taken a wound" (98).

The friction Rabbit encounters from Nelson is compounded by yet another intersection he has reached in life—middle age. Harry feels somewhat like the huge cars of his youth which have now been junked in favor of new, cheap imports like the Toyotas he sells. Facing his own advance in years, Rabbit reflects on American consumerist society in which something no longer useful is discarded: "Who in this day and age keeps a car much longer than four years?" he asks (12). Rabbit does not want to be disposed of so easily. Trapped between two generations, he yearns for youth, for the oozing sexuality of Cindy Murkett or of Nelson's girlfriends, yet he simultaneously rejects the culture of the young: "When Rabbit first began to drive the road was full of old fogeys going too slow and now it seems nothing but kids in a hell of a hurry, pushing" (30). Everyone is in a hurry. Everyone has some place else to be—people to meet, places to go—yet ironically, in spite of this constant movement, America is experiencing an energy shortage.

Harry wonders if the country he once knew has also been discarded: "Here we're supposed to be Automobile Heaven and the foreigners come up with all the ideas," he exclaims (13). The America of Ike and of Camelot has been tarnished by Vietnam and Watergate, and the emergent nation is one Harry sees clearest in terms of its loss of automotive supremacy. Nelson reflects on the condition of America as a loss of individual identities, the byproduct of standardization: "The country's the same now wherever you go. The same supermarkets, the same plastic shit for sale. There's nothing to see" (70). Nelson feels as alienated as Harry did in *Rabbit, Run* when he asked: "Is it just these people I'm outside, or is it all America?"

Nelson's automobile accidents reflect his attempts to burst forth from this standardized stagnation he perceives. Perhaps his actions originate from his frequent television watching, which provides evidence of purposive intersectional collision that can lead to resolution: "Charlie's angels are chasing the heroin smugglers in a great array of expensive automobiles that slide and screech, that . . . finally collide with one another, and then another, tucking into opposing fenders and grilles in a great slow-motion climax of bent metal and arrested motion and final justice" (137). Nelson learns, though, as did Rabbit on his sojourn south in *Rabbit, Run*, that final justice is not so easily obtained, that all life is an intersection of ideas, cultures, and practices, unguided by traffic lights or directional signals—a potential wreck.

The friction between Harry-and-Nelson/Harry-and-youth climaxes head on in the final Rabbit novel, *Rabbit at Rest* (1990), as Rabbit faces the ultimate medial friction—death. The novel opens with Rabbit, now a semi-retired Floridian transplant, on the road to the airport to pick up the visiting Nelson and his family. Though Nelson, now a cocaine addict, "has made him uneasy for thirty years," Harry feels more uneasy about the sense that he is on the way to meet "his own death" (1-2). In retirement-capital Florida, signs of death surround him: consumerist living intermixes with consumer dying as cremation societies and cardiac rehabilitation centers alternate along the highway with K-Marts and Taco Bells. Rabbit observes, "Any time you get somewhere down here without a head-on collision is a tribute to the geriatric medicine in this part of the world . . ." (106). Such images of death and decay pervade the novel. Perhaps Updike best summarizes this sense of mortality in his description of America's deteriorating highway system, an apt metaphor for Rabbit's impression of his own demise: "All the roads and bridges are falling apart at once" (400).

The nation, like Rabbit's health, has continued to deteriorate. No longer a world leader, America has taken a second seat following the lead of Japan: "Everybody's tailgating, that's the way we move along now," Rabbit observes (12). Nelson proclaims: "Americans want to go back to fins and convertibles and the limo look and these Japs are still trying to sell these tidy little boxes" (36). America would like to return to "the good old days" of the Fifties, the era of Rabbit's youth, but this age no longer exists (if it ever did), nor is it possible to reclaim. America is dying, a victim of spiritual emptiness. This notion is keenly expressed in Nelson's profession of the kind of car he prefers: "Infiniti's are fan*ta*stic, there's no car in them, just birds and trees, they're selling a *con*cept" (406). The ultimate empty signifier, "Infiniti" aptly represents for Updike the moral and spiritual vacuity of American civilization at the end of the Reagan Eighties, an era in which symbol prevails over substance.

Not only is Rabbit, like America, facing death head on, he also faces the culmination of the friction he has experienced with his son. Nelson and Harry's medial opposition is obvious in their curt exchanges, such as this one begun by Harry: "You've damaged enough cars in your life." "Yeah, and you've damaged enough lives in yours" (25). Both their lives have fallen victim to numerous damages from collisions, some accidental, some self-inflicted. The ultimate collision between father and son occurs when Harry sleeps with his daughter-in-law, Pru. This act seems almost fated; since his affair with Ruth, we have observed Rabbit's sexual obsession, his inability to place common decency above his own urges. In fact, we have frequently felt that Rabbit's misuse of women would lead to his final downfall, and his sexual adventure with Pru and the trickery of his granddaughter, which brings about his heart attack, do.

Pru's confession of their liaison to Nelson and Janice proves too difficult for Harry to face, so once again he flees southward in his car, driving along the same route he had previously traversed for escape in *Rabbit, Run*, searching his radio dial (now digitalized) once more for old tunes. The oldies station soon fades out, however, replaced by realities of the Eighties: news of the PTL scandal, talk shows about AIDS, reports on Japanese stocks. And after thirty years, the terrain along his southern route has changed significantly. The store where he once stopped to ask for directions has now been turned into a "slick little real-estate office" (438); the gas pumps are now an asphalt parking lot; the once wooded country lane is now lined with Pizza Huts, Minit Markets, and Smorgasbords—all made possible by the car.

Eventually Rabbit makes it to the Gulf; however, its warm waters do not heal nor bring about a baptism into forgiveness, rather they represent the geriatric Florida that only reminds him of his own mortality. The plain fact facing Rabbit is the one we all must face: our inability to escape death and dying. Rabbit's entire existence can be seen as an attempt to circumvent, ward off, ignore, and deplore his own demise, yet in spite of all his attempts, his life comes full circle. As he tries to escape south in the beginning of the first novel, he tries again in the end of the last; and as we first witness him in *Rabbit, Run* playing basketball, harkening back to his days as a high-school hero, in the end of *Rabbit at Rest* he again seeks to renew his sense of self through a game of hoops. This time, however, his actions place him on his death bed, a result of his weakened heart. A victim of years of hard driving and high mileage, Rabbit is simply worn out. "Enough," he thinks in the end.

Enough—with this final word Updike ends the literary cycle of Rabbit Angstrom. Collectively in the four Rabbit works Updike has catalogued the friction of the middle-class, white American male in his interactive rubbings with the traffic of American society throughout the past four decades. In movement, friction is inevitable, and in the movements of Rabbit through the American briar patch, we see how his scrapes and collisions have both strengthened and ravaged him. Rabbit has endured the internal-stream friction resulting from self-conflict over the direction of his own life, the marginal friction coming from the nation's vast social changes over the past thirty years, and the intersectional friction emanating from his struggles to maintain a sense of home and family, all to face supremely the medial friction of his own death. Amidst the friction, Updike has used metaphors of automobility to correspond to Rabbit's journey because the automobile, the ultimate generator of America's traffic, is at the heart of the American middle-class experience. Paralleling Rabbit's demise, the all-American, gas-guzzling Fifties' automobile has disappeared, out of gas, and has been replaced by, as Nelson says, not even a car, but a concept. With America beginning the decade of the Nineties with yet more friction—from the conflict in the Gulf precipitating from protecting oil for automobiles to the increased friction resulting from the nation running out of money to grease the gears of its banks and industries—Rabbit will speak no more. One can hope for a miracle (for both America and Harry), but short of one, readers will have to imagine how a banged-up Rabbit might continue to be driven through the traffic jam of the American *fin-de-siècle*.

Crossing the White Line

Rabbit's question to Skeeter: "Why do so few American Negroes want to give up their Cadillacs and . . . go back to Africa?" bluntly addresses the role of automobility in the African-American experience. While Rabbit presents a picture of automobility in the life of the middle-class white male, the story of the auto in the history of African Americans is quite different. As Brenda Jo Bright observes, "A lesson many learned prior to the publicized beating of Rodney King is that a man of color is not necessarily free to move about the city as he pleases. . . . Blacks have long been subject to strict surveillance and delimited mobility" (91). Thus a seeming norm in American literature finds the coupling of automobiles and blacks leading to calamity: in *Invisible Man* (1952) the protagonist is expelled from college for driving a white trustee across "the white line dividing the highway" to the black side of town (38); in *Native Son* (1940) Bigger Thomas murders Mary Dalton ultimately as a consequence of his position as a chauffeur; and as early as Arna Bontemps's "A Summer Tragedy" (1933) black sharecroppers use their car to commit suicide. White authors coupling blacks and cars have created equally disastrous results: Coalhouse Walker, Jr., of E. L. Doctorow's *Ragtime* (1975) loses his life over the restoration of his Model T Ford, for example. Henry Ford's dictum concerning paint choice on his Model T, "Any color as long as it's black," may identify the primary reason for these characters' travails—the color of their skin. These recurring calamities suggest that to these authors the automobile, the most visible machine in American society, embodies a larger machine—that of racism and its byproducts of discrimination, exploitation, and alienation.

Arna Bontemps

"A Summer Tragedy" chronicles the final hours of Jeff and Jenny, aging black sharecroppers who decide to end their lives rather than continue with the infirmities of old age and the difficulties imposed on them by their hard-driving landlord. Their method of demise is their automobile, an aging Model T, which they drive off a cliff into a raging river. On several occasions, Bontemps parallels the increasingly decrepit bodies of Jeff and Jenny with the mechanical condition of "the little rattle-trap car," the Ford becoming emblematic of the couple's condition: "The engine came to life with a sputter and bang that rattled the old car from radiator to tail light. . . . The sputtering and banging increased. The rattling became more violent. That was good. It was good banging, good sputtering and rattling, and it meant that the aged car was still in running condition" (139). Jeff's and Jenny's bodies correlate to the mechanical clamor of the car: "The suggestion of the trip fell into the *machinery* of his mind like a wrench. . . . When he took his hands off the wheel, he noticed that he was *trembling* violently. . . . A few moments later she was at the window, her voice *rattling* against the pane like a broken shutter" (139—emphases added). Jeff's heart beats like "the little pounding motor of the car," which "worked harder and harder. The puff of steam from the cracked radiator became larger" (145). Even the shed which houses the car is likened to the house of the old couple and metaphorically to the couple themselves; "miraculously, despite wind and downpour, it still stood" (139).

Clearly Bontemps wishes us to view the old couple in much the same vein as the vehicle: both have existed for a service function, and both have been literally driven into the ground. Jeff comments how his landlord feels that one mule is enough to plow forty acres and how such a philosophy has resulted in the deaths of many mules—and many men, he adds. He is proud to have survived such a rigorous existence. Yet like the Model T, his and Jenny's radiators are cracked: he is partially crippled by a stroke, Jenny is blind, and both fear they will end up like a discarded mule, or a junked automobile. They therefore choose to do what they perceive they must do to die with dignity.

Neither Jeff nor Jenny can bear the loss of each other: he is her eyes, she his hands. The old couple and the car also have a symbiotic relationship. Jeff and Jenny could have chosen a more passive role for the car in their suicides, for example, using it for carbon monoxide poisoning. Instead, they have the car "die" with them, and Bontemps leaves us, not with the couple, but with the image of the torn car: "In another instant the car hit the water and dropped immediately out of sight. A little later it lodged in the mud of a shallow place. One wheel of the crushed and upturned little Ford became visible above the rushing water" (148). The couple regarded the car as "a peculiar treasure" (139). Like most farmers of the Thirties, they also found it indispensable. The automobile was their one link to the outside world, their source of mobility, particularly since old age had crippled the mobility of their own bodies. Yet in spite of the car, they are unable to escape from their condition, neither physically nor economically, and this compounds their desperate state. Before his death, Jeff remembers especially one event in his life: the time he took a trip to New Orleans, the last time he really left the farm behind. Now the old couple goes on one final journey, a journey to their deaths made possible by the car.

The story of one old couple may seem insignificant, as Bontemps relates in this image: "Chugging across the green countryside, the small, battered Ford seemed tiny indeed" (140); yet since their story is called a tragedy, the two are obviously meant to be seen as heroic figures. They exemplify the untold stories of countless lives worn out as cogs in a machine exploiting them for cheap labor and holding them captive in indebtedness. In the story's conclusion we are torn between rejoicing over the couple's ability to die in a manner they see befitting dignity and outrage over the harshness of a life which has led them to make such a decision. Like a Model T, Jeff and Jenny have been pushed to their limits and discarded, products of a cycle of exploitation. Steinbeck writes, "There was one nice thing about Model T's. The parts were not only interchangeable, they were unidentifiable" (*Cannery Row* 76). So like a Model T, the story of Jeff and Jenny could be interchanged with that of hundreds of other share-cropper families, all of whose lives remain sadly unidentifiable to the larger world.

In another story from the same year, "Saturday Night: Portrait of a Small Southern Town, 1933," Bontemps again uses automobiles to illuminate racial oppression in his society. In this story the narrator speaks from his car as he drives through town on a Saturday evening. A white man has been killed by a hit-and-run driver, leading one character to remark: "We know right well that it *was* a colored man who was driving that car. . . . That driver refused to stop because he feard a mob" (164). On another occasion a political speaker remarks: "Take Macon County fer'n instance. Down yonder there's seven niggers to every white man. . . . Yet 'n still they got heap better roads 'n we got here in Madison County" (159). Both quotations clearly demonstrate prevailing racist attitudes, but by far the most prominent incident involving an automobile recounts the story of two black men helping a white driver:

> [A]t the turn of the Pike there is an automobile stuck in the heavy mud. We slow down. The white driver beckons to two blacks who are about to pass him without stopping: "Come here boys, give me a push." They do not speak but come quietly and set their muscles against the weight of the car. Presently it gets away. The driver does not pause or look back. . . . Apparently neither they nor the driver have been aware of anything irregular in the episode that summoned them to push a carload of able men out of the mud and left them ankle deep in the spot as the others drove away. Apparently there is no pang, no tragedy. (168-9)

These incidents involving automobiles clearly show the second-class life of blacks in a small Southern town—they are left in the mud while whites use them and drive away. Bontemps would have us feel a pang and see these stories as the tragedies they are.

Richard Wright

Richard Wright's *Native Son* moves from Bontemps's rural settings to urban Chicago, but the protagonist, Bigger Thomas, is also victimized, unable to escape. Again the automobile is connected to his plight. Early in the novel Wright uses passing cars to illustrate the restlessness of Bigger and his unemployed companions. Like Bontemps's two men in the mud, Bigger and his friends are left behind as those empowered by the automobile drive by: "They waited leisurely at corners for cars to pass; it was not that they feared cars, but they had plenty of time" (31). Bigger has too much time on his hands, and in that time his growing sense of alienation and anger festers. He wishes he could escape. As a symbol of this desire, he steals auto tires, the wheels for his flight. Potential relief comes in his job as driver for the "philanthropic" Daltons, a position which allows Bigger to dream of escape. When he first gets the job, he imagines his vehicle: "He hoped it would be a Packard, or a Lincoln, or a Rolls Royce. Boy! Would he drive! Just wait! Of course, he would be careful when he was driving Miss or Mr. Dalton. But when he was alone he would burn up the pavement; he would make those tires smoke!" (60-1). Marsh and Collett write in *Driving Passion: The Psychology of the Car*: "For many individuals, driving a car is one of the few opportunities to escape from a life of routine submission. . . .The car is, for them, a technological leveler. . . . Challenges . . . can be taken up and symbolic battles won" (165). The car provides such an opportunity for Bigger; it furnishes the only real feeling of power he has ever had: "He had a keen sense of power when driving; the feel of a car added something to him. He loved to press his foot against a pedal and sail along, watching others stand still, seeing the asphalt road unwind under him" (63).

Bigger sees the automobile as a way out of his depressed existence, yet paradoxically, it is responsible for his plight. His situation represents the condition of many inner-city blacks after the automotive revolution. Economic opportunities increased because of the automobile, yet such opportunities were often located out of the reach of those without cars. Dan Lacy elaborates in *The White Use of Blacks in America*:

> The very ease of private automobile transportation led to a decay and abandonment of public transportation even where it existed, and there was little incentive for the establishment of new transit or bus lines to serve the new areas. Blacks who could not afford to own and maintain cars in the city were hopelessly blocked from employment in precisely those types of plants in which opportunities were largest and most promising. (216)

Unable to find good jobs, inner-city blacks like Bigger worked at unskilled labor or in domestic positions, if they had jobs at all.

Bigger's dreams of power through the automobile quickly crumble when wealthy Mary Dalton asks him to drive her to the black side of town: "It was a shadowy region, a No Man's Land, the ground that separated the white world from the black that he stood upon. He felt

naked, transparent . . ." (67-8). Mary's request violates Bigger's sense
of order, thereby making him vulnerable. Wright describes Bigger's
sense of losing control: "He was not driving; he was simply sitting and
floating along smoothly through darkness" (77-8). This darkness
engulfs Bigger, and ultimately it leads him to smother Mary in his
panic over being caught in her bedroom and then to burn her body in
the Dalton's furnace, acts which eventually result in his execution.[36]

Ralph Ellison

Like Bigger Thomas, the protagonist of *Invisible Man* is ruined by
driving a white person. Wright tells of Bigger's proximity to Mary that
"never in his life had he been so close to a white woman" (68), and the
invisible man finds himself in the same position with Mr. Norton, the
white trustee of the college: "I had never been so close to a white
person before," he asserts (84). Like Bigger, the invisible man is
initially elated by the power he feels in commanding an automobile, yet
he also has a sense of impending doom because of his proximity to
whiteness: "We were driving, the powerful motor purring and filling
me with pride and anxiety" (37), he declares; "Riding here in the
powerful car with this white man who was so pleased with what he
called his fate, I felt a sense of dread" (40).

The invisible man fears the crossing of the white line: both
entering into the territory of power and wealth which society has taught
him is reserved for white people and taking someone from the white
world into the true world of the African-American community, the
world of Trueblood and of the Golden Day. "I suddenly decided to turn
off the highway, down a road that seemed unfamiliar," the invisible
man narrates of the journey to Trueblood's (40). Down this unfamiliar
road they approach "a team of oxen hitched to a broken-down wagon,"
a clear contrast to the symbol of success and power of the automobile
(40).[37] The white line of the highway becomes the symbol for this line
of division between black and white in society: "I wished we were back
on the other side of the white line, heading back to the quiet green
stretch of the campus," the narrator declares (49); and on another
occasion he states, "The wheel felt like an alien thing in my hands as I
followed the white line of the highway" (96). The trip to the Golden
Day further compounds the crossing of the line, and symbolically the
invisible man drives there on the wrong side of the road. As with
Bigger, this act of crossing the white line leads the invisible man to

lose control of his destiny: "I had a sense of losing control of the car and slammed on the brakes in the middle of the road . . . ," he declares (97). The invisible man's fate is best represented by Ellison's description of an insect that "crushed itself against the windshield, leaving a yellow, mucous smear" (44). He is crushed, destroyed by the circumstances of this encounter, an encounter that demonstrates little real change in the social position of African Americans since emancipation. Indeed, when we last see the car, it has stopped "in front of a small building with white pillars like those of an old plantation manor house," seemingly indicating times have not changed at all (98).

Jean Rosenbaum asserts that the automobile "is more than a convenience; it is a symbol . . . of belonging to a group, and it brings group recognition" (2). The invisible man wants to be part of "the group." At one point with Mr. Norton he thinks: "[W]ith the car leaping leisurely beneath the pressure of my foot, I identified myself with the rich man reminiscing on the rear seat . . ." (39). This identification suggests that the invisible man wishes to appropriate whiteness, and his emulation of the hegemony of the white superstructure, as represented by Mr. Norton, leads to his downfall. Only after realizing he must embrace blackness and not try to appropriate whiteness and objects connected to the white power structure, such as fancy cars, does the invisible man become self-actualized.

E. L. Doctorow

Ragtime demonstrates that writers other than African Americans also tie automobiles to the demise of black characters. Like the invisible man, Doctorow's character, Coalhouse Walker, Jr., also wants to belong to the power group. Driving a new Model T and wearing goggles and a duster, Walker appears at the home of a white family housing Sarah, the mother of his child. The family's father finds Walker's status exceptional: "It occurred to father one day that Coalhouse Walker Jr. didn't know he was a Negro" (185). Walker, however, knows that "as the owner of a car he was a provocation to many white people" (199). The 1910 auto race between white race-car driver Barney Oldfield and black heavyweight champion Jack Johnson exemplifies Walker's sentiments. When Oldfield won the race, the *New York Sun* ran the headline, "White Race Saved." Johnson had been harassed by policemen throughout the country, particularly for driving white women around in his vehicle. One Indianapolis theatre owner threatened to kill him for this practice. Historian Clay McShane concludes that during this time period, "Nothing infuriated whites concerned with limiting status symbols more than black drivers" (134). One such white infuriated by Walker's driving, the racist fire chief Will Conklin, asks Walker for a toll to pass his firehouse. Walker leaves to get a policeman, and upon returning discovers his car muddied, torn, and defecated on. He demands reparation, but in the ensuing exchange the officer arrests him. The following day he returns to find the car thoroughly vandalized, pushed into a pond, wires ripped from the engine: "Waterlogged and wrecked, it offended the sensibilities of anyone who respected machines and valued what they could do" (274).

Walker becomes obsessed with justice over the restoration of his car, yet he is unable to obtain it because of Conklin's judicial connections. Then, another incident involving an automobile compounds his rage. Sarah attempts to plead Walker's case before the visiting U.S. Vice President, and as he exits his Panhard limousine, she bolts toward him. Suspected of being an assassin, she is mortally wounded by a blow from a gun. Ironically, an expensive automobile much like that which carried the Vice President bears her to her funeral: "a custom Pierce Arrow Opera Coach with an elongated passenger compartment and a driver's cab open to the weather. . . . The car was so highly polished the boy could see in its rear doors a reflection of the entire street" (223). Walker then becomes a vigilante, burning down firehouses and leaving the demand: "I want my automobile returned to me in its original condition. If these conditions are not met I will continue to kill firemen and burn firehouses until they are" (243). He forms a gang that executes terrorist activities in quick strikes from automobiles, and those acts lead the New York legislature to enact an automobile registration law so that vehicles might be traced. Eventually the gang takes over the J. P. Morgan Library, and Conklin is forced to restore the car on the street in front of the edifice. Walker ultimately surrenders, but upon exiting the building is needlessly shot and killed.

To Walker, the struggle for racial equality begins with justice over the destruction of his Ford. He feels "with an enemy as vast as an entire nation of the white race, the restoration of a Model T automobile was as good a place to start as any" (337). That Walker owns a Model T is interesting, not only because of *Ragtime*'s structural emphasis on the interchangeability of parts, as the Model T had, but also because of Henry Ford's dealings with black employees in Detroit. August Meier and Elliott Rudwick's *Black Detroit and the Rise of the UAW* addresses this association. At one time Ford was the largest employer of African Americans in Detroit. He saw "in black America an eager reservoir of workers committed to the American system" (14); however, "In Ford's view negroes, like these other disadvantaged groups, were social outcasts who needed and would appreciate his help" (11). His *Ford Guide*, published in 1917, advised that "Black people came from Africa where they lived like other animals in the jungle. White men brought them to America and made them civilized" (Batchelor 50-1). Ford's racist and patronizing attitude, like that of Wright's "philanthropic" Daltons and *Invisible Man*'s Mr. Norton, did not promote equality and opportunity, but rather reupholstered the notion of the superiority of white society, positioning whites as saviors of the downtrodden black community. Walker's assertion that the restitution of his Ford is as good a place to start as any thus can extend beyond the car to Ford himself and particularly to the enterprises practiced by the white capitalist elite.

Jeff and Jenny, Bigger Thomas, the invisible man, and Coalhouse Walker are all associated with the automobile, perhaps the most visible symbol of the machine age. They are also victimized by another machine—racism. All are victims of the alienation, discrimination, and exploitation of a racist system; and all die, except the invisible man, who recognizes the turnings of the machine before it grinds him to death in its cogs. While associations between automobility and racism are prominent in these works by Bontemps, Wright, Ellison, and Doctorow, they are not the only writers to have made such a connection. Alice Walker, for one, in *The Color Purple*, demonstrates the hatred felt by racist whites over blacks who own cars, much like the feelings expressed by Conklin against Coalhouse Walker. In this novel, Sofia drives a new car into town. There, Millie, the white mayor's wife, approaches her and asks her to become her maid. Her reply of "hell, no" in conjunction with bitter sentiments whites hold against Sofia for driving such a nice car and not seeming to know her proper place in society leads to a fist fight between her and the mayor, an action which results in her being beaten, imprisoned, and eventually assigned as maid to Millie as punishment. The mayor then buys Millie a new car and says that "if colored could have cars then one for her was past due," but Sofia has to teach her how to drive it (100). After learning, Millie announces she will drive Sofia to see her children, but Sofia must now sit in the back seat because, as Millie observes, "This *is* the South. . . . Have you ever seen a white person and a colored sitting side by side in a car, when one of 'em wasn't showing the other how to drive it or clean it?" (101-02). Her visit lasts only fifteen minutes, however, because Millie strips the gears in the vehicle and makes Sofia go with her to get a mechanic because she "couldn't ride in a pick-up with a strange colored man" (103). Once again, in this text the car becomes a vehicle through which instruments of racism manifest themselves.

Ragtime's Father "said it was ridiculous to allow a motorcar to take over everyone's life as it now had" (217); nevertheless, the car is the most visible mechanical symbol of empowerment in our society. Jeff, Jenny, Bigger, the invisible man, Coalhouse, and Sofia all want to have power, the power they feel society owes them as human adults. Owning or even driving a car gives them a sense of having made it, of being part of the economic power structure. Yet it is a short-lived and unfounded sense for all. In spite of the symbolic power of the automobile, it imparts no real economic nor political empowerment. Despite their car, Jeff and Jenny can escape the system which ensnares them only in death; both Bigger and the invisible man's cars carry them on destructive paths; and Coalhouse Walker pays for his Model T with his life. In the works of Bontemps, Wright, Ellison, Doctorow, and Walker, the automobile assumes a larger-than-life role as a precipitator of doom, an emblem of the racial injustices of America.

V

"Where We Are in America":
Contemporary Representations of
Automobility

Rot like this cannot be stayed.

—Joy Williams

The invisible man, Jeff and Jenny, and Bigger Thomas all seek to escape the realities of their existence. As such, they resemble Rabbit Angstrom and Sal Paradise, characters who also see the automobile as providing the possibility of escape, yet who learn that while the car can sometimes provide a physical escape, it seldom can provide an emotional or spiritual one. As a recent pamphlet entitled "Kill the Car!" declares, "When they purchase a car, people aren't simply obtaining needed transportation, but pseudo-identity, and the illusion of freedom." Though not in all current fiction (*The Widows' Adventures*, e.g.), contemporary representations of automobility, such as in the fiction of Harry Crews, Joy Williams, Ann Beattie, and Louise Erdrich, tend to focus on these pseudo-identity and illusory qualities that the automobile provides.

Also, contemporary women writers have now clearly appropriated the traditionally masculine domain of automobility. An advertisement for the 1966 Corvette captioned with the title, "The day she flew the coupe," tells the story of a young couple who have recently purchased a 'Vette: "not once had he offered to let her drive. His excuse was that this, uh, was a big hairy sports car. Too much for a woman to handle . . . . That's why she hid the keys, forcing him to seek public transportation. Sure of his departure, she . . . was off for the hills . . . . Hard to drive. What propaganda" (Stern). Seven years after this ad,

General Motors vice president John DeLorean resigned, declaring: "The automobile industry has lost its masculinity" (Stern 108). Whether this assertion rings true or not, women writers have obviously moved beyond engendered notions of automobility handed down for over fifty years and have made the automobile a utilitarian vehicle in their fiction, something only their sister Flannery O'Connor had done to any extent before them. Like the young Corvette owner, Beattie, Williams, and Erdrich have plainly abandoned masculine propaganda and driven off in a new direction with their textual vehicles.

Rotting Birds and Blue Convertibles: Joy Williams's Failed Escapes

Joy Williams writes in her novel *Breaking and Entering* (1988): "He can go anywhere, just has to learn to drive. 'Escape' I told him. Escape was my advice" (261). Her collection of short fiction, the appropriately entitled *Escapes* (1990), presents characters influenced by such advice, characters who struggle to achieve transformation in their lives, to escape from their difficulties, limitations, and decay. In their efforts to escape, these characters become obsessed with cars and travel, and the automobile becomes to them a means of power to insulate or isolate them from reality. Such attempts at escape usually meet with futility, and the very mode of escape becomes a means of entrapment. The automobile, often their method of transport, ensnares them and serves as the agent of "rot," the malady of contemporary American life.

This paradigm is best exemplified in "Rot." In this story, Lucy's husband Dwight develops a morbid obsession for owning an old black Ford Thunderbird when he discovers it in a parking lot, a dead man at the wheel. Despite the car's connection to death, Dwight feels he must own it because to him the car represents a nostalgia for a better age and the possibility of restoration. The car, however, turns out to be junk. Its paint—hearselike black—covers rust and the original color—the sanguine Starmist Blue. One mechanic recommends repair parts might be found through a service whose name suggests spiritual rebirth, *The T-Bird Sanctuary*; however, the existential repairman Boris offers different advice: "This car is unrestorable. It is full of rust and rot. Rust is a living thing, it breathes, it eats and it is swallowing up your car. . . . Rot like this cannot be stayed. This brings us to the question, What is man? with its three subdivisions, What can he know? What ought he do? What may he hope? . . . Once rot, then nothing" (23). Like Boris, Williams uses the automobile metaphorically as an extension of the human condition, paralleling the condition of the car to the conditions of Dwight and Lucy themselves.

In response to Boris's philosophical comments, Dwight says to Lucy, "You never used to hear about rust and rot all the time. It's new, this rust and rot business" (24). Ironically, rust and rot are not new to Lucy and Dwight; they are just now becoming aware of the detritus around them, of the junkyard condition of their world. Like the car, their world is full of rot: a baby seal at the Aquarium is put to sleep, born too ugly for children to see; the television reports a shooting and murder; the paper tells of toxic waste. In addition, Dwight and Lucy are surrounded by the decay of Dwight's past. They live in the same town as three of his old lovers, all of whom are degenerating: for instance, Daisy has had a leg amputated, and Rosette finds life with her new husband "a long twilight of drinking and listless anecdote" (27). And like the car, Dwight's own marriage is rotting. Lucy and the car are connected early in the story when Dwight declares: "I knew I just had to have this car, it was just so pretty. It's the same age as you are darling. That was the year the good things came out" (18). Like his desire for the car, Dwight developed an abnormal obsession for Lucy at first sight: even though he was twenty-five and she was only four months old, he declared he would one day marry her, and he did. Now, like the car, she needs restoration and new life. One day she tells her desires to the Thunderbird as if it were a genie: "I'd like a Porsche Carrera. . . . I would like a little baby" (30). Earlier, Daisy responded to Lucy's news of the T-Bird as if Lucy were pregnant: "So! You're going to have another car!" (25). But the car does not provide a new generation for Lucy; she remains unfulfilled.

Dwight cannot let go of his pipedreams for the car, so he decides to bring it into the living room of the house to preserve it from the elements. "It didn't look bad inside the house at all and Lucy didn't mind it being there, although she didn't like it when Dwight raised the hood. . . . They would sit frequently in the car, in their house, not going anywhere, looking through the windshield out at the window and through the window to the street" (29). Their lives become more isolated: they invite no one over; Dwight begins to sit alone in the car more and more. Through their windshield perception, they watch a television set which has no sound, and Dwight presses the rim of the car's horn, which does not work. Nothing in their world functions as it should. In the story's conclusion, the couple sit in the car, an emotional tomb, peering out the windshield and through the living-room picture window to the rain falling outside. Twice removed from the regenerative possibilities of the rain and the outside world, they are, as Lucy says, not a part of everything.

The car functions as a signifier, but it does not signify what Dwight intended. He nostalgically thinks the old car will elicit a better age. Instead, it mires them deeper into the true condition of their present lives. Dwight confuses the Thunderbird with the Phoenix, the mythical bird which rises brilliantly from ashes to new life. Instead of freeing them or providing new possibilities, the Thunderbird traps them; they become consumed by its rust and sit entombed in it, just like the dead man whom Dwight finds in the parking lot. The car thus epitomizes everything wrong in their lives and everything decadent about the world in which they live. The '50s Thunderbird comes from an age of optimism and growth in American economy and society. Today the sites of that unparalleled period of industrial output have become an economically depressed area of the country—the Rust Belt, as it has come to be known. Once powerful machines of industry tower over depressed cities and towns, ghosts of an age of productivity. And Dwight's car, once majesty of the American highway, personifies this lost age.

As evidenced in "Rot," automobiles in Williams's fiction foremost represent failed means of escape, lost periods of fulfillment, be they societal or personal. Williams's cars are often rusting or rotting, similar to the environment surrounding her stories' characters. While these cars should either elicit feelings of nostalgia or promise the hope of restoration, in fact they are often beyond repair, as are the lives of their owners. The automobile entraps, isolates, and detaches, suffocating those around. The car is thus often connected to death or dying. Such elements are clearly seen in "Rot," and "The Route," "Escapes," and "The Little Winter" present variations on these themes.

In "The Route" a young wife and her middle-aged husband seek escape from their marital problems by means of an automobile trip from New York to Key West. "We had the car so we went," the wife begins matter of factly (97). Her narration consists of comments made at obscure but suggestive destinations along their trip south—Alert, North Carolina, for example. Again, discussion of the car substitutes for an analysis of the relationship: "This car takes a lot out of one," the wife says, "It is exhausting and seems to have intentions of its own. . . . We are traveling in a straight line but he is struggling with the wheel" (100-01). Both relationship and vehicle are out of control, aimless. And again, the car evokes the sense of decay. The husband obsesses over his theory concerning sharks, and associatively the car takes on a sharklike quality, described as fishy in look and smell: "It is a Buick with big fins. . . . It has a strange odor about the right hubcap. Now I have heard pranksters . . . put dead fish or something awful there," declares the wife (100). Finally the smelly Buick literally and violently falls apart, as the wife graphically recounts:

> A worn battery cable shorted out on the frame, setting fire to the engine at the same time an electrode from the spark plug fell into the combustion chamber, disintegrating the piston. The tires went flat the transmission fluid exploded the gas tank collapsed an armature snapped shooting the generator pulley through the hood the brake shoes melted the windshield cracked and the glove compartment flew open spilling my panties into the street. (106)

The decay in their own relationship is represented by this smelly, disintegrating car and also by rotten things they encounter on the trip: pools full of algae, motels serving bad meat, a bat biting the husband, Santa Claus telling them to "Fuck off!" As they encounter more and more rot and decay, they journey towards a more violent disintegration of their own relationship and lives, culminating with the disintegration of the car and the infection of the husband.

After the bat bite, the husband changes, becoming desperately amorous, rabid, vampiric. The function of the car changes, too: they now use it for sex. Parking beside an old shack, they leave the engine running and rush inside to make love; discovering the house occupied, they make love in the car. Contiguous to the husband's transformation, the couple replaces the crumbled Buick with a "mean machine": "It has air extractors, a shaker hood, six spoilers, four pipes, a 400-cubic-inch Ram Air V-8 and four-barrel carbs" (107). They blast past everyone on the road, but as the wife realizes, "I know not forever" (107). She realizes their destructive level of energy cannot be sustained. This new car cannot sustain their relationship; it will burn out just as the rabid husband does. The "new" car is a quick-fix, not a solution.

Eventually their escape takes them to Key West, where they can drive no further. They have reached the end of the road, the southernmost point in America: "All the streets are dead ends," the wife says (108). By now, the husband has lost his faculties, so they kiss a final time, awaiting the sharks which will devour him as the couple swims in the ocean. Like Lucy and Dwight, whom rust and rot eat away, this couple is also consumed. Their relationship is a consumer relationship in a consumer society, of which both sharks and Buicks are emblematic. Images of violent destruction and consumption surround them: sharks, bats, monstrous automobiles. They cannot escape this world; the "mean machine" will fail them just as the Buick did. They have reached the end of the line—the termination of U.S. 1—and their escape has failed. Unlike Dwight and Lucy's Thunderbird, this automobile does lead to some short-lived respite, but as in "Rot," it ultimately fails as an object of hope and promise and leads to detachment and death.

"Escapes," the collection's title story, and "The Little Winter" unite the motif of escape found in "The Route" with the image of rust and decay seen in "Rot." Once again, automobiles serve as signifiers. Psychologist Jean Rosenbaum has written about women patients who buy convertibles to express feelings of freedom and to overcome their sense of being inhibited and unloved (19). In "Escapes," Lizzie's mother fits the role of such a woman. She wants to escape her own problems, including her husband's desertion.[38] Alcohol is her chief means of diversion, but she also buys a convertible to help free her spirit. The "blue" convertible, however, epitomizes Lizzie's mother's inability to be free: she cannot make use of its retractable roof because she lives in Maine and it is winter. Furthermore, as with Dwight's Thunderbird, this car has been devoured by rust; freezing air rushes in through rusted holes in the floorboard, chilling the car's occupants. Lizzie's dream about the car—she and her mother try to drive to another house in it but keep circling back to the same one—best illustrates her mother's entrapment.[39]

The central action of the story concerns the drunken mother's embarrassing interruption of a magician's act in her attempt to learn the escape artistry of her hero, Houdini.[40] Following this incident, mother and daughter return home in the car, the daughter recollecting "the soft, stained roof ballooning up in the way I knew it looked from the outside" (14). Lizzie and her mother are trapped within her mother's ballooning difficulties. Lizzie, however, is one day able to transcend the situation and look on from the outside, while her mother remains caught up in her problems, as epitomized by the car. Lizzie concludes,

"I got out of it, but it took me years" (14), referring both to getting over her mother's eventual suicide (which perhaps took place in the car) and to the vehicle itself, which to her has become representative of her mother. The vehicle in this story underscores the mother's problems. This blue convertible cannot convert the mother; it only compounds her frustrated desire to escape her sorrow, loneliness, and despair.

The cold air of "Escapes" rematerializes in "The Little Winter." In this story, death and dying are prevalent: the protagonist, Gloria, is dying of a brain tumor; cars have killed two of her dogs. Driving a rental car to a friend's home, she finds the landscape by the highway morbidly parallel to her condition: cemeteries and obelisks shroud the roadside; dying trees line the median. The trip becomes a metaphor for her life. As she travels toward her impending death, she remembers the time of year she once called "the little winter," the brief cold period before the lengthy winter season sat in. She now endures this preliminary cold period in her own life as she awaits the deep cold of death. All about her this sense of cold rushes in, just as the freezing air pours into the blue convertible of Lizzie's mother.

Gloria travels to visit her friend Jean and Jean's daughter Gwendal. On the way, she spends a night in a motel shaped like a teepee and drives to a monastery where dogs are raised. She is on a twilight-zone vacation, her story a surrealist travelogue much like the one in "The Route." Jean, seemingly not able and not desirous to abandon the rot of her own life, lives in the same town as three of her ex-husbands, her situation being similar to that of Dwight in "Rot." Her daughter Gwendal, however, does wish to escape. Gwendal wants to be kidnapped and driven around America in a van; so Gloria takes her, and they escape on the back roads of America, kidnapping a monastery dog and stopping at little motels, such as the aptly named Motel Lark. Gwendal refers to Gloria's condition as "The Great Adventure," a title both descriptive of their trip and of Gloria's own dying, yet she finds Gloria ill-prepared for life, to say nothing of her impending death: "I bet you don't even know how to check the oil in that car," Gwen says to her (92). Gwen equates Gloria's lack of knowledge concerning the car with her lack of insight towards life, a substitution further bringing into focus the use of the automobile trip in this story to embody the journey of life, a life, in Gloria's case, with little direction.

Two other stories in *Escapes*, "Health" and "The Last Generation," contain interesting uses of the automobile. Young Pammy of "Health," like Gloria, is not well, having been infected with tuberculosis bacteria contracted while on vacation in Mexico. She now lives seemingly securely protected by the innocence of childhood and by the care of her parents. As the story opens, she travels in her father's car to her tanning session, realizing how outwardly safe her world is: her father drinks from a no-spill coffee cup; he drives cautiously; antiseptic is sprayed on the tanning bed. Each scene of the story shows Pammy encased, kept from the outside world: first in her father's car, then in the tomblike tanning bed, and finally in her mother's car. At the end of the story "she unlocks the car's door. Pammy gets in and the door locks again" (122). She is locked away from all experiences that might harm her, but as the tuberculosis germs demonstrate, one cannot live protected from all things. This fact is most clearly demonstrated in the story when a man looks in on Pammy while she sits undressed in the tanning room. The innocence of childhood is invaded just as the tuberculosis germs have already invaded her seemingly healthy life.

Pammy would like to grow up and break free from this frozen world; she looks forward to the end of innocence, to new knowledge. This is represented by her desire to learn to drive: "Pammy looks forward to learning how to drive now, but after a few years, who knows? She can't imagine it being that enjoyable after a while. . . . Morris had given Pammy a lesson in driving the Jeep. He taught her how to shift smoothly, how to synchronize acceleration with the depression and release of the clutch" (112-13). Though Pammy is taught to shift smoothly, we realize as adults that not all of life is easy shifting—there are times of depression as well as release.

Perhaps Pammy, unlike many of Williams's characters, will learn to manage her times of difficulty and depression rather than try to escape from them. Once, Pammy saw a radical skater leaping cars in a mall parking lot; "'I don't fall,' the boy said, . . . 'because I've got a deep respect for the concrete surface and because when I make a miscalculation, instead of falling, I turn it into a new trick'" (120). Williams's main characters lack this ability to take a miscalculation and turn it into something positive. Instead, they sit trapped amidst their difficulties like Pammy locked inside her mother's car. No matter how much Williams's characters wish they could escape their problems, their pasts, their deaths, they cannot—especially not by running (nor driving) away from them. Gloria recognizes the danger of such false hope early in "The Little Winter" when she says of the duck decoys which Jean's ex-husband Bill carves, "[T]hey are objects designed to lure a living thing to its destruction with the false promise of safety, companionship, and rest" (87). Her assessment of Bill's decoys could easily be applied to her adventure in the rental car, to Dwight's Thunderbird, to Lizzie's mother's convertible, or to the "mean machine" of "The Route"—all these objects promise power, warmth, security, yet they fail to deliver on these promises and, in fact, promote destruction.

The destructive power of the automobile is seen in most of Williams's stories, but particularly in "The Last Generation."[41] In this story, nine-year-old Tommy's mother has been killed in a car wreck. Ironically, an ambulance is responsible for her death when she quickly stops so that it might proceed through a red light at an intersection. In doing so, a truck rear-ends her. Her family's close association with automobiles compounds the irony: her husband works as an automobile mechanic; Tommy builds and paints model cars; and her son Walter drives a truck which he had taken to the stock-car races, the destination of the ambulance, speeding not because of an emergency, but because it was late for the start of the race. Walter keeps a compass in the cab of his truck to help him with direction, and a compass placed on Williams's story would surely point in the direction of death. As in "The Little Winter," this story's tone portends doom: not only the mother, but fish and birds are all found dead. "They would know that it [a living thing] had existed because they had found it dead," states the narrator (168). And we sense from this, the final story in the collection, that we are all somehow a part of this "last generation, the ones who would see everything for the last time" (168).

As one of Williams's characters says in *Breaking and Entering*, "Things had purposes for which they were not intended certainly" (19). At the heart of these purposes is Williams's recognition of the automobile as an icon central to contemporary American culture. The car has been at the spine of this culture, but Williams's stories indicate a vertebral atrophy of society and the individual. Perhaps the decline of automobility parallels societal degeneration. The message of *Escapes* would seem to be: "Rot like this cannot be stayed"—it cannot be escaped. However, the promotion of escape permeates American society; "Get away in a Chevrolet," we are told. Williams's characters cannot get away in their Chevrolets. As Julian Smith writes: "Automobility has been consciously marketed and both consciously and subconsciously embraced by the American public as a form of emotional *transport*, the state or condition of being transported by ecstasy, of being enraptured" (182). In Williams's work, however, automobiles inevitably fail as methods of emotional transport; they emotionally entrap and confine characters instead. These characters— like Duane in *Breaking and Entering*, who "had just mounted four new tires—Pro Trac 60's. He had longed for those bit meats for a long time and now he possessed them. The big meats thrilled him, but he knew he was not as happy as he should have been" (106)—ultimately find the car unfulfilling. Williams's stories make clear the failure of the automobile as an external alleviation of internal disorder and point to the loss of real transformation in contemporary society, a condition resulting from people's dependence on material conveyance. In *Escapes* the car may provide transport, but it cannot provide transcendence. To depend on it for escape leaves one like Dwight or Lucy, entombed in the junkyard of the soul.

"Useful Junk": Louise Erdrich's Mystical Vehicles

Like Joy Williams, Louise Erdrich also writes about characters seeking escape from their present conditions, characters searching for transcendence in their otherwise listless lives. In addition, these characters are Native American. But for many of them, as with Williams's Anglo characters, the car becomes only a momentary enabler in their quest, and ultimately not a spiritually satisfying one. In the collection of stories which comprise *Love Medicine* (1984), we find numerous examples of such characters, and automobiles appear on nearly every other page of the novel. As one character notes, "It was as if the car was wired up to something" (22), seemingly indicating that cars in this text have some sort of overt supernatural or symbolic powers associated with them. Throughout the novel, Erdrich's characters view cars as special, even sacred, possessions. Characters remember with respect their old vehicles, recalling them like venerated elders (10). Sometimes they even stuff their real elders into the tiny back seats of their sports cars (14). These cars have been part of people's lives since childhood, sometimes even serving as playhouses for them (17).

Erdrich's automobiles have not gone unnoticed by literary critics. Marvin Magalaner writes:

> In *Love Medicine* the car is used by the author as a multipurpose tool
> to exhibit her Indian families adjusting (or failing to adjust) to their

twentieth-century role. Required for life on and off the reservation, the car is at once as familiar as a hat or as a grocery bag, but, at the same time, invested with a mystique that engenders the awe and respect once reserved for venerated natural spirits. (102)

Magalaner concludes that "if water is the all-pervasive symbolic link with the past, with time past and to come, and with the natural environment, then the unnatural present is epitomized by the automobile" (101). Examining the "mystique" of cars in Erdrich's fiction reveals automobiles connected to violence, death, escape, sex, characters' personalities, and even nature. As such, these textual vehicles serve sacrificial, spiritual, sacramental, and sanctuarial functions in her Native world.

From the onset of the novel, vehicles are imbued with sacramental qualities, the first being that of sexual union. To June Kashpaw, a truck is personified as a lover of sorts. She has sex in a truck with a mud engineer named Andy, whom she picks up in a local bar. As Andy makes love to her on the vehicle's seat, his hands accidentally turn on the heater. "She felt it open at her shoulder like a pair of jaws, blasting heat, and had the momentary and voluptuous sensation that she was lying stretched out before a great wide mouth. The breath swept across her throat, tightening her nipples" (5). The vehicle's breath, not the man's, satisfies her, yet only momentarily. In the end of this first chapter, she escapes from both, forcing the truck door open after her human lover falls asleep atop her and pins her down. She falls out the truck door into the cold snow beneath. The truck heater only momentarily warms her inner self; the outside reality she literally falls into is an icy, cold world. The mud engineer proves to be no more than "boom trash," the type of man who drives "around the state in big pickups that are loaded with options" (9). While the trucks may have options, the men provide none. Nor does June believe that she any options for her life. In the next chapter, we discover that she has frozen to death in the snow, far away from the warm breath of the truck's heater.

Later in the novel, a car again serves as a bedroom when Nector Kashpaw and Lulu Lamartine make love amidst melting butter they are delivering in the "soft inside, deep cushioned and cool" of her Nash Ambassador (96). Yet for Nector, this secret affair leads to more than he bargained for: "The more I saw of Lulu the more I realized that she was not from the secret land of the Nash Ambassador, but real . . . with a long list of things she needed done or said to please her" (101). Nector discovers that their love affair cannot be contained unreally within the doors of the car. He finds that he cannot escape the relationship, and he discusses his predicament in terms of an automotive metaphor: "I tried to let things go, but I was trapped behind the wheel. Whether I liked it or not I was steering something out of control" (104).

In another relationship, the car provides sanctuary for one character and becomes a violent substitute for her husband. Lynette takes the car keys and locks herself inside their Pontiac to escape her husband, King's, raging temper.

> Lynette was locked in the Firebird, crouched on the passenger's side. King screamed at her and threw his whole body against the car, thudded on the hood with hollow booms, banged his way across the roof, ripped at antennae and side-view mirrors with his fists, kicked into the broken sockets of the headlights. Finally he ripped a mirror off the driver's side and began to beat the car rhythmically, gasping. But though he swung the mirror time after time into the windshield and side windows he couldn't smash them. (32)

This Firebird, a religious symbol to the Chippewa (Magalaner 102), has been purchased with the life insurance money from his mother June's death, and after his rampage, King cries out how cold she now must be in her grave. The car provides sanctuary for Lynette, but we sense that King's violence against it is perhaps a venting of the anger he feels over his mother's senseless death. The car thus serves as a substitute on whose body he expresses his suppressed feelings of anger about and towards his mother.

Others in the family will not ride in the Firebird because to them it represents the reality of June's tragedy all too concretely. The spirit of the dead woman is seemingly reincarnated in the vehicle. The narrator, Albertine, comments:

> So the insurance explained the car. More than that it explained why everyone treated the car with special care. Because it was new, I had thought. Still, I had noticed all along that nobody seemed proud of it except for King and Lynette. Nobody leaned against the shiny blue fenders, rested elbows on the hood, or set paper plates there while they ate. . . . It was as if the car was wired up to something. As if it

might give off a shock when touched. Later, when Gordie came, he brushed the glazed chrome and gently tapped the tires with his toes. He would not go riding in it, either, even though King urged his father to experience how smooth it ran. (22)

Perhaps they feel the Firebird too connected to the spirit of June, or too emblematic of her demise. Nonetheless, there is a clear sense that the car represents something far more than just a new auto.

In the chapter entitled "The Red Convertible," frequently reprinted on its own as a short story, we find another car closely associated with the spirit of a character who dies. Lyman Lamartine begins the story: "I was the first one to drive a convertible on my reservation. And of course it was red, a red Olds. I owned that car along with my brother Henry Junior . . . . Now Henry owns the whole car, and his younger brother Lyman (that's myself) . . . walks everywhere he goes" (143). From the first moment the boys see the car, they believe it to be much more than an inanimate object: "There it was, parked, large as life. Really as *if* it was alive. I thought of the word *repose*, because the car wasn't simply stopped, parked, or whatever. That car reposed, calm and gleaming . . ." (144). Henry and Lyman take the car on a series of road trips suitable for a Kerouac novel until Henry joins the Marines and is shipped to Vietnam. While he is gone, the car functions for Lyman as a remembrance of his brother. Lyman says: "I kept him informed all about the car"; "I always thought of it as his car while he was gone" (147); and "I thought the car might bring the old Henry back somehow" (149).

When Henry does return home, he suffers from post-traumatic stress syndrome. In an effort to shake him out of his condition, Lyman takes a hammer and trashes the car:

> By the time I was done with the car it looked worse than any typical Indian car that has been driven all its life on reservation roads, which they always say are like government promises—full of holes. It just about hurt me, I'll tell you that! I threw dirt in the carburetor and I ripped all the electric tape off the seats. I made it look just as beat up as I could. (149)

In many ways, this car, which reminds Lyman so much of his brother, now resembles on its exterior the condition of his brother inside. Lyman's ploy seems to work, though, as one day soon after, Henry comments: "But when I left, that car was running like a watch. Now I don't even know if I can get it to start again, let alone get it anywhere near its old condition." "After that I thought he'd freeze himself to death working on that car," says Lyman (149-50).

After Henry returns the car to mint condition, he and Lyman drive to the river. Henry tells his brother that he knows what he has done for him, and he offers the newly repaired vehicle to Lyman for good. He then jumps into the river and drowns himself. Lyman tries to save his brother, but to no avail. The story ends with a conclusion reminiscent of Bontemps's "A Summer Tragedy." Lyman recounts:

> I walk back to the car, turn on the high beams, and drive it up the bank. I put it in first gear and then I take my foot off the clutch. I get out, close the door, and watch it plow softly into the water. The headlights reach in as they go down, searching, still lighted even after the water swirls over the back end. I wait. The wires short out. It is all finally dark. And then there is only the water, the sound of it going and running and going and running and running. (154)

The red convertible, so closely connected to Henry, now drowns a silent death along with him, and the spirits of both return to the sacred waters. When Lyman returns home, he tells everyone that the car went into the river in an accident and that only he escaped. The truth is also covered over just like brother and car.

Such accidents, almost like sacrifices, occur other places in the novel. We are told of Henry Senior's death in 1950 when a train struck his car, parked on the railroad tracks. Whether an act of drunkenness or suicide remains unknown, but the deaths of both father and son are connected to their cars. In another incident, Gordie, drinking and grieving over June's death, believes his dead wife is pursuing him through the house. He grabs the keys to the Malibu and takes off. "He drove with slowness and utter drunken care, craning close to the windshield, one eye shut so that the road would not branch into two before him" (178). But in his daze, he hits a deer. He wishes to put the dead animal in the car's trunk, but he only has the key to the ignition. He thinks to himself: "He had never really understood before but now, because two keys were made to open his one car, he saw clearly that the setup of life was rigged and he was trapped" (179). So he puts the deer in the back seat. The deer turns out merely to be stunned, but when it wakes up, it too feels trapped like Gordie. To keep the animal from going wild, he takes a crow bar and smashes in its skull, and in the process, smashes the car's interior as well. In the spirit of sacrifice, "She saw how he'd woven his own crown of thorns," Gordie thinks of the deer (180). After the act, Gordie believes he has slaughtered June in the back seat, not a deer, an ironic substitution given June's own death after having made love on a vehicle's seat. Once again, the car is connected to a psychological substitution in which violence against the non-human or the inanimate displaces violence against a person. The car thus serves as a sacrificial offering of sorts.

As seen above, automobiles hold a visible position in *Love Medicine* from the start and throughout, and the novel ends with a classic post-war image of automobility—the use of the car to escape. The auto as escape agent has been hinted at in scenes such as Gordie's attempt to run from June's spirit or in the story of Beverly Lamartine (Henry Senior's brother), a traveling salesman, who dreams of escaping: "One night he saw himself traveling. He was driving his sober green car westward, past the boundaries of his salesman's territory, then over the state line and on across to the casual and lonely fields, the rich, dry violet hills of the reservation" (79). The most prominent escape image, though, comes in the final chapter, "Crossing the Water," as Lipsha, June's son, drives away in the Firebird he has won from King in a poker game. Lipsha describes this car, bought with June's life insurance money:

> The car was stove-in on the right bumper so that one headlight flared off to the side. I had seen there was nicks and dents in the beautiful finished skin. I ran my hand up the racy invert line of the hood as I drove the tangled highways in a general homeward direction. . . . I was free as a bird, as the blue wings burning on the hood. . . . The buzzing yellow arc lamps of the city were soon left behind, and the air began turning bold and sweet with the smells of melting earth. . . . I thought I would never quit driving I felt so good. (266)

The car provides an idyllic physical and emotional transport for Lipsha, the comfort from the vehicle personified so much that the car has "skin."

As Lipsha drives, he thinks of his father, Gerry, who has recently escaped from police custody. However, a knocking sound coming from the rear end of the car interrupts his solace. Lipsha believes the jack must not be properly secured in the trunk. "But then the knocking would start up, so I'd have to bare down and speed. . . . I didn't want to stop, but I thought I'd have to just pull over and tie the jack in tight. So I stopped, and soon as I did I knew there was something strange going on, because the knocking started up fast and furious" (267). When he opens the trunk, he discovers his father. Lipsha then drives Gerry to the Canadian border, and on the way they have a serious father-son talk, perhaps their first. The two connect, and Lipsha feels "There was a moment when the car and road stood still" (271). After dropping off his father, he returns home, and he finds that "A good road led on" (272). The novel ends with the Firebird providing the literal means of escape for Gerry, after it has served as his sanctuary. And for Lipsha, the newly acquired vehicles makes possible an almost mystical connection with his father and the world of the reservation.

Joy Williams's observation that "things had purposes for which they were not intended" seems a perfect analysis of automobiles in Erdrich's fiction. Marvin Magalaner also examines Erdrich's next novel, *The Beet Queen*, and finds the car in it to represent a means of escape, isolation, enclosure, and entrapment as well (104). In *Love Medicine* Erdrich writes that in Lulu's backyard, "The ground is cluttered with car parts . . . and other useful junk" (108); and cars do seem to be useful junk to her writing. For her Native Americans, the car functions sacramentally, sacrificially, spiritually, and as sanctuary. It perhaps takes the place of more traditional items that may have served these functions in the past—one type of Firebird has replaced another. Magalaner writes that "the natural has not been abandoned by the modern Indian; the natural has been perverted" (104), perverted to coincide with automobility's takeover of the culture. Sometimes (and quite often) the car fails her characters, but the lucky ones, like Gerry, use it as deliverance to a life of freedom.

Ann Beattie's Shifting Symbols

Along Erdrich and Williams, Ann Beattie has tapped the power of the automobile as a complex signifier more than any fiction writer since Flannery O'Connor. In fact, in a letter to James Plath, Beattie recognizes the kinship:

> I think of Flannery O'Connor's essay in which she explains "Good
> Country People" and says that although Hulga's wooden leg comes

to signify the wooden-ness of her soul, it isn't just a symbol: first and foremost, it's a wooden leg. That's the way I feel about cars: first and foremost, they've got to be cars. The reader has got to believe that he or she can get in them and drive them.

And Beattie does so herself, adding humorously: "I have a 1968 aqua Mustang V-8. Symbolically, my husband had it restored for my 40th birthday." Beattie says in conclusion that the cars of her characters, as in real life, "will not be a constant, but a shifting symbol, depending on circumstance" (Plath, "My Lover" 118, 117). The circumstances of Beattie's characters from four collections of her stories—*Distortions* (1976), *Secrets and Surprises* (1978), *Where You'll Find Me* (1986), and *What Was Mine* (1991)—can provide a fuller understanding of the textual vehicles found in the fiction of another contemporary woman writer.

At the onset of his excellent article outlining the role of the car in Beattie's short story, "A Vintage Thunderbird," James Plath briefly introduces several uses of automobiles in Beattie's other fiction: as plot turners (a car stealing opens "Friends," a drive through the Holland Tunnel precipitates "High School," a cross-country trip sets up "Colorado," a long drive controls "Summer People"); as places in which to get lost ("Friends," "Spiritus," "Where You'll Find Me"); as a refuge ("Summer People," "Coney Island"); and as "instruments of disaster" (*Love Always*, "The Lawn Party") (113-14). In addition to Plath's examples of instruments of disaster, "Gaps" features a woman found dead in the driver's seat (*Distortions* 220); "Honey" starts by mentioning Henry's car accident; "Television" begins with the story of a car falling in a hole at a car wash (*What* 31 & 91); and a car runs over the title character in "Starley" (*Secrets*). Plath concludes that Beattie uses automobiles as instruments of accident and disaster, narrative tools, places to get lost inside of, refuges, and, most prominently, extensions of personality and symbols of power, particularly sexual. To Plath's list, I would add: instruments of transition, symbols of nostalgia, cultural referents, possessions, emotional tombs, means of escape to freedom, and signifiers of consumption and interchangeability.

Plath primarily views the car in "A Vintage Thunderbird" as an extension of the characters' personalities, perhaps its predominant use in Beattie's stories. The Thunderbird in this story, as in Williams's "Rot," represents the only tangible connection in a male-female relationship, this one between Nick and Karen.[42] Plath argues that Beattie's male and female characters have so little in common that "objects become as important for them as 'having babies' traditionally was" (115). The car is their one common and visible bond. For instance, when Karen enters a new relationship, she offers the car to Nick as a substitute for herself: "The first time she went away with a man for the weekend . . . she stopped by . . . and gave him [Nick] the keys to her Thunderbird. She left so quickly . . . he could feel the warmth of the keys from her hand" (*Secrets* 4, Plath 116). The car signifies a number of historic moments in their relationship. As David Laird suggests, cars often serve as "tokens to spend again in nostalgic reflection and celebration" (247). Thus, when Nick reflects on the Thunderbird, he remembers these occasions nostalgically:

> He remembered the day she had bought the Thunderbird. It was the day after her birthday, five years ago. That night, laughing, they had driven the car through the Lincoln tunnel and down the back roads in Jersey, with a stream of orange crepe paper blowing from the radio antenna, until the wind ripped it off. . . . He had driven, then she had driven, and then he had driven again. . . . Years later he had looked for the road they had been on that night, but he could never find it. (7, 8)

To Nick, their drives together represent their former relationship; and as the relationship begins to suffer damage, so does the car: "He had begun to think he had driven the Thunderbird for the last time. She had almost refused to let him drive it again after the time, two weeks earlier, when he tapped a car in front of them on Sixth Avenue, making a dent above *their* left headlight" (6—emphasis added). Note the use of *their* even though "the car they drove was hers—a white Thunderbird convertible" (3), a clear indication as to how the car for Nick is seemingly indistinguishable from his relationship to Karen. At one point we are told, "Every time he drove the car, he admired it more. She owned many things that he admired . . ." (3). Separating himself from this sense of possession proves very difficult.

The car represents a personified extension of Nick's and Karen's personalities and thus their relationship itself. As such, when their relationship collapses, Nick yearns nostalgically and romantically for the Thunderbird: "If he had the keys, he could be heading for the Lincoln Tunnel. Years ago, they would be walking to the car hand in hand, in love. It would be her birthday. The car's odometer had five miles on it" (14). But the odometer now shows high mileage. In fact, Karen feels it is time for a trade-in, of both car and relationship. In the story's conclusion,

> He turned to her, wanting to say that they should go out and get the Thunderbird. . . . But the Thunderbird was sold. She had told him the news while they were sitting in the waiting room of the abortion clinic. The car had needed a valve job, and a man she met in Bermuda who knew all about cars had advised her to sell it. . . . If she had been more careful, they could have been in the car now . . . . She had no conception—she had somehow never understood—that Thunderbirds of that year, in good condition, would someday be worth a fortune . . . . (20)

"I'm going to get a new car," Karen concludes (20). Rather than work on their relationship, she would rather acquire a new model. She does not share Nick's desire to preserve what is old. The conspicuous consumption Americans apply to their vehicles is also applied by Karen to the men in her life. Her disposable consumerism is much like that of Penelope in "Colorado": "She had flunked out of Bard, and dropped out of Antioch and the University of Connecticut, and now she knew that all colleges were the same—there was no point in trying one after another. She had traded her Ford for a Toyota, and Toyotas were no better than Fords (*Secrets* 132). Relationships, colleges, cars—all are interchangeable parts.

"A Vintage Thunderbird" is not the only story in which a car serves as an extension of characters' personalities. For example, similar to Erdrich's "The Red Convertible," in "It's Just Another Day in Big Bear City, California" (*Distortions*), "Big Bear" cannot get rid of a '65 Peugeot because it is too closely associated with its former owner, his wife's brother, who was killed in Vietnam. In "Shifting," the condition of Larry's car corresponds with his personality, his emotional life, and thus his relationship to his wife, Natalie:

> There was never any clutter in the car. Even the ice scraper was kept in the glove compartment. . . . He vacuumed the car every weekend, after washing it at the car wash. . . . She would lean against the metal wall of the car and watch him clean it. . . . It was expected that she would not become pregnant. . . . It was also expected that she would

keep their apartment clean, and keep out of the way as much as possible . . . . (*Secrets* 56)

Later in the story we are told that Natalie "had trouble shifting" (63), an obvious comment on her personal life as well, especially since Larry has told her somewhat patronizingly, "It's not an automatic shift. You don't know how to drive it" (59). Characters often have self-awareness about such substitutions between their lives and cars. In "La Petite Danseuse de Quatorze Ans," Diana accuses Griffin of crashing a car his famous father gave to him as a way of getting back at his parents. "But surely crashing it into a tree at high speed was an extreme response," she surmises (*Secrets* 86). And in "Tuesday Night" the narrator Diane, who drives a 1966 Mustang convertible, concludes the story with this observation: "I remember Henry saying to me, as a way of leading up to talking about divorce, that going to work one morning he had driven over a hill and had been astonished when at the top he saw a huge yellow tree, and realized for the first time that it was autumn" (*Secrets* 292).

Diane also daydreams about a time she "parked on the little road and necked. Sometimes the boy would drive slowly along on the country roads looking for rabbits" (290). But these nostalgic remembrances do not end romantically: "[W]henever he saw one . . . he floored it, trying to run the rabbit down" (290). Difficulties with relationships are thus frequently connected to driving. In "Octascope" the female narrator first describes her relationship with Nick in terms of his car, "his old Mercedes, with a velvet-covered, foam-padded board for a front seat" (*Secrets* 100). She then states that when they first met, "Nick and I drove for hours, going in circles, because he was a strange man I had just met and I was afraid to go anywhere with him" (100). Like their drive to nowhere, so goes their relationship. Such metaphoric use of the car closely resembles the failed escapes of Joy Williams. When the nostalgia of the past or the failures of the present cannot comfort characters, often they take off, expecting to find fulfillment by driving. In "Home to Marie," every time couples fight, they take off in their cars. In fact, the narrator concludes, "My thought, when I hear a car streaking off, is always that a person is leaving home" (*What* 67). Beattie writes that these characters have "an unarticulated longing for change," and they believe "that travel is an expedient way . . . to make that change" (Plath, "My Lover" 114).

Escape through casual sex or illicit relationships is another means. Christina Murphy writes: "Characters search for the love they do not possess by involving themselves in temporary liaisons they know will not keep them secure (or even desired) for long. The romances and attractions seem to be only temporary stays against confusion, distractions from the deeper pain of those characters' lives . . ." (26-7). These liaisons are frequently associated with cars. "Parking Lot" provides a classic example. In this story the unnamed protagonist meets a man in the parking lot at work who offers to drive her to her car, which she always parks at a distance. Instead, they drive to a bar and then a motel to make love, a routine they continue to repeat. On the phone, she tries to tell her husband about the relationship by beginning, "There's a man . . ."; but thinking she is delayed because the car has broken down, his thoughts focus only on the car, as he continues her sentence, "Who's going to fix it." In the end, "She gets out of the car and stands in the parking lot. Standing there, she thinks of her lover, gone in one direction, and of Jim, in another" (*Distortions* 196).

Perhaps the best example comes from "Shifting," in which a teenager who teaches Natalie to drive a stick-shift Volvo despite her husband's desire to sell the car becomes her lover after she successfully completes her lessons. As a sign of the inappropriateness of her act, Natalie returns to her car to find "a white parking ticket clamped under the windshield wiper, flapping in the wind" (*Secrets* 68). Beattie associates sex with the car in a number of other stories: for example, in "Secrets and Surprises," where the noisy tailpipe of a car announces the arrival of a former lover, and in "When Can I See You Again?" (*Where You'll Find Me*) as Arnie plays with Martha's toes as if they are a stick-shift. On his dashboard, Arnie keeps a swan, a form Zeus used to seduce Leda (Plath, "My Lover" 117). In "Hale Hardy and the Amazing Animal Woman" Beattie even makes a reference to the archetypal American textual vehicle associated with sex when Hale receives a copy of *Lolita* from his former English teacher, a gift which makes him conclude (in classic escapist fashion): "it might be a good idea to pick up some woman and drive across the country with her . . ." (*Distortions* 100).

In addition to escaping *with* their cars, other characters escape *within* them. In "When Can I See You Again?" Martha and Annie often sit in Arnie's car.

A glass swan he had bought in Atlantic City was glued to the dashboard. It was a prism, and in the day light shot through it and threw colors all over the interior. Sitting in the front seat was like reclining in a Jackson Pollock. Sometimes, on their lunch hour, Martha and Annie left the office where he was a pasteup man and she was an editor and sat in his car in the garage, eating take-out food and looking at the spots of light. His parking place was by a window, and the light streamed in at noon. (*Where* 61)

The characters go nowhere—they just sit, watching the world with windshield perception. In "Deer Season" Elena sits in the car, frozen like a deer in headlights, staring "at the guide lights without counting, as the car moved slowly along the highway" (*Secrets* 188). In "Hale Hardy," Gloria sits in her car at the Grand Canyon, refusing to get out and look. And in "Summer People" (*Where You'll Find Me*) Byron keeps his sleeping bag with him in the car, preferring to stay there rather than socialize. These characters seemingly believe that the car can protect them from outside realities. [43]

Just as the mirrored roadster of Jay Gatsby reflects back an image of his age, so too do the automobiles of Beattie. Liz in "High School" "flips down the visor and looks at herself" (*Where* 77), and the narrator in "Octascope" describes Nick's car as follows: "Inside the car were little square mirrors. . . . I could cock my head and see my profile in the mirror glued on the passenger-side window, or bend forward . . . and see my eyes in the mirror on the dashboard" (*Secrets* 100). I think it no coincidence that Nick is the name of a character in this story. This Nick is reminiscent of an earlier literary one. Christina Murphy concurs. She believes that Beattie's characters

> are Nicks or Gatsbys, either lost in the decadence . . . or searching vainly after a Platonic idea . . . . Like Fitzgerald's characters, they see through the emptiness of their era, at the same time they are products of the era they find so vacuous and spiritually unfulfilling. If Fitzgerald was the social historian, the literary chronicler, of the generation that came to consciousness in the 1920s, Beattie is the same type of historian and chronicler of the generation whose sense of self . . . was defined by the values and beliefs of the 1960s. (122)

As with Fitzgerald, the auto becomes a convenient vehicle through which to house Beattie's chronicles. The narrator of "Parking Lot" observes, "People keep so much junk in their cars" (*Distortions* 190); and in her fiction, Beattie certainly puts a great deal of "junk" into her automobiles. In an interview with James Plath, she says, "I'm not very interested in looking at the surfaces of things except as starting points"; "I tend to write about things that are so-called 'real' only to the extent that they begin to transform" (361, 371). Like Fitzgerald, she transforms her fictional cars into agents signifying many facets of the lives and relationships of those who dwell in her society. As James Plath concludes, to Beattie "the car is even more than a symbol. It is an instrument of power/status/wealth/creativity/escape/control, and as such the automobile occupies a central position in Beattie's fiction, forever defining and redefining relationships between her males and females . . ." ("My Lover" 118).

Williams, Erdrich, and Beattie illustrate a recurrent phenomenon in post-war literature: the failure of the automobile as an ultimate means of empowerment and escape. Not all things associated with the car are negative. In *Love Medicine*, for instance, the car does occasionally offer momentary deliverance, but in at least one writer's work, Charles Dickinson's *The Widows' Adventures*, the car is also portrayed as responsible primarily for positive change.

On the Road—Revisited

If the 1950s saw the explosion of the younger generation, then the 1980s saw the outpouring of the older. Gray power grew in importance as an increasing number of Americans became retirees. Quite often the norm for depicting automobility among the older generation has been the image of the little old lady behind the wheel creeping along the freeway at forty miles per hour. Floridians in particular have perpetuated this image (as Updike sets forth in *Rabbit at Rest*). However, Charles Dickinson's *The Widows' Adventures* (1989) offers a different picture. In this novel, two seventy-year-old sisters, Helene and Ina, undertake a cross-country auto trip from their home in Chicago to visit family in California. Ina never learned to drive, so she leaves the driving to her sister; but there is one problem—Helene is blind! Dickinson deserves much credit for making this implausible plot work; however, more interesting than his skill as a writer is the theme the book conveys about how these women use the automobile as a source of empowerment, quite a different message from that of other contemporary works.

Ina and Helene, both widows, live in a decaying section of Chicago. Though Dickinson does not address this point, the automobile is partly responsible for this decay (as we saw in *Native Son*). Automobility has made commuting to more distant suburbs possible; thus the blight of the sisters' neighborhoods: thieves and vandals break into their houses while "dangerous boys" drive by cruising for trouble. The vehicular activities of these young miscreants are nothing like those the sisters remember. They reminisce about the times they went with their husbands on long rides away from the city. But those times are no more. Helene now sits in her Olds Omega letting the engine run while she relives old feelings. Ina remembers her husband Vincent's LTD, which once left oil stains on the garage floor. Vincent viewed the stains "like clouds. Abe Lincoln's profile. A lion. A woman bent over a dog. A tree. Two men reading one newspaper. The car leaked oil like an artist, but Vincent never did anything to fix the problem. He enjoyed the pictures" (31). To Vincent the car held imaginative powers, and the novel concerns how the two sisters come to adopt such a view for themselves.

One day Ina finds Helene sitting in the garaged Olds with the engine running. She first fears her sister is committing suicide, but Helene announces she wishes to drive the car to her daughter Amanda's home, a short distance away. She wants Ina to be her "eyes" and to navigate for her. At first Ina wants no part of this undertaking, but she begins to see the importance of the act to her sister, who feels worthless because of her age and the blindness which has overtaken her. A potentially destructive act, the drive instead rejuvenates Helene. She reanimates the dormant car: "Helene had given it life, set it in motion" (91); and the car sets her life in motion again, revitalizing her by making her once more feel young and worthy.

What Helene does not see on the drive to Amanda's are the young neighborhood boys who disrespectfully spit on the car's windshield and jump on the hood, tyrannizing Ina. Ina decides she has had enough of this "country *crawling* with crooks, killers, rapists, child-molesters, con artists, pickpockets, second-story men, sex-torturers, arsonists, cat burglars, car thieves, psychopaths, pederasts, armed robbers" and "white-collar crime." Ina's constant fear, particularly of all young people, drives her to concoct a seemingly irrational plan to head west, traveling cross-country with her sister, driving at night on the bluest of highways to avoid traffic. After a great deal of coaxing, Helene agrees, and the two head west. "Roads in the west were perfect for their needs, running wide and forgiving and lacking in surprises" (233), yet the journey taxes them more than either had realized it would: "In her planning she [Ina] had not foreseen the vastness of the land they would be crossing. It had been merely maps spread before her, a distance large in theory, even imposing" (234).

The two are often overwhelmed by their seeming insignificance on the vast landscape. The sisters want desperately to escape into the West's spaciousness, but they have internal conflicts a continental trek cannot drive away: Ina is an alcoholic; Helene's husband abused her. If Jack Kerouac had written for *The Golden Girls*, he might have envisioned a plot like this. But *The Widows' Adventures* is more than a septuagenarian *On the Road*. The deeper adventure of the novel is the discovery these women make about themselves and the often rocky relationship they have had with each other over the years. The strength they obtain from controlling the car and conquering the obstacle of driving west empowers them and enables them once more to deal with a world in which they have felt immaterial. It provides Ina with the compulsion to face her alcoholism, and it furnishes Helene with the determination to undertake learning Braille.

In the 1950s *On the Road* gave us a picture of the road west and its attraction to America's youth. Nearly forty years later (Sal Paradise could now be a retiree) Dickinson drew a comical, touching, but often disturbing look at what the road west had become for the nation's elderly. Is west their direction of sunset or the horizon for new adventures? One thing we learn from Helene and Ina—it's not just a sentimental journey. Helene declares in the end of the novel: "We are farther west than anyone we know from our shrinking circle of acquaintances." Like Sal, the sisters have accomplished the American dream of heading west, and the automobile makes this transformation possible. In contrast to the illusion of "go west, young man" as seen by Sal, the sisters do not encounter disillusionment in the process; and unlike Williams's or Beattie's characters, they ultimately realize that their redemption does not lie in the vehicle itself, but rather in the movement they make with the car. Though geographically this movement is toward the west and the open road, spiritually and psychically it is a movement toward self-worth, self-mobility. Perhaps because of their age and experience, Helene and Ina are able to separate the method of their auto-mobility from its consequences and to value the goal of their journey over their means of transport. Their ability to do so makes them somewhat exceptional in contemporary fiction.

"Where We Are in America": Harry Crews's *Car*

Finally, we come to Harry Crews's *Car*. Written in 1972, earlier than *Escapes*, Beattie's stories, *Love Medicine*, *The Widows' Adventures*, or the latter two Rabbit novels, this novel, nonetheless, summarizes the place of automobility in today's society perchance better than any other work. *Car* depicts the culminating forces of automobility and conspicuous consumption in contemporary America, the natural evolution of the very unnatural driving machine, which has infiltrated every possible aspect of culture and history. From countryside to city street, from business to home, from bedroom to bathroom—the car is everywhere. Though set in the South, *Car* moves beyond regionalism to depict all of America consumed in and by automobile culture, eaten by the car and eater of it.

Car focuses on the Mack family of Jacksonville, Florida. Father Easy owns Auto-Town, a euphemistically named junkyard. His son Mister runs the car crusher and dreams of one day owning a Cadillac: "You show me a man who can trade in for a new Cadillac in October of every year and I'll show you a man in the mainstream of America," he declares (2). Daughter Junell drives an eight-ton wrecker called Big Mama and makes out in police cruisers at the scene of wrecks. Finally, Mister's twin brother, Herman, automotive entrepreneur, attempts his latest enterprise, eating an entire car, a Ford Maverick, to be specific. Why eat a car? "The car is where we are in America. . . . I'm going to eat a car because it's there," Herman announces (27). And what symbolizes the automobile's contribution to mass consumption more than the actual act of eating a car itself? Herman's stunt radically enacts the aphorism taught in health class to every school child in the 1970s: "You are what you eat!" And America *is* the car. Yet as unrealistic as the premise of Crews's fiction may sound, the story is possibly based on a real event (Willis 9). In his column from *Saturday Review* dated 5 November 1966, Cleveland Amory tells the story of Leon Samson, 28, of Ballarat, Australia:

Mr. Samson, who bills himself as "the man with the steel stomach," recently made a $22,000 wager that he could, within five years, eat an automobile. A family-sized car, too. Already Mr. Samson has consumed one front fender, one tire, and one carburetor . . . . [H]e's also potentially a mighty weapon to have to help rid the countryside of all those unsightly automobile graveyards.

Whether based on a true story or not, the fictional America that Crews depicts is a real nation voraciously consuming automobiles. Herman's feat is simply an (il)logical extension of the obvious.

From the novel's onset, Crews depicts a nation overflowing with vehicles. *Car* opens with Mister atop a monstrous car crusher smashing (eating?) Cadillacs, his revered icons of prosperity. "On three sides his horizon was mountains of wrecked cars. Every possible kind of car in every possible kind of attitude" (4). Is this not a true American panorama? Crews continues his description from the vantage point of the second floor of the hotel where Herman is staging his auto ingestion: "'You don't see a tree down there' . . . . Herman liked it, liked the bumper-to-bumper cars there below, liked the noseburning, eyewatering emissions from hundreds of smoky tailpipes" (28).

Herman loves the car, and he ultimately fails in his task of devouring the vehicle because of this love and the kinship he feels with the Maverick. He is also a maverick, and his maverick act challenges people's sense of propriety: people threaten his life; Ford Motor Company sues to prevent the carnage. Jean Rosenbaum asserts that "men do not want to associate oral qualities with their cars." Oral qualities associated with cars are usually negative ones: for example, a car that "eats" gas. As another example, the failure of the Edsel could be attributed to its front grille resembling a huge open mouth (8). Ironically, though the car is not a natural object, people do not want anything unnatural done to it—eating a car disturbs their psychic perception of the car's place and function. But Herman does not view his act as unnatural. In fact, in his dreams he imagines himself at one with the car: when he gets hot, he can turn on his own air-conditioner; if the world outside bothers him, he can tint his windshield, and so forth.[44] He becomes like the Futurists' mechanomorph. Herman, however, abandons his stunt essentially because he realizes he no longer needs to eat a car to attain self-worth. Margo, the hotel whore, accepts him unconditionally, acting as a mother to him. (In fact, the only mention of a mother at all in the novel is Big Mama, the massive tow truck. The mother-of-all-tow-trucks perhaps serves as mother to the family.) In the end of the novel, Herman takes Margo deep within the cavernous piles of Auto-Town's cars to a wrecked Rolls-Royce, a special site where Herman has not returned since his childhood when he used to hide there with a young girl until she was killed, crushed trying to get to the hideaway. This incident has consumed Herman so much that he attempts to devour a car, the source of his guilt. McLuhan has suggested that the car is like a womb, and in the novel's conclusion Herman lies with Margo in the womblike refuge of the Rolls, his twin brother having taken his place eating the Maverick.

Mister hones in on the publicity and profit generated by Herman's stunt, using his brother as a source of income to achieve his lifelong goal of owning a Cadillac. While Herman consumes the car physically, Mister does so economically and spiritually. He worships the Cadillac as an icon of prosperity. In fact, both brothers epitomize America's worship of the car as god. Their view conforms well with that espoused by America's renowned cultural critic, Lewis Mumford, who has called automobility an American religion. Crews himself makes the same observation in an essay entitled "The Car": "We have found God in cars, or if not the true God, one so satisfying, so powerful and awe-inspiring that the distinction is too fine to matter" (96). Larry Vonalt considers Herman's eating of the car a form of theophagy, the practice of ingesting a god as a means of worship (132 ff.) (perhaps a subtle rite intoning "This Body by Fisher do in remembrance of me"). However, Mister's form of worship is more aligned with that of the average American. The religious signification of automobiles manifests itself repeatedly throughout the novel, as, for instance, when a massive pile-up on the expressway above Auto-Town is cleared as wreckers push the cars off the elevated roadway right into the junkyard, and Easy Mack sees this act like manna falling from heaven.

Easy, however, does not see his son's consumption of the automobile as theophagy, but rather as sacrilege. Easy venerates automobiles too much to eat one; each time Herman ingests a piece of the car, Easy chokes at the thought of it. Easy once said the car would save them all, "that America was a V-8 country, gas-driven, and water-cooled, and that it belonged to the men who belonged to cars" (79). Proud of his cars, Easy is offended by and does not comprehend Lady Bird Johnson's so-called beautification plan for America, which causes him to have to erect a fence around the junkyard. He exalts automobility, but Herman's act compels him to question his values.

The distress this event causes him is best represented by his obsession with a tiny squeak in the Cadillac which Mister buys (an act reminiscent of Sinclair Lewis's contention that "even the littlest squeak . . . drives me crazy"). Easy disassembles the entire car in his effort to find the rattle: "He had opened up that Cadillac car and looked behind the instrument panel, and he had felt his own mortality in a way that he had never felt it before. . . . God Himself would have been amazed and confounded before such a thing" (103). When Mister takes over for his twin and nearly dies ingesting a piece of the car and passing it, Easy's world becomes so dissociated that he takes his own life—the final sound of the novel comes as he pulverizes himself in the car crusher.

For the Mack family, the car is life (and death). In their own separate ways they each consume the automobile. Together they represent a nation bound up in automobility. "'Everything that's happened in this goddam country in the last fifty years,' said Herman, 'has happened in, on, around, with, or near a car'" (12). From the powerful influence of Ford to the assassination of John F. Kennedy in a motorcade, a great deal of twentieth-century American history can be seen relative to automotive history. Herman's first automotive exhibition highlights this fact. He creates CAR DISPLAY: YOUR HISTORY ON PARADE, an assemblage of various makes and models of cars arranged chronologically so that visitors might sit in these vehicles and relive significant events in their lives. "SEE THE CAR IT HAPPENED IN—THE EVENT THAT CHANGED YOUR LIFE," proclaims CAR DISPLAY's huge billboard located, where else, beside the expressway (12). People associate the major events of their lives with cars, Herman believes.[45] Even our very existence is perhaps affiliated with one: "How many of the American people do you think fucked for their children in the back seat of a car?" Herman asks (11).

Sex for his sister Junell is certainly dependent on the automobile. She meets her beau Joe, a state trooper, only at wrecks, where the two of them neck in his cruiser, Junell becoming excited over Joe's orgasmic discussion of the vehicle: "Junell loved to hear about that car, that Chrysler Cruiser. . . . His voice would get high and urgent as he put together the story of a chase: laying a hundred-yard streak of rubber, a curve taken in" (42). When the two are finally alone and away from the cruiser (Joe is assigned to guard Herman's car-eating exhibit), they are unable to act sexually, that is until Junell gets the idea to make love in the Maverick. Like Junell, Margo also finds cars arousing. She tells Herman the story of a high-school football player who date-rapes her on the hood of his Corvette, but she declares, "He didn't get me, the Vette did." "I wish I could eat it, too, swallow it all," she swears (56). Like Herman, she bears her guilt obsessively, she says, by trying to "fuck everybody." Her consumption of men equates with Herman's consumption of the car. Indeed, masculinity and automobility are often interchangeable identities in American culture. Dr. Joyce Brothers maintains that cars are a phallic extension, "a powerful symbol of masculinity" (D. Lewis, "Sex" 127). Certainly Margo's declaration to "swallow it all" can be read in this light.

Beyond religious and sexual connections, the car also embodies American culture's penchant for violence. Writing on automobile racing, Tom Wolfe suggests that people come to stock-car races to see wrecks; hence the birth of the demolition derby, "a piece of national symbolism" (30). Crews also conveys this morbid fascination Americans have with automobile accidents in his description of a six-year-old girl mangled in automobile wreckage, a stick-shift driven through her pelvis. The remainder of her family lies unrecognizable as humans in the debris. Junell and others pursue such wrecks at which the onlookers are somehow enlivened by the horrific violence and massive destruction of which the car is capable while simultaneously being seemingly unaffected by the human loss.[46] This wreck, the car crusher, and the junkyard itself all bear witness to the car's latent destructive powers, not to mention the destruction being done to the environment by the "noseburning, eyewatering emissions" or the decimation of small towns because of the growth of superhighways.

Jennifer Randisi asserts that three of Crews's novels begin with scenes of towns made obsolete by the modern superhighway (213). These superhighways lead to a sort of automotive Darwinism, a survival of the auto-fittest. *Car* depicts this evolution of American automobility, which Crews parallels to the evolution of life itself: "Then the first evidence of a fin began to appear. . . . It swam through all the garages from Canada to Mexico. It went upstream . . . to the headwaters of the American heart. And there it remained" (3). Though the seeds of the automobile culture were already well sown, the coming of Cadillac's tail fin in the 1950s did spawn monumental automania. Then came the Interstate, which plowed through wilderness and civilization alike, wrapping itself around the edges of Auto-Town itself. Auto-Town could just as well be Every-Town, masses of rotting automobiles encircled by superhighways (as Joy Williams would probably concur). *Car* presents America as prophesied by Faulkner: the wilderness of forests replaced by the wilderness of roads.

Harry Crews is the descendant of four score years of American automobile culture, and his novel pays homage to the literature of automobility preceding him. "I refuse to have my life measured out in cars," cries Herman (49), echoing Eliot's Prufrock, whose life is measured out in coffee spoons. Crews parodies Prufrock's parlor, replacing it with Herman's garage, yet Eliot himself ushered in the automobile age in *The Waste Land* with "the sound of horns and motors" bringing Sweeney to Mrs. Porter, his verse a parody of yet another era in which "a noise of horns and hunting" brought Actaeon to Diana (see Eliot's note to lines 197-98). Finally, in addition to its biblical reference, the last sentence of *Car*, "Motes of dust rose in front of them and hung in the dead air," could also pay homage to another writer whose works teem with automobility, Flannery O'Connor. Her Motes, Hazel Motes of *Wise Blood*, lives for his Essex, blinding himself when his car is destroyed, just as Easy crushes himself when his automobile belief system fails him.

"Power was everywhere" in the Cadillac Mister buys (87), and the power of the automobile as signifier is evident everywhere in *Car*. Crews's novel makes a fitting finale to this study because it embodies numerous elements of the historical development of automobility in American literature. In and of itself, it serves as a sort of CAR DISPLAY: HISTORY ON PARADE. Paralleling early perceptions of the automobile in American culture, the Mack family members all begin their lives as automobile romanticists, but gradually they realize the power of the car is not blindly benign. As with Sinclair Lewis in his later works or Fitzgerald in *The Great Gatsby*, Crews uses the automobile to satirize the conspicuous consumption of Americans, but rather than showing off the glittering reflections of his Rolls-Royce, Crews hides his Rolls in the center of a pile of wrecked vehicles. In addition to mocking the Rolls, Crews also parodies Ford's Model T, the affordable car, substituting instead Ford's Maverick, the edible car. Similar to *The Grapes of Wrath*, *Car* is a novel about the undervalued American family and their car, and Crews, like Steinbeck, demonstrates how ultimately the car does not serve to save the family but rather to sunder it. As in Faulkner's work, within the Mack family, embodiments of two Souths exist: Easy Mack, a good ol' boy, representing the South of tradition, and Mister, encompassing the new greed of consumerism, a greed which nearly kills him. The vehicles in

Car can also be seen as extensions of the characters' personalities, as cars are in Beattie's works. Finally, in *Car*, as in *Escapes*, the automobile is seen as a central image of a decaying society. Though more an object of laughter in Crews's work, the car is nonetheless deadly. "For Harry Crews the automobile is a complex metaphor of the culture that produced it" (Randisi 213). Like Lewis, Fitzgerald, Steinbeck, Faulkner, O'Connor, Updike, Beattie, and Williams, Harry Crews knows the automobile is the driving machine of American culture.

The automobile remains a progressive force in the literature of contemporary writers such as Updike, Doctorow, Williams, Beattie, Erdrich, Dickinson, and Crews. One could add to this list Paul Auster, Joan Didion, Steve Heller, Paul Hemphill, Greg Matthews, Larry McMurtry, Toni Morrison, Sam Shepard, Hunter S. Thompson, Tom Wolfe, and assuredly many others. "Can't live with it; can't live without it!" and "No Exit" these contemporary writers seem to say about the car. In a positive light, the automobile in contemporary literature shows the effects of a one-hundred-year-old marriage which just will not break; but in a negative sense, it is a cancer too greatly metastasized for removal. Feeding off the culture, the culture feeding off of it, the car and the nation consume each other. Though the car has promised escape and deliverance, those promises remain unfulfilled. The union holds; the promises fail. This is where we are in America.

A Complex and Inescapable Symbol

Everything in life is somewhere else, and you get there in a car.

—E. B. White

Even before the automobile's invention, American literature espoused the principles of automobility: the quest for movement and the desire for individual mobility. Likewise, before the automobile, tensions between the forces lauding technological progress and those warning of depersonalization and dehumanization were also at play. This tension highlights the difficulty of blending the manufactured into the natural order, and in the literature of automobility we see a continued playing out of this dynamic. The automobile is a machine in the garden of America, and as such, the simultaneous desires to cultivate and to prune it exist.

Early twentieth-century works primarily upheld the voice of progressivism, embracing the car and its novel possibilities. This view of the romantic/pastoral vehicle, seen in works such as Sinclair Lewis's early writings, integrates the car into the romantic mythologies of Arthurian legend or the myth of the American West; but the romance of auto-tourism gave way to a greater realization of the car's remaking of American culture, not always for the better. The growth of mass consumption and inveterate consumerism troubled many writers who saw the automobile as displacing fundamentally higher virtues and values. Stuart Chase and F. J. Schlink's *Men and Machines* (1929) adopts such a satirical view of automobility:

> The motor car . . . is the most powerful prime mover we possess; it is the outstanding exhibit in mass production; it is the rock upon which the whole structure of American "prosperity" is founded; it is the

171

chief creator of the new labor burden; the mightiest reason for the
congestion of cities and the desolation of the countrysides; and the
leading national plaything. (257)

Yet Chase and Schlink's contemporary, Simeon Strunsky, argued that

> the more things American change under the impact of the
> automobile, the more they remain American. This new machine
> which has laid hold on the American home, factory, school, shop and
> forum, and which threatens the very existence of the old America, as
> so many good people have found reason to fear, proves on closer
> inspection to be only an affirmation of the old America. The
> automobile embodies a vigorous restatement of basic national
> principles. The automobile cannot undermine the old American way
> of life because it is a product of that way of life and of the spirit that
> shaped it. . . . The throb of its engine is the beat of the historic
> American tempo. (172-73)

In spite of Strunsky's assurances, suspicions of the car continued to
grow: Lewis and Tarkington satirized the standardization of automobile
culture; Fitzgerald unmasked the decadence of the limousine-set;
Sinclair and Dos Passos exposed the realities of mass production.

As the car became integrated into more and more aspects of
culture, its complexity as a cultural icon and signifier increased.
Automobility's fundamental importance to the American economy of
the Great Depression is dramatically demonstrated in *The Grapes of
Wrath*. Steinbeck presents us with the portrait of an American family
whose very existence is maintained by their vehicle yet whose plight is
directly respondent to the economic byproducts of mass production and
assembly-line technology, the essence of automotive industrialism.
With the Joads, tourism evolved into vagabondage. The Joads readily
demonstrate how the internal-combustion engine radically altered farm
life, and Faulkner and Caldwell carry on to depict a rural South
rewritten under the influence of a mobility made possible by the car.
Yet in their portraits, this automotive deliverance also dispenses a
throng of detriments which undermine the very essence of Southern
character.

Faulkner saw the car as "the mechanised, the mobilised, the
inescapable destiny of America" (*Reivers* 71), and the works of post-
World War II writers focus on the inescapability of automobility and

the unfulfilled promises of its union with America. Flannery O'Connor saw the tremendous paradoxical possibility of the car as a signifier. While clearly a profane representation of mordant secularity in her stories, it simultaneously hierophanically transcends the culture of consumption. However, in most post-war literature the car ultimately fails as a means of salvific experience. Kerouac, Nabokov, and other Fifties' writers reflected the dominance of the automobile in their society. Kerouac worshipped the vehicle as a symbol of psychic transport yet came to realize such an exalted view as disillusioned. Arna Bontemps, Richard Wright, Ralph Ellison, and E. L. Doctorow demonstrated that for African Americans the car was no savior either. Though often looked to as a means of escape, it ultimately failed to deliver; and in fact, left those dependent on it disenfranchised, or even dead.

With Rabbit Angstrom, John Updike plumbs the 1950s' penchant for automobility as it has evolved through three subsequent decades of American culture. Updike, along with numerous current writers, portrays the automanic-depression of contemporary American culture. Ann Beattie's characters seem inseparable from their vehicles. Joy Williams finds the automobile at the rotting core of a society bent on impossible escape; meanwhile, Harry Crews sees the auto as the ultimate embodiment of our consumptive culture. While Louise Erdrich portrays some characters having positive experiences with their vehicles, Charles Dickinson seems to stand alone in his faith in the car as a catalyst of transformation, but even to him the car is a catalyst only, not an active ingredient of transcendence in and of itself.

In *Driving Passion* Marsh and Collett assert that

> the fundamental symbolism of the car is both complex and inescapable. It conjures up images of speed, excitement, and vitality. At the same time it also communicates a sense of cosy seclusion—a womb-like refuge. Its potential deadliness gives it an air of aggression while its power and shape endow it with a sense of sexual potency. It is precisely because the car can communicate with such a variety of messages that it has captured our imagination. (26)

The automobile *is* a complex and inescapable symbol, a crucial icon of American culture; thus, not surprisingly, it is at the heart of American literature as well. Because of its paradoxical complexity, the automobile has captured the imagination of many of America's best writers. These novelists, playwrights, poets, and short-story writers, well aware of the cultural importance of the automobile, have used the car as a vehicle in their literary creations, manipulating the signifier in a myriad of significations throughout the broad range of twentieth-century literature and molding America's literary landscape into a literary motorscape.

The car is America's primary vehicle of transport, perhaps both physically and imaginatively; yet despite beliefs to the contrary, Marsh and Collett argue, the idea that the car is primarily a means of transport is a very false notion (210). Instead, the car culture, which Tom Wolfe calls "an esoteric world of arts and sciences" (35), has become a religion; "the opium of the American people" (Agee 54); an arbiter of windshield perception; an embodiment of racism; a forger of mechanomorphism; a promoter of interchangeability and standardization; an emblem of desire; a place for sex (and an aphrodisiac itself); both an extension of the phallus and a substitute for the womb. One recent pamphlet goes so far as to say, "The car and car culture are integral to nearly every destructive pathology in modern capitalism" ("Kill").

Quintessentially, the car is "an article of dress without which we feel uncertain, unclad, and incomplete" (McLuhan, *Understanding* 217). As Williams's mechanic Boris extols: the automobile leads us to the existential questions of life itself. Booth Tarkington prophesied that "men's minds are going to be changed in subtle ways because of automobiles" (275), and without a doubt, the mind of every American has been. For a culture bent on speed and escape, the car proves to be the ideal mythic signifier, a complex and inescapable symbol of our paradoxical age.

Notes

1. Gillespie and Michael Rockland write in their analysis of the Jersey Turnpike that Marx's contrast of pastoral and industrial views is nowhere more explicit (and ironic) than in the text written on New Jersey license plates—"The Garden State" (6-7).

2. I became intensely aware of this fascination while watching televised reports of the missiles used in the Persian Gulf War. The phenomenal technology involved in the pinpoint guidance of these massive weapons of destruction was brilliantly captured through the televised signals from these weapons' video cameras. Caught up in the awe of the technology, we overlooked the genuine reality of the unbelievable destruction wrought by their impact.

3. Adams's correlation of religion and the machine is echoed in the title of Chapter 1 of Henry Ford's *My Philosophy of Industry*: "Machinery, the New Messiah."

4. For my discussion of automobile history I am deeply indebted to James J. Flink's *The Automobile Age*.

5. Lewis also reflects on this trip in "Travel Is Broadening" from *The Man Who Knew Coolidge*.

6. See Julian Smith's "A Runaway Match" for a detailed discussion of these early automobile romance movies. Also, Kenneth Hey's "Cars and Films in American Culture" details further connections between the automotive and motion-picture industries.

7. Aurilla's comments substantiate those of her real-life contemporary, Lord Montague, who extolled the attraction of an automobilist to a woman: "Just as the fair sex adores the actor, the singer, or the author, so she adores a man of action who does things, controls things. The sense of being absolutely dependent upon the man

at the wheel has a peculiar fascination and results in a sense of trust broadening sometimes into senses of other things" (Anderson 203).

8. Images of speed were not exclusive to the works of the Italian Futurists. In 1910 Barney Olds commissioned William Foster to do an automobile painting. Foster's work, which depicts a speeding car racing a train, the two melding into one, became a famous American image of the unification of the automobile and speed.

9. For a detailed discussion of the effects of automobiles on health care, see Berger 175-92, or consider E. B. White's humorous assessment, which appeared in *Harper's Magazine*:

> Today this town doesn't even have a doctor. It doesn't have to have a doctor. If you chop your toe off with an axe you get into somebody's car and he drives you ten miles to the next town where there is a doctor. For movies you drive twenty-five miles. For a railroad junction, fifty. For a mixed drink, twenty-five. For a veterinary, twenty-five. For a football game, fifty, or one hundred or two hundred, depending on where your allegiance lies. . . . Everything in life is somewhere else, and you get there in a car. (Cohn 197)

10. Sinclair Lewis, too, highly esteemed his own car. An article in the *Carmel (CA) Pine Cone-Cymbal* discusses how on a visit of Lewis's to Carmel he cherished his Ford so much he "kept it spotless and at night and in bad weather kept it enclosed in a white nightie" (G. Lewis 107).

11. In the same year as *Dodsworth*'s publication, *Middletown*, a chronicle of Muncie, Indiana in the 1920s, also appeared. *Dodsworth*'s newfound appraisal of speed is echoed in *Middletown* in the perceptions of an adolescent Sunday-schooler who replies to his teacher's question, "Can you think of any temptation we have today that Jesus didn't have?" by rejoining—"Speed!" (Lynd 258).

12. Similar uses of the automobile appear in other works of the period, most notably John O'Hara's *Appointment in Samarra*, in which Julian English, a Cadillac dealer, commits suicide in his car in his garage after his business and marriage fall apart. O'Hara blatantly confesses his allegiance to Fitzgerald in this passage: Joe Montgomery "had known Scott Fitzgerald at Princeton, and that made him in Caroline's eyes an ambassador from an interesting country, full of interesting people whom she wanted to meet and see in action. She did not know, of course, that she was a member in good standing of the

community which she thought Joe Montgomery represented, which Fitzgerald wrote about" (133). Joe owns a red Jordan roadster, perhaps a reflection of Fitzgerald's Jordan Baker. The Englishes' world revolves around automobiles: consider his wife Caroline's name, which even begins with c-a-r. And in O'Hara's society, as in Fitzgerald's, people are also treated as commodities, sometimes even with less respect: Julian "treated his car more considerately" than Caroline, for example (262).

Fitzgerald went on to use the car as a central metaphor in other works, most notably the short story, "The Family Bus," published in 1933. In this story young Dick Henderson's life experiences are shaped by a 1914 roadster his family purchased when he was four: a brother dies in the car; he courts his lover in it; a cruel fraternity prank is played on him by painting the car; and in the end an experimental carburetor installed on it at the factory in 1914 revolutionizes the cars built by the auto company for whom Dick becomes an engineer twenty years later. In the story's conclusion, he rides off into the sunset in the car, his lover at his side (Bruccoli).

13. "In 1922 Ford purchased the Wayside Inn at Sudbury, Massachusetts, to preserve it from destruction. Celebrated by the poet Henry Wadsworth Longfellow, the old inn appealed to Ford as a symbol of pioneer days. . . . But a new highway ran too near. . . . So, turning against the age he helped to create, Ford had the state highway rerouted around the shrine at a cost of $250,000" (Nash 160).

14. Ford's exaltation to lordship is clearly set forth in this letter written to him from an Alabama farmer (May 1923):

> We of the South affectionately acclaim you, instead of Lincoln, as the Great Liberator. Lincoln has freed thousands, you have freed your ten thousands. The rutted roads on mountain sides and water sogged wheel tracks on low lands have been smoothed, that the wheels of Fords may pass. The sagged barbed wire gates of barren cotton patches and blighted corn fields have been thrown open that brainblinded and soulblinded recluses might ride joyously into the world with their families in Fords. An army of white clad serfs on small Southern farms in Ford cars and trucks are pushing onward and upward into a conscious heirship. (Wik 125)

15. In addition, Doctorow also writes about the event which precipitates World War I, the assassination of Archduke Ferdinand,

which takes place in an automobile. Doctorow's version of the event accentuates the flukish nature of the assassination. The Archduke and his wife escape injury when a bomb aimed at them explodes, but after their escape their chauffeur makes a wrong turn. "As it happened the car stopped beside a young Serbian patriot who was one of the same group who had tried to kill the Archduke by bomb but who had despaired of another opportunity. The patriot jumped on the running board of the touring car, aimed his pistol at the Duke and pulled the trigger" (362).

16. The negative impact of new highways appears in other works of the period, for example, Louise Armstrong's play *Good Roads* (1929). In this drama, Mr. and Mrs. Gordon live in the country by the side of a new macadam road to the city. On the night a bank has been robbed, a stranger named Harry Fall pretending to be on the lookout for the crooks appears at the house. Claiming he will get the sheriff, Fall actually steals the car. The sheriff asserts that good roads are bringing bad city dwellers into the country. Mr. Gordon agrees, exclaiming that he has had no peace of mind since the road was built. In spite of the incident, however, Mrs. Gordon says she still enjoys watching the numerous different cars drive by.

A specifically Southern negative reaction to the good-roads movement appears in *I'll Take My Stand* (1930) in Andrew Nelson Lytle's judgment that "good-road programs drive like a flying wedge and split the heart" of the rural South (234 ff.).

17. In *Blue Highways* William Least Heat Moon echoes this man/machine connection. He writes: "[O]n the road, I again became part of the machine: generator, accelerator, humanator. I knew nothing. A stupefied nub on the great prairie" (281).

18. For more on the concept of "motorcentrism" see Folke Kihlsted's "The Automobile and the Transformation of the American House."

19. Because of the extensive appearance of automobiles in Faulkner's writings, several scholars, most notably Carey, Dettelbach, Milum, and Waldron (see references), have made note of them. While the observations of these scholars bear repeating, none have attempted to make a comprehensive synthesis of the car's role in Faulkner's works, choosing instead to focus on individual texts or concepts. I acknowledge my debt to their insights and hope to extend their arguments further.

20. See also Glenn Carey's "William Faulkner on the Automobile as Socio-Sexual Symbol."

21. In developing Boon's infatuation with the car, perhaps Faulkner recalled ads such as that for the 1949 Buick Roadmaster, which declares that the Buick is "Ready, Willing—and Waiting" for you. McLuhan insists that this ad, among others, presents the automobile as "a date with a dream" (*Mechanical* 83-84). Perhaps also Faulkner (as well as Buick's ad campaigners) could be reflecting on Karl Shapiro's poem "Buick" (1942) in which the poet exalts his car as a

> warm-hearted beauty, you ride, you ride,
> You tack on the long curves with parabola speed and a kiss of goodbye,
> Like a thoroughbred sloop, my new high-spirited spirit, my kiss.
> . . . you leap in the air with your hips of a girl. (14)

22. In a review of *Test Pilot* (1935) Faulkner provides additional insight into his conceptions of machines and speed by addressing our obsession with "the folklore of speed" which pushes human beings

> a good deal nearer to the . . . limit at which blood vessels will burst and entrails rupture." He writes: "Perhaps they [future Americans] will contrive to create a kind of species or race . . . who flies more than four hundred miles an hour . . . children culled by rules or even by machines from each generation and cloistered and in a sense emasculated and trained to conduct the vehicles in which the rest of us will hurtle from place to place.

He continues, suggesting instead that perhaps these vehicles will be

> peopled not by anything human or even mortal but by the clever willful machines themselves carrying nothing that was born and will have to die or which can ever suffer pain, moving without comprehensible purpose toward no discernible destination, producing a literature innocent of either love or hate and of course of pity and terror, and which would be the story of the final disappearance of life from the earth. I would watch them, the little puny mortals, vanishing against a vast and timeless void filled with the sound of incredible engines, within which furious meteors

moving in no medium hurtled nowhere, neither pausing nor flagging, forever destroying themselves and one another. ("Folklore" 371-2)

23. In *A Wreck on the Road to Damascus* Brian Ragen does an outstanding job discussing the role of the automobile in *Wise Blood*, and I do not wish to duplicate his argument here; therefore, I will confine my analysis to O'Connor's short stories.

24. This is not the only story in which traits of a character are portrayed using automotive terminology, for example, the description of Mrs. Freeman in "Good Country People":

> Besides the neutral expression that she wore when she was alone, Mrs. Freeman had two others, forward and reverse, that she used for all her human dealings. Her forward expression was steady and driving like the advance of a heavy truck. Her eyes never swerved to left or right but turned as the story turned as if they followed a yellow line down the center of it. She seldom used the other expression because it was not often necessary for her to retract a statement, but when she did, her face came to a complete stop. . . . (271)

25. In a similar fashion O'Connor uses the bus in "Everything that Rises Must Converge" as a microcosm of the social condition of the South. (The trolley car of "The River" and the train in "The Artificial Nigger" can be seen in the same vein.)

26. In "Good Country People" Glynese also judges people based on their automobiles. O'Connor humorously chides such suppositions:

> She [Mrs. Freeman] said he owned a '55 Mercury but that Glynese said she would rather marry a man with only a '36 Plymouth who would be married by a preacher. The girl asked what if he had a '32 Plymouth and Mrs. Freeman said what Glynese had said was a '36 Plymouth. Mrs. Hopewell said there were not many girls with Glynese's common sense. (282)

27. Interestingly, in 1958, five years after the publication of this story, John Keats turned to the imagery of the biblical prophet Nahum for the title of his anti-automobile book, *The Insolent Chariots*:

The chariots shall rage in the streets,
They shall justle one against another in the broad ways:
They shall seem like torches,
They shall run like the lightnings. . . .

28. Just as the Misfit enters the scene in his hearse-like auto, characters in other stories appear in vehicles, frequently bringing evil tidings with them: in "The Lame Shall Enter First" police cars repeatedly deliver the malevolent Rufus Jones to Sheppard's door; in "A Circle in the Fire" a truck brings the three delinquent boys to Mrs. Cope's farm; in "The Comforts of Home" "the little slut" emerges from Thomas's mother's car as the story opens; and in "The River" Mr. Paradise, "a huge old man who sat like a humped stone on the bumper of a long ancient gray automobile," interrupts Bevel's baptismal gathering (166).

29. Such connections are also intimated in "A Circle in the Fire" when the three boys discuss how they would make a parking lot out of the farm.

30. Similarly, O'Connor several times depicts Mr. Paradise in "The River" as being connected to his car's bumper. In addition, he sits inside a store, drinking an orange drink, while outside is an orange gas pump, seemingly indicating both man and car drink from the same source.

31. Chris Challis claims that in naming his character Dean Moriarty, "Kerouac fused the method actor whose love of fast driving was to kill him with the alter ego of fiction's most famous detective" (115).

32. In his discussion of the automobile's place in the history of film, Arthur Penn also maintains that "in American Western mythology, the automobile replaced the horse in terms of the renegade figure" (360).

33. A poem such as Allen Ginsberg's "Hiway Poesy LA-Albuquerque-Texas-Wichita" additionally substantiates the Beats' assimilation of corporate advertisement into their depiction of America: "'This is Ford Country what are *you* driving,' Be a Ford dealer?" the poet speaks.

34. Challis writes that "Kerouac enjoyed the drive a lot more than the driving" (65), and Charters's biography confirms that Kerouac was so enamored by Cassady's skill as a driver parking cars in New York

City that he had Neal get him a job as a fellow parking lot attendant (71).

35. In *U.S. 40 Today* Thomas and Geraldine Vale address the changes the growth of the Interstate system brought to driving. They assert that Interstates leave drivers "isolated from the landscapes through which they pass," cut off by fences, gullies, medians, and a lack of roadside businesses (7).

36. Bigger's cremation of Mary Dalton in the furnace may be an ironic twist on his position as her chauffeur. *Chauffeur*, as noted in a previous chapter, derives from a French verb meaning "to stoke up or fire up a boiler or engine."

37. "Saturday Night" contains a similar scene of contrast. The narrator of Bontemps's story drives his car through a procession of ramshackle wagons headed to town for the evening's festivities. "Here the going is the thing," writes Bontemps, "Whatever one does, the romance of the journey is unpremeditated" (159).

38. Even Lizzie's name suggests an automobile: the Tin Lizzie, Ford's Model T.

39. In "The Skater" a father trying to get over the death of his daughter also dreams of escaping in his car. In his dream the car will not stay on course because it is skidding across treacherous patches of ice.

40. This connection of automobiles and Houdini is reminiscent of the opening of Doctorow's *Ragtime*, where Houdini crashes his car in front of the home of Mother and Father but escapes uninjured.

41. Accidents occur in other stories. In "White" a woman driving a Triumph convertible rear-ends Bliss and Joan in their own driveway. They invite the woman to a party, where they learn the Triumph belongs to her husband, who has had a stroke and is divorcing her. And in "The Blue Men" Bomber, May, and Edith flip their car twice, crushing the roof and fenders. They land upright and keep on driving. A policeman who observes the accident stops them, and May says to him: "I thought it was just a dream, so I kept on going" (150).

Also, accidents abound in *Breaking and Entering*: characters discuss the death of James Dean in his "sinister" Porsche (5), a Mercedes goes into a lake (16), BMWs are rear-ended (38), birds are flattened by cars (26), sedans are blown up (102), and children are paralyzed in wrecks (183). Characters even define their lives by accidents: "I've lived in this town my whole life. Smashed up my first car in this town," says Duane (39).

42. The Thunderbird has been an object of interest to a number of writers. Perhaps most humorously is David Ives's rewriting of Wallace Stevens's "Thirteen Ways of Looking at a Blackbird" as "Thirteen Ways of Looking at a Thunderbird." Consider, for instance, stanza three: "The sticker price / Is nothing. / The Thunderbird / Is everything." In his introduction to the poem, Ives writes that the poem has been "reimagined to reflect his [Stevens's] position as an American consumer and longtime devotee of Classic Car Digest" (72).

43. The protagonist in Paul Auster's *The Music of Chance* shares this feeling of protection provided by the car. Auster writes: "The car became a sanctum of invulnerability, a refuge in which nothing could hurt him anymore. As long as he was driving, he carried no burdens, was unencumbered by even the slightest particle of his former life" (12).

44. In an essay entitled "The Car" Crews writes of his own sensual fusing with his first automobile: "In the mystery of that love affair, the car and I merged" (99).

45. Poe, a character in Joy Williams's *Breaking and Entering*, would concur with Herman's view:

> I delivered a baby once. It was in an automobile graveyard in Alabama where I was looking for a bumper for my Studebaker. A cheerful and filthy child escorted me through the yard, reciting the history of his favorite wrecks. There was the VW van with the canvas sunroof through which a motorcycle had hurtled, decapitating a passenger when the van failed to negotiate a curve. There was the Buick that had held six in a thunderstorm, all killed when a lightpole fell on them. There was the Olds 88 where the woman lingered for hours while they tried to carve the twisted metal way from her legs. (183)

All the events important to this character are associated with cars.

46. Karl Shapiro draws an early literary portrait of the violence of an automobile accident in "Auto Wreck" (1942). He writes that the auto wreck "spatters all we know of denouement / Across the expedient and wicked stones" (6).

Bibliography

Adams, Henry. *The Education of Henry Adams*. 1918. Boston: Houghton, 1961.

Agee, James. "The Great American Roadside." *Fortune* Sept. 1934: 53+.

Amory, Cleveland. "First of the Month." *Saturday Review* 5 Nov. 1966: 6+.

Anderson, Rudolph E. *The Story of the American Automobile: Highlights and Sidelights*. Washington: Public Affairs, 1950.

Armstrong, Louise van Voorhis. *Good Roads*. New York: Samuel French, 1929.

Asch, Nathan. *The Road*. New York: Norton, 1937.

Auster, Paul. *The Music of Chance*. New York: Viking, 1991.

Barthes, Roland. *Mythologies*. Trans. Annette Lavers. New York: Hill, 1972.

Batchelor, Ray. *Henry Ford, Mass Production, Modernism, and Design*. New York: Manchester UP, 1994.

Beattie, Ann. *Distortions*. 1976. New York: Vintage, 1991.

———. *Secrets and Surprises*. New York: Random, 1978.

———. *What Was Mine*. New York: Random, 1991.

———. *Where You'll Find Me*. New York: Linden, 1986.

Belasco, Warren James. *Americans on the Road: From Auto-camp to Motel, 1910-1945*. Cambridge: MIT P, 1979.

———. "Commercialized Nostalgia: The Origins of the Roadside Strip." Lewis and Goldstein 105-22.

Berger, Michael. *The Devil Wagon in God's Country: The Automobile and Social Change in Rural America, 1893-1929*. Hamden, CT: Archon, 1979.

Bontemps, Arna. *The Old South: "A Summer Tragedy" and Other Stories of the Thirties*. New York: Dodd, 1973.

Bowers, Q. David. *Early American Car Advertisements*. New York: Bonanza, 1966.

Bright, Brenda Jo. "Remappings: Los Angeles Low Riders." *Looking High and Looking Low*. Eds. Brenda Jo Bright and Liza Bakewell. Tucson: U of Arizona P, 1995. 89-124.

Brinkley, Douglas. Introd. *A Hoosier Holiday*. By Theodore Dreiser. Bloomington: Indiana UP, 1997.

Brownell, Blaine. "A Symbol of Modernity: Attitudes Towards the Automobile in Southern Cities." *American Quarterly* 24 (1972): 20-44.

Bruccoli, Matthew. *The Price Was High: The Uncollected Stories of F. Scott Fitzgerald*. New York: Harcourt, 1979.

Caldwell, Erskine. *Around about America*. New York: Farrar, 1964.

———. *God's Little Acre*. 1933. New York: Signet, 1961.

———. *Tobacco Road*. 1934. New York: Signet, 1962.

Carey, Glenn O. "William Faulkner and the Automobile as Socio-Sexual Symbol." *CEA Critic* 36.2 (1974): 15-17.

Catanzaro, Mary F. "The Car as Cell in *Lolita*." *Kansas Quarterly* 21.4 (1989): 91-96.

Challis, Chris. *Quest for Kerouac*. London: Faber, 1984.

Charters, Ann. *Kerouac: A Biography*. New York: Warner, 1974.

Chase, Stuart, and F. J. Schlink. *Men and Machines*. New York: MacMillan, 1929.

Cleveland, Reginald M., and S. T. Williamson. *The Road Is Yours*. New York: Greystone, 1951.

Clough, Rosa Trillo. *Futurism*. New York: Philosophical P, 1961.

Cohn, David L. *Combustion on Wheels: An Informal History of the Automobile Age*. Boston: Houghton, 1944.

Corso, Gregory. *Gasoline*. San Francisco: City Lights, 1958.

Crews, Harry. *Car*. New York: Morrow, 1972.

———. "The Car." *Blood and Grits*. New York: Harper, 1979.

Dettelbach, Cynthia Golomb. *In the Driver's Seat: The Automobile in American Literature and Popular Culture*. Westport, CT: Greenwood, 1976.

Dickinson, Charles. *The Widow's Adventures*. New York: William Morrow, 1989.

Doctorow, E. L. *Ragtime*. New York: Random, 1975.

Doolittle, James Rood. *The Romance of the Automobile Industry*. New York: Klebold, 1916.

Dos Passos, John. *The Big Money*. Boston: Houghton, 1946.

Dreiser, Theodore. *A Hoosier Holiday*. 1916. Westport, CT: Greenwood, 1974.

Echevarria, Luis Giron. "The Automobile as a Central Symbol in F. Scott Fitzgerald." *Revista Alicantina de Estudios Ingleses* 6 (1993): 73-78.

Eliade, Mircea. *The Sacred and the Profane.* 1957. Trans. Willard R. Trask. New York: Harper, 1961.

Eliot, T. S. *The Complete Poems and Plays, 1909-1950.* New York: Harcourt, 1971.

Ellison, Ralph. *Invisible Man.* 1952. New York: Random, 1972.

Erdrich, Louise. *Love Medicine.* 1984. New York: Bantam, 1987.

Estrin, Barbara L. "Recomposing Time: *Humboldt's Gift* and *Ragtime.*" *Denver Quarterly* 17.1 (1982): 16-31.

Faulkner, William. "Country Mice." *New Orleans Sketches.* 1958. London: Sidgwick, 1959. 191-207.

———. "Folklore of the Air." Rev. of *Test Pilot*, by Jimmy Collins. *The American Mercury* 36 (1935): 370-72.

———. *Intruder in the Dust.* New York: Random, 1948.

———. *Light in August.* 1932. New York: Random, 1972.

———. *The Mansion.* New York: Random, 1959.

———. *Pylon.* 1935. London: Lehman, 1950.

———. *The Reivers.* 1962. New York: Signet, 1969.

———. *Requiem for a Nun.* New York: Random, 1950.

———. *Sanctuary.* 1931. New York: Vintage, 1958.

———. *Selected Letters.* Ed. Joseph Blotner. New York: Random, 1977.

———. *The Sound and the Fury.* 1929. New York: Random, 1954.

———. *The Town.* New York: Random, 1957.

Felsen, Henry Gregor. *Hot Rod.* New York: Dutton, 1950.

Field, Edward. *A Six-Cylinder Courtship.* New York: Grosset, 1907.

Fitzgerald, F. Scott. *The Great Gatsby.* New York: Scribner's, 1925.

Flink, James J. *The Automobile Age.* Cambridge: MIT P, 1988.

———. *The Car Culture.* Cambridge: MIT P, 1975.

———. "Three Stages of American Automobile Consciousness." *American Quarterly* 24 (1972): 451-73.

Flower, Raymond, and Michael Wynn Jones. *100 Years on the Road: A Social History of the Car.* New York: McGraw, 1981.

Ford, Henry. *Today and Tomorrow.* Garden City, NY: Doubleday, 1926.

Foster, Mark S. "The Automobile and the City." Lewis and Goldstein 24-36.

Friedman, Melvin J. "Flannery O'Connor's Sacred Objects." *The Added Dimension: The Art and Mind of Flannery O'Connor.* Ed. Lewis A. Lawson. New York: Fordham UP, 1966. 196-206.

Fugin, Katherine, Faye Rivard, and Margaret Sieh. "An Interview with Flannery O'Connor." Magee 58-60.

Gentry, Marshall Bruce. "*Ragtime* as Auto Biography." *Kansas Quarterly* 21.4 (1989): 105-112.

Ginsberg, Allen. *The Fall of America*. San Francisco: City Lights, 1972.

Goldberg, Vicki. "Four Wheels, and Off to New Horizons." *New York Times* 30 May 1997: B1+.

Grigsby, John L. "The Automobile as Technological Reality and Central Symbol in John Dos Passos's *The Big Money*." *Kansas Quarterly* 21.4 (1989): 35-41.

Hassan, Ihab. *Selves at Risk*. Madison: U of Wisconsin P, 1990.

Hey, Kenneth. *Cars and Films in American Culture, 1929-59*. Lewis and Goldstein 193-205.

Hicks, John D. *Republican Ascendancy*. New York: Harper, 1960.

Hindus, Maurice. "Ford Conquers Russia." *Outlook* 146 (1927): 280-83.

Hipkiss, Robert A. "*On the Road*: Kerouac's Transport." *Kansas Quarterly* 21.4 (1989): 17-21.

Hokanson, Drake. *The Lincoln Highway: Main Street Across America*. Iowa City: U of Iowa P, 1988.

Hoover, J. Edgar, with Courtney Ryley Cooper. *American Magazine* Feb. 1940: 14+.

Interrante, Joseph. "The Road to Autopia." Lewis and Goldstein 89-104.

Ives, David. "Thirteen Ways of Looking at a Thunderbird." *The New York Times Magazine* 28 Aug. 1994: 72.

Jardim, Anne. *The First Henry Ford: A Study in Personality and Business Leadership*. Cambridge: MIT P, 1970.

Jennings, Jan, ed. *Roadside America: The Automobile in Design and Culture*. Ames, IA: Iowa State UP, 1990.

Jordan, Philip D. *The National Road*. New York: Bobbs-Merrill, 1948.

Kazin, Alfred. *On Native Grounds*. New York: Reynal, 1942.

Keats, John. *The Insolent Chariots*. Philadelphia: Lippincott, 1958.

Kerouac, Jack. Introd. *The Americans*. By Robert Frank. New York: Grossman, 1969.

———. *On the Road*. New York: Signet, 1957.

———. *Visions of Cody*. New York: McGraw, 1972.

Kihlsted, Folke T. "The Automobile and the Transformation of the American House, 1910-1935." Lewis and Goldstein 160-75.

———. "A Bridge between Engineering and Architecture." Jennings 3-14.

"Kill the Car—No More Roads!" Detroit: Fifth Estate, 1996.

Lacey, Robert. *Ford: The Men and the Machine*. Boston: Little, 1986.

Lacy, Dan. *The White Use of Blacks in America*. New York: Atheneum, 1972.

Laird, David. "Versions of Eden: The Automobile and the American Novel." Lewis and Goldstein 244-56.

Lawrence, D. H. *Studies in Classic American Literature*. 1923. New York: Viking, 1964.

Leonard, Jonathan N. *The Tragedy of Henry*. New York: Putnam's, 1932.

Lewis, David L. "Sex and the Automobile: From Rumble Seats to Rockin' Vans." Lewis and Goldstein 123-33.

——, and Lawrence Goldstein, eds. *The Automobile and American Culture*. Ann Arbor: U of Michigan P, 1983.

Lewis, Grace Hegger. *With Love from Gracie: Sinclair Lewis, 1912-1925*. New York: Harcourt, 1955.

Lewis, Sinclair. *Babbitt*. 1922. New York: NAL, 1980.

——. *Dodsworth*. New York: Harcourt, 1929.

——. *Free Air*. New York: Harcourt, 1919.

——. *Main Street*. New York: Harcourt, 1920.

——. *The Man Who Knew Coolidge*. New York: Harcourt, 1941.

——. "Speed." *Selected Short Stories*. New York: Literary Guild, 1935. 301-20.

Lhamon, W. T., Jr. *Deliberate Speed: The Origins of a Cultural Style in the American 1950s*. Washington: Smithsonian, 1990.

Liebs, Chester H. *Main Street to Middle Mile*. Boston: Little, 1985.

Lindsay, Vachel. *Collected Poems*. New York: MacMillan, 1967.

Lynd, Robert S. and Helen Merrell. *Middletown: A Study in American Culture*. New York: Harcourt, 1929.

——. *Middletown in Transition*. New York: Harcourt, 1937.

Lytle, Andrew Nelson. "The Hind Tit." *I'll Take My Stand: The South and the Agrarian Tradition*. 1930. Gloucester, MA: Peter Smith, 1976.

McLuhan, Marshall. *The Mechanical Bride: Folklore of Industrial Man*. New York: Vanguard, 1951.

——. *Understanding Media*. New York: McGraw, 1964.

McNally, Dennis. *Desolate Angel: Jack Kerouac, the Beat Generation, and America*. New York: Random, 1979.

McShane, Clay. *Down the Asphalt Path*. New York: Columbia UP, 1994.

Magalaner, Marvin. "Louise Erdrich." *American Women Writing Fiction*. Ed. Mickey Perlman. Lexington: UP of Kentucky, 1989.

Magee, Rosemary M., ed. *Conversations with Flannery O'Connor*. Jackson: U of Mississippi P, 1987.

Mailer, Norman. *The Naked and the Dead*. New York: Holt, 1948.

Marsh, Peter, and Peter Collett. *Driving Passion: The Psychology of the Car.* London: Cape, 1986.

Marx, Leo. *The Machine in the Garden: Technology and the Pastoral Ideal in America.* New York: Oxford, 1964.

———. *The Pilot and The Passenger: Essays on Literature, Technology, and Culture in the United States.* New York: Oxford, 1988.

Meier, August, and Elliott Rudwick. *Black Detroit and the Rise of the UAW.* New York: Oxford, 1979.

Meikle, Jeffrey L. *Twentieth Century Limited: Industrial Design in America, 1925-1939.* Philadelphia: Temple UP, 1979.

Milum, Richard A. "Continuity and Change: The Horse, the Automobile, and the Airplane in Faulkner's Fiction." *Faulkner, The Unappeased Imagination.* Ed. Glenn O. Carey. Troy, NY: Whitson, 1980. 157-74.

Moon, William Least Heat. *Blue Highways.* New York: Fawcett, 1982.

Mumford, Lewis. *The Highway and the City.* New York: Harcourt, 1963.

Murphy, Christina. *Ann Beattie.* Boston: Twayne, 1986.

Nabokov, Vladimir. *Lolita.* 1955. New York: Capricorn, 1972.

Nash, Roderick. *The Nervous Generation: American Thought, 1917-1930.* Chicago: Rand, 1970.

Nevins, Allan, and Frank Ernest Hill. *Ford: Decline and Rebirth: 1933-1962.* New York: Scribner's, 1963.

Norris, Frank. *The Octopus.* New York: Doubleday, 1901.

O'Connor, Flannery. *The Complete Stories.* New York: Farrar, 1971.

———. *The Habit of Being.* Ed. Sally Fitzgerald. 1979. New York: Farrar, 1988.

———. *Wise Blood.* 1952. *Three by Flannery O'Connor.* New York: Signet, 1983. 1-120.

O'Hara, John. *Appointment in Samarra.* New York: Duell, 1934.

Ostrander, Gilman M. *American Civilization in the First Machine Age. 1890-1940.* New York: Harper, 1970.

Patton, Phil. *Open Road: A Celebration of the American Highway.* New York: Simon, 1986.

Penn, Arthur. "*Bonnie and Clyde*: Private Morality and Public Violence." *Hollywood Directors: 1941-1976.* Ed. Richard Koszarski. New York: Oxford, 1977. 360-64.

Pettifer, Julian, and Nigel Turner. *Automania: Man and the Motorcar.* London: Collins, 1984.

Plath, James. "Counternarrative: An Interview with Ann Beattie." *Michigan Quarterly Review* 32 (1993): 359-79.

———. "My Lover the Car: Ann Beattie's 'A Vintage Thunderbird' and Other Vehicles." *Kansas Quarterly* 21.4 (1989): 113-19.

Post, Emily. *By Motor to the Golden Gate*. New York: Appleton, 1916.

"Private Historian." *Time* 10 August 1936: 51-52.

Rae, John B. *The American Automobile: A Brief History*. Chicago: U of Chicago P, 1965.

Ragen, Brian Abel. *A Wreck on the Road to Damascus: Innocence, Guilt and Conversion in Flannery O'Connor*. Chicago: Loyola UP, 1989.

Randisi, Jennifer L. "The Scene of the Crime: The Automobile in the Fiction of Harry Crews." *Southern Studies* 25 (1986): 213-19.

Recent Social Trends in the United States. Report of the President's Research Committee on Social Trends. New York: McGraw, 1933.

"Recent Southern Fiction: A Panel Discussion." Magee 61-78.

Reck, Franklin M. *A Car Traveling People: How the Automobile Has Changed the Life of Americans—A Study of Social Effects*. Detroit: Automobile Manufacturer's Assn., 1945.

Ristoff, Dilvo I. *Updike's America*. New York: Lang, 1988.

Rose, Albert C. *Historic American Roads: From Frontier Trails to Superhighways*. New York: Crown, 1976.

Rose, Mark. *Interstate: Express Highway Politics, 1941-1956*. Lawrence: Regents P of Kansas, 1979.

Rosenbaum Jean. *Is Your Volkswagen a Sex Symbol?* New York: Hawthorn, 1972.

Rothschild, Emma. *Paradise Lost: The Decline of the Auto-Industrial Age*. New York: Random, 1973.

Sanford, Charles L. *Automobiles in American Life*. Troy, NY: Rensselaer, 1976.

———. "'Woman's Place' in American Car Culture." Lewis and Goldstein 137-52.

Scharff, Virginia. *Taking the Wheel: Women and the Coming of the Motor Age*. New York: Free, 1991.

Schneider, Kenneth R. *Autokind vs. Mankind*. New York: Norton, 1971.

Schneider, Kenneth and Blanche, eds. *The Quotable Car*. Berkeley: U of California P, 1973.

Sears, Stephen W. *The American Heritage History of the Automobile in America*. New York: American Heritage, 1977.

Shapiro, Karl. *Collected Poems, 1940-1978*. New York: Random, 1978.

Silk, Gerald, et al. *Automobile and Culture*. New York: Abrams, 1984.

Sinclair, Upton. *The Flivver King: A Story of Ford-America.* Pasadena: Upton Sinclair, 1937.

Smith, Julian. "A Runaway Match: The Automobile in the American Film, 1900-1920." Lewis and Goldstein 179-91.

Stein, Gertrude. *The Autobiography of Alice P. Toklas.* New York: Harcourt, 1933.

Steinbeck, John. *Cannery Row.* New York: Viking, 1945.

———. *The Grapes of Wrath.* 1939. New York: Viking, 1958.

———. *Travels with Charley: In Search of America.* New York: Viking, 1962.

Stern, Jane and Michael. *Auto Ads.* New York: Random, 1978.

Strunsky, Simeon. *The Living Tradition: Change and America.* New York: Doubleday, 1939.

Susman, Warren. *Culture as History: The Transformation of American Society in the Twentieth Century.* New York: Pantheon, 1984.

Tarkington, Booth. *The Magnificent Ambersons.* Garden City, NY: Doubleday, 1918.

———, and Harry Leon Wilson. *The Man from Home.* New York: Harper, 1908.

Tate, J. O. "The Essential Essex." *The Flannery O'Connor Bulletin* 12 (1983): 47-59.

Tichi, Cecelia. *Shifting Gears: Technology, Literature, Culture in Modernist America.* Chapel Hill: U of North Carolina P, 1987.

Updike, John. *Rabbit at Rest.* New York: Knopf, 1990.

———. *Rabbit Is Rich.* 1981. New York: Fawcett, 1982.

———. *Rabbit Redux.* 1971. New York: Fawcett, 1972.

———. *Rabbit, Run.* 1960. Greenwich, CT: Fawcett, 1962.

Vale, Thomas R. and Geraldine R. *U.S. 40 Today: Thirty Years of Landscape Change in America.* Madison: U of Wisconsin P, 1983.

Vaughan, David K. "The Automobile and American Juvenile Series Fiction, 1900-40." Jennings 74-81.

Vonalt, Larry. "The Other End of Love: Harry Crews's *Car.*" *A Grit's Triumph: Essays on the Works of Harry Crews.* Ed. David K. Jeffrey. Port Washington, NY: Associated Faculty P, 1983. 132-39.

Waldron, Randall. "Faulkner's First Fictional Car—Borrowed from F. Scott Fitzgerald?" *American Literature* 60 (1988): 281-85.

Walker, Alice. *The Color Purple.* 1982. New York: Washington Square, 1983.

Wells, Joel. "Off the Cuff." Magee 85-90.

West, Thomas Reed. *Flesh of Steel: Literature and the Machine in American Culture.* Nashville: Vanderbilt UP, 1967.

Wharton, Edith. *A Backward Glance.* New York: Appleton, 1934.

———. *A Motor-Flight through France*. New York: Scribner, 1908.

Whitman, Walt. *Leaves of Grass*. Eds. Harold K. Blodgett and Sculley Bradley. New York: New York UP, 1965.

Widmer, Kingsley. "The American Road." *U of Kansas City Review* 26 (1960): 309-17.

Wik, Reynold M. *Henry Ford and Grass-Roots America*. Ann Arbor: U of Michigan P, 1973.

Williams, Joy. *Breaking and Entering*. New York: Vintage, 1988.

———. *Escapes*. New York: Atlantic Monthly, 1990.

Willis, Lonnie. "Harry Crews' *Car*: A Possible Source." *Notes on Contemporary Literature* 12.5 (1982): 9-10.

Wolfe, Tom. *The Kandy-Kolored Tangerine-Flake Streamline Baby*. New York: Farrar, 1965.

Wright, Richard. *Native Son*. 1940. New York: Harper, 1966.

Index

—A—

Adams, Henry, 16, 17, 19, 175
Agee, James, 9
Amory, Cleveland, 164
Anderson, Rudolph, 23, 31, 34,
   35, 57, 176
Asch, Nathan, 121
assembly line, 7, 55, 57-59, 61,
   63, 64-69, 77, 99, 172
Auster, Paul, 9, 170, 183
automania, 95, 168
automobile
   advertisements, 10, 27, 29, 30,
      31, 37, 63, 110, 179, 181
   and African America, 8, 65, 97,
      129, 132-137, 173
   and Broadway, 23
   and city, 4, 17, 19, 38, 44, 52,
      70, 123, 133
   and death, 21, 51, 52, 72, 79,
      82, 83, 87-89, 140, 142, 144,
      147, 149, 150, 152, 153
   and escape, 8, 41, 74, 95, 99,
      101, 107, 120, 122, 125,
      128, 133, 139, 142, 144,
      145, 148-50, 153, 154, 155,
      159, 161, 170, 173
   and film, 71, 75, 76, 92, 175,
      181
   and freedom, 30, 31, 41, 82, 98,
      99, 105, 115, 144
   and health, 29, 37
   and masculinity, 9, 10, 139,
      140, 168
   and Mexican America, 5
   and mobility, 75, 100
   and Native America, 148, 154
   and nostalgia, 8, 40, 93, 140,
      142, 155, 158
   and physicians, 22
   and religion, 45, 47, 48, 73, 74,
      166, 174
   and romance, 6, 7, 19, 24, 26,
      27, 33-36, 83, 110, 117, 175
   and rural life, 4, 7, 15, 27, 32,
      43, 60, 70-75, 81, 82, 88, 90,
      172, 177, 178
   and satire, 7, 38-41, 56, 83, 93,
      169, 171
   and sex, 85, 86, 98, 107, 122,
      143, 149, 159, 167, 174
   and speed, 17, 29, 30, 32, 35-
      38, 40, 47, 85, 87, 88, 93,
      97, 173, 176, 179
   and the South, 7, 70, 71, 74, 82,
      88, 90, 93, 99, 107, 172,
      177, 178, 180

and tours, 22-24
and women, 8-11, 27, 30, 31,
    144
as complex signifier, 7, 55, 93
chauffeurs, 22, 30, 35, 129,
    178, 182
history, 19
Automobile Magazine, 34
automobility, 4-8, 10, 13, 15, 18-
20, 22, 24, 25, 27, 33, 35, 39,
41, 48, 49, 52, 53, 55, 58, 65,
70, 71, 73, 77, 78, 82-84, 91,
93, 95-97, 107, 112-14, 119,
129, 137, 139, 147, 153, 154,
161, 162, 164, 166-69, 171-173

—B—

Barthes, Roland, 11, 47
Beats, 97, 108, 109, 111-14, 116,
    117, 121
Beattie, Ann, 8, 139, 140, 154-56,
    158-61, 164, 170, 173
"A Vintage Thunderbird", 155,
    157
"Colorado", 155, 157
"Coney Island", 155
"Deer Season", 160
"Friends", 155
"Gaps", 155
"Hale Hardy and the Amazing
    Animal Woman", 159-60
"High School", 155, 160
"Home to Marie", 158
"Honey", 155
"It's Just Another Day . . .", 157
"La Petite Danseuse de
    Quatorze Ans", 158
"Octascope", 158, 160
"Parking Lot", 159-160

"Shifting", 157, 159
"Spiritus", 155
"Starley", 155
"Summer People", 155, 160
"Television", 155
"The Lawn Party", 155
"Tuesday Night", 158
"When Can I See You Again?",
    159
"Where You'll Find Me", 155
Distortions, 155, 157, 159, 161
Secrets and Surprises, 155-60
What Was Mine, 155, 158
Where You'll Find Me, 155,
    159, 160
Bedford's Hope, 23, 27
Belasco, Warren, 17, 28, 81
Berger, Michael, 74
bicycle, 15, 20
BMW, 182
Bontemps, Arna, 8, 97, 129-32,
    138, 173, 182
"A Summer Tragedy", 129-30,
    152
"Saturday Night", 131, 182
Bright, Brenda Jo, 5, 129
Brinkley, Douglas, 24
Brothers, Joyce, 168
Brownell, Blaine, 11
Buick, 42, 143, 144, 179
Burroughs, William, 108

—C—

Cadillac, 106, 110, 123, 129, 164-
69, 176
Caldwell, Erskine, 7, 70-72, 74,
78, 88, 90, 93, 97, 172
God's Little Acre, 70-72, 74
Tobacco Road, 70-72, 74

Carey, Glenn, 179
Cassady, Neal, 108, 111, 112, 115
Catanzaro, Mary, 119
Challis, Chris, 112, 181
Charters, Ann, 108-11, 115
Chase, Stuart, 55, 171
Chevrolet, 27, 29, 63, 96, 147
Chrysler, 96, 103, 125, 167
Clough, Rosa, 19, 36
Collett, Peter, 15, 20, 32, 36, 48,
    133, 173, 174
consumerism, 7, 15, 43, 47, 49,
    53, 63, 72, 77, 88, 93, 95, 100,
    117-19, 127, 144, 155, 157,
    164, 166, 169, 171, 173
convertible, 96, 125, 127, 144,
    145, 147, 151, 152, 156-58,
    182
Corso, Gregory, 114
Corvette, 4, 139, 140, 168
Cowley, Malcolm, 92
Crews, Harry, 8, 9, 139, 164-66,
    168-69, 170, 173, 183
Cunningham, Walter, 59

—D—

DeLorean, John, 10, 140
Detroit, 22, 56, 57, 60, 62, 85,
    116, 137
Dettelbach, Cynthia, 76, 89, 178
Dickinson, Charles, 161-63, 170,
    173
Dickinson, Emily, 14, 28
Didion, Joan, 170
Doctorow, E. L., 56, 65-69, 97,
    129, 135, 138, 170, 173, 177,
    178

Ragtime, 7, 56, 65, 66, 69, 129,
    135, 136, 138, 182
Dodge, 96
Doolittle, James, 13, 21, 29, 38
Dos Passos, John, 7, 67, 68, 172
    The Big Money, 67
Dreiser, Theodore, 24, 25, 28, 35
Duryea, 3, 20, 21

—E—

Echevarria, Luis, 50
Eisenhower, Dwight D., 111, 122,
    126
Eliade, Mircea, 101
Eliot, T. S., 169
Ellison, Ralph, 8, 97, 135, 138,
    173
    Invisible Man, 129, 134, 137
Emerson, Ralph Waldo, 3
Erdrich, Louise, 8, 139, 140, 148,
    149, 154, 157, 170, 173
    Love Medicine, 148, 153, 154,
        161, 164
    The Beet Queen, 154
Essex, 98, 99, 169
Estrin, Barbara, 66
Evans, Oliver, 13, 19

—F—

Faulkner, William, 7, 70, 82-93,
    97, 113, 169, 170, 172, 178,
    179
    "Country Mice", 82, 83, 87
    Intruder in the Dust, 83, 85-87,
        92
    Light in August, 90
    Pylon, 90-91

Requiem for a Nun, 83
Sanctuary, 86, 89, 91, 140
Sartoris, 87, 88, 93
The Mansion, 85, 88
The Reivers, 82-85, 88, 90-92
The Sound and the Fury, 86, 89
The Town, 84, 89, 90
Felsen, Henry, 114
Hot Rod, 114, 115
Field, Edward, 34, 35, 37
Fitzgerald, F. Scott, 35, 50, 51,
    52, 53, 83, 160, 161, 169, 170,
    172, 176, 177
    "A Night at the Fair", 35
    "The Family Bus", 177
    The Great Gatsby, 7, 50-53, 83,
        160, 169
Flink, James, 6, 15, 56, 58-61, 74,
    75, 175
Ford, 4, 6, 8, 9, 25, 31, 42-44, 46,
    55, 56, 78, 87, 89, 99, 110,
    113, 123, 130, 131, 136, 137,
    157, 165, 176, 177, 181
    Model T, 32, 55, 58-60, 65, 69,
        89, 99, 129-31, 135-38, 169,
        182
Ford, Henry, 7, 21, 45, 53, 55-69,
    93, 99, 129, 137, 167, 175, 177
Foster, Mark, 17, 20
Freidman, Melvin, 101
Futurists, 9, 18, 36, 37, 165, 176

—G—

Gardner, Ethellyn, 30
General Motors, 10, 21, 45, 95,
    99, 122, 140
Gentry, Marshall, 65, 67
Ginsberg, Allen, 108, 113, 114,
    181

Goldberg, Vicki, 6
Grahame, Kenneth, 50
Great Depression, 60, 74-76, 80,
    172
Grigsby, John L., 67
Guthrie, Janet, 10

—H—

Harding, Warren G., 3
Harpham, Geoffrey, 65
Hassan, Ihab, 5
Hawkes, John, 9
Heller, Steve, 9, 170
Hemphill, Paul, 170
Hey, Kenneth, 71, 175
Hicks, John, 121
Hitler, Adolph, 61
Hokanson, Drake, 14, 25
Holmes, John Clellon, 108
Hoover, J. Edgar, 81
Horseless Age, 4, 22
Houdini, Harry, 65, 144, 182
Huck Finn, 14, 108, 110
Hudson, 76, 80, 111
Huxley, Aldous, 69

—I—

I'll Take My Stand, 87, 178
Infiniti, 127
interchangeability, 53, 64, 66-69,
    137, 174
Interrante, Joseph, 74, 75
Ives, David, 183

—J—

James, Henry, 48
Jeep, 146

Jordan Playboy, 31, 52
Jordan, Philip, 26
Josephson, Matthew, 69

—K—

Kazin, Alfred, 68
Keats, John, 6, 85, 180
Kerouac, Jack, 97, 108, 109, 111,
  112, 114-16, 118, 120, 151,
  163, 173, 181
  Big Sur, 116
  On the Road, 8, 84, 97, 108,
    110-16, 161, 163
  Visions of Cody, 112
Kihlsted, Folke, 178

—L—

Lacey, Robert, 63
Lacy, Dan, 133
Laird, David, 81, 84, 87, 102
Lawrence, D. H., 18
Leonard, Jonathan, 56, 57, 59, 63,
  65
Levitt, Dorothy, 30, 32
Lewis, Grace, 25, 26
Lewis, Sinclair, 7, 24-28, 30, 33,
  35, 38, 39, 41, 42, 44, 45, 48-
  50, 53, 71, 96, 112, 167, 169-
  72, 175, 176
  "Speed", 24, 35, 38-41, 47, 114
  Babbitt, 30, 41, 44-46, 48, 53
  Dodsworth, 41, 45-49, 71, 100,
    176
  Free Air, 7, 24, 26, 27, 30, 33,
    34, 38, 39, 41, 49, 84, 110
  Main Street, 25, 41, 42, 45, 48,
    49

The Trail of the Hawk, 25
World So Wide, 49
Lhamon, W. T., 117
Liebs, Chester, 92
Lincoln, 133
Lincoln Highway, 14, 25, 26
Lindsay, Vachel, 33
Lynd, Robert and Helen, 76
  Middletown, 64, 75, 176
Lytle, Andrew Nelson, 87

—M—

Maeterlinck, Maurice, 16
Magalaner, Marvin, 148-50, 154
Mailer, Norman, 69
Malibu, 152
Marinetti, Filippo Tommaso, 36
Marsh, Peter, 15, 20, 32, 36, 48,
  133, 173, 174
Marx, Leo, 14-16, 19, 110, 111,
  175
mass production, 7, 17, 58-60, 77,
  79, 99, 171, 172
Matthews, Greg, 170
Maverick, 164, 166, 167, 169
McClintock, Miller, 119
McLuhan, Marshall, 11, 33, 85,
  166, 174, 179
McMurtry, Larry, 9, 170
McNally, Dennis, 116
McShane, Clay, 9, 10, 50, 136
mechanization, 46, 62, 75, 87,
  104, 105, 107
Meier, August, 137
Mercedes, 158, 182
Mercury, 180
Milum, Richard, 89, 178

mobility, 3, 7, 13, 14, 17, 70, 72,
    77, 82, 85, 97-99, 120, 126,
    131, 163, 171, 172
Moon, William Least Heat, 109,
    178
Morgan, J. P., 66, 136
Morrison, Toni, 170
Motocycle, 4, 22
Mumford, Lewis, 48, 100, 166
Murphy, Christina, 159, 160
Mustang, 124, 125, 155, 158

—N—

Nabokov, Vladimir, 116, 117, 173
    Lolita, 96, 116-19, 159
Nader, Ralph, 8, 96
Nash, Roderick, 29, 56, 61, 177
Nazism, 61, 104
Nelson, Willie, 14
New York Sun, 23, 135
New York Times, 6, 60
Norris, Frank, 28

—O—

O'Connor, Flannery, 8, 97-104,
    106-08, 140, 154, 169, 170,
    173, 180, 181
    "A Circle in the Fire", 181
    "A Good Man Is Hard to Find",
        98, 102
    "A Temple of the Holy Ghost",
        107
    "A View of the Woods", 98,
        106-07
    "Everything that Rises Must
        Converge", 180
    "Good Country People", 107,
        154, 180

    "Greenleaf", 98, 105
    "Parker's Back", 98, 101
    "The Artificial Nigger", 180
    "The Comforts of Home", 107,
        181
    "The Displaced Person", 98,
        103
    "The Lame Shall Enter First",
        181
    "The Life You Save May Be
        Your Own", 98, 101
    "The Partridge Festival", 107
    "The River", 180-81
    Wise Blood, 98, 99, 107, 169,
        180
O'Hara, John, 176-77
Oldsmobile, 21, 22, 31, 96, 151,
    162
Ostrander, Gilman, 115

—P—

Packard, 44, 65, 133
Panhard, 136
Patton, Phil, 14, 109, 117
Penn, Arthur, 181
Pettifer, Julian, 33, 35, 39
Pierce Arrow, 136
Plath, James, 154-56, 158, 159,
    161
Plymouth, 180
Pontiac Firebird, 150, 151, 153,
    154
Porsche, 123, 141, 182
Post, Emily, 10, 24, 30
Pynchon, Thomas, 9

—R—

Ragen, Brian, 98, 109, 180

railroad, 3, 14-16, 20, 23, 27, 28,
    34, 38, 44, 152, 176, 180
Randisi, Jennifer, 168, 170
Reader's Digest, 50
Reck, Franklin, 41
Ristoff, Dilvo, 120
Rolls-Royce, 48, 50, 83, 133, 166,
    169
Rosenbaum, Jean, 11, 84, 85, 135,
    144, 165
Rudwick, Elliott, 137

—S—

Sanford, Charles, 11, 45
Saturday Evening Post, 26, 39
Scarrett, Winthrop, 70
Schneider, Kenneth, 16, 19, 29,
    50, 70
Sears, Stephen, 56, 60, 95
Shapiro, Karl, 179, 183
Shaw, George Bernard, 23
Shepard, Sam, 170
Silk, Gerald, 18, 69
Sinclair, Upton, 56, 62-66, 68,
    172
    The Flivver King, 7, 56, 62, 63,
        65, 67
Sloan, Alfred P., 45
Smith, Julian, 147, 175
standardization, 17, 43-46, 48, 53,
    68, 79, 89, 112, 126, 172, 174
Stein, Gertrude, 8, 10
Steinbeck, John, 7, 70, 74, 76-78,
    80, 82, 93, 104, 105, 108, 113,
    131, 169, 170, 172
    Cannery Row, 55
    The Grapes of Wrath, 74, 76,
        77, 81, 82, 84, 169, 172

Travels with Charley, 76
Stevens, Wallace, 183
Strunsky, Simeon, 76, 93, 172
Studebaker, 183
Susman, Warren, 43, 56

—T—

Tarkington, Booth, 7, 23, 39-41,
    172, 174
    The Magnificent Ambersons,
        39-40
Tate, J. O., 98
Thompson, Hunter S., 170
Thunderbird, 4, 140-42, 144, 147,
    155-57, 183
Tichi, Cecelia, 68
Toyota, 120, 124, 125, 157
tractor, 57, 59, 79, 80, 101, 102,
    104
Triumph, 182
truck, 76-79, 90, 102, 105, 113,
    147, 149, 166, 177, 180, 181
Turner, Nigel, 33, 35

—U—

Updike, John, 8, 97, 119, 120,
    123, 125, 127-29, 161, 164,
    170, 173
    Rabbit at Rest, 119-20, 126,
        128, 161
    Rabbit Is Rich, 120, 124
    Rabbit Redux, 120, 122, 124
    Rabbit, Run, 119-22, 124, 126,
        128

—V—

Vale, Thomas and Geraldine, 182
Vietnam, 120, 122, 123, 126, 151,
     157
Volkswagen, 10, 58
Volvo, 159
Vonalt, Larry, 166

—W—

Waldron, Randall, 83, 178
Walker, Alice, 137-38
Walker, Timothy, 15, 129, 136
Warren, Robert Penn, 9
Wells, Joel, 98
West, Thomas, 69
Wharton, Edith, 8, 10, 26, 30
White, E. B., 171, 176
Whitman, Walt, 3, 14, 17-19, 112
Widmer, Kingsley, 114, 116
Williams, Joy, 8, 139-42, 146-48,
     154, 158, 161, 163, 168, 170,
     173, 174
     "Escapes", 142, 144-45

"Health", 145
"Rot", 140, 142, 144, 145, 155
"The Blue Men", 182
"The Last Generation", 145,
     147
"The Little Winter", 142, 144-
     47
"The Route", 142, 144-45, 147
"The Skater", 182
"White", 182
Breaking and Entering, 140,
     147-48, 182, 183
Escapes, 8, 30, 140, 145, 147,
     148, 164, 170
Williams, William Carlos, 9
Wilson, Woodrow, 50
Winton Flyer, 84, 85
Winton, Alexander, 21, 22
Wolfe, Tom, 74, 119, 168, 170,
     174
World War II, 7, 60, 82, 93, 108,
     172
Wright, Richard, 8, 97, 132, 134,
     138, 173
Native Son, 129, 132, 162

A native of South Carolina, Roger Casey is an Associate Professor of English at Birmingham-Southern College in Birmingham, Alabama, where he also serves as Director of General Education and Instruction. He teaches courses in cultural theory, contemporary drama, American literature, and leadership studies. In addition, he co-directs the Associated Colleges of the South Teaching and Learning Workshops and is a Kellogg National Fellow. He received his Ph.D. in English from Florida State University and his B.A. from Furman University. He is married to Robyn Allers, a writer. They have five cats and three Fords.